K9 Spirit Guides

The Healing Power of Man's Best Friend

HEATHER LEIGH STROM

BALBOA.PRESS
A DIVISION OF HAY HOUSE

Copyright © 2023 Heather Leigh Strom.

All rights reserved. No part of this book may be used or reproduced by any means, graphic, electronic, or mechanical, including photocopying, recording, taping or by any information storage retrieval system without the written permission of the author except in the case of brief quotations embodied in critical articles and reviews.

Balboa Press books may be ordered through booksellers or by contacting:

Balboa Press
A Division of Hay House
1663 Liberty Drive
Bloomington, IN 47403
www.balboapress.com
844-682-1282

Because of the dynamic nature of the Internet, any web addresses or links contained in this book may have changed since publication and may no longer be valid. The views expressed in this work are solely those of the author and do not necessarily reflect the views of the publisher, and the publisher hereby disclaims any responsibility for them.

The author of this book does not dispense medical advice or prescribe the use of any technique as a form of treatment for physical, emotional, or medical problems without the advice of a physician, either directly or indirectly. The intent of the author is only to offer information of a general nature to help you in your quest for emotional and spiritual well-being. In the event you use any of the information in this book for yourself, which is your constitutional right, the author and the publisher assume no responsibility for your actions.

Artwork by Alex Florin

Print information available on the last page.

ISBN: 979-8-7652-4070-0 (sc)
ISBN: 979-8-7652-4072-4 (hc)
ISBN: 979-8-7652-4071-7 (e)

Library of Congress Control Number: 2023906073

Balboa Press rev. date: 05/10/2023

Contents

Foreword ix
Preface xi
Introduction xiii
Prologue xv

SECTION 1: THE BASICS

Chapter 1   What Is a K9 Spirit Guide? 1
Chapter 2   Who Am I? 4
Chapter 3   How This Book Is Organized 6

SECTION 2: ANTHEA

Chapter 4   My Little Indian Puppy 19
Chapter 5   The Flare of Betrayal 24
Chapter 6   Tori Emerges 28
Chapter 7   The Flare of Persecution 35
Chapter 8   We Find Our Stride 37
Chapter 9   Flare of Inadequacy 40
Chapter 10   A Welcome Change of Pace 42
Chapter 11   A Surge of Inadequacy 48
Chapter 12   A Bunch of Rocks 51
Chapter 13   I Just Knew 53

Chapter 14	The Beast Inside Her	55
Chapter 15	The Irony of Tori	59
Chapter 16	Living at Church	65
Chapter 17	Sally as a Mother	69

SECTION 3: ÖSKAR

Chapter 18	The Day Care Center	81
Chapter 19	Church Camp	84
Chapter 20	The Scoop on My Father	87
Chapter 21	My Big German Shepherd Dog	93
Chapter 22	Flares of Worthiness	98
Chapter 23	A Peek into My Destiny	100
Chapter 24	Anthea Returns	107
Chapter 25	Their Shadow Sides	111
Chapter 26	Like Father, Like Son	114
Chapter 27	The Closing of a Chapter	118
Chapter 28	Consequences	123
Chapter 29	The Ultimate Truth	125
Chapter 30	Nick Comes Home	131
Chapter 31	The Rage That Lies Beneath	134
Chapter 32	The Power of Energy Healing	141
Chapter 33	A Painful Parting	144
Chapter 34	The Power within You	149
Chapter 35	Waiting for Me	152
Chapter 36	Dialing In	155
Chapter 37	Zozzo Delivers	157

SECTION 4: OERAGON

Chapter 38	The Light of My Soul	173
Chapter 39	The Butterfly Emerges	177
Chapter 40	Apachi Shines!	180
Chapter 41	Apachi Knows Best	182

Chapter 42 Embracing New Growth 184
Chapter 43 The Dichotomy of Sisters 187
Chapter 44 Tying Up Loose Ends 189
Chapter 45 Running from Myself 191
Chapter 46 Apachi's Broken Heart 195
Chapter 47 Nikki Isn't Who I Think She Is 201
Chapter 48 A Psychic Dental Emergency 204
Chapter 49 Avoidance 208
Chapter 50 The Swap Out 210
Chapter 51 My Black Panther 213
Chapter 52 Apachi Comes Home 216
Chapter 53 Aged Wisdom 219
Chapter 54 Nikki as Queen 222
Chapter 55 Cosmic Shift 227
Chapter 56 An Old Awakening 231

SECTION 5: DÄMEON JA'LAR͠ON HÉRIC

Chapter 57 The Gift of Gigi 249
Chapter 58 Nikki Takes a Tumble 254
Chapter 59 Gigi's Spirit Emerges 256
Chapter 60 Seeking Knowledge 259
Chapter 61 Nikki Prepares Her Departure 261
Chapter 62 Apachi Hands over the Reigns 265
Chapter 63 My First Experience with Héric 271
Chapter 64 Behold the Next Seven Years! 274
Chapter 65 Karma Comes Knocking 276
Chapter 66 Alternate #7 278
Chapter 67 Medical Disaster 281
Chapter 68 Blinded by the Darkness 284
Chapter 69 Spiritual Counsel 286
Chapter 70 Last Chance 291
Chapter 71 The Pieces Finally Come Together 294
Chapter 72 A Resurrection 297

Chapter 73 Mo's Shift Comes to a Close 300
Chapter 74 A Familiar Dog...305
Chapter 75 Winding Curves Ahead 308
Chapter 76 A New Direction from a Powerful Force..................312
Chapter 77 Moving On... 314
Chapter 78 The Wheels Begin to Turn.. 319
Chapter 79 The Beginning of a New Adventure 321
Chapter 80 Journey into the Unknown 324
Chapter 81 Missing Pieces..328
Chapter 82 Are You My Father? 332
Chapter 83 Ancestral Entanglement..335
Chapter 84 Rage 339

SECTION 6: THEIR GIFT TO HUMANITY

Chapter 85 In Summary 345
Chapter 86 A Revolution of Awareness.......................................348

Epilogue.. 351
Acknowledgments 353

Foreword

If you have picked up this book, you have been guided here for a reason.

I have worked with animal spirits, in many ways and in many forms, for over thirty years and I am always amazed by their guidance, teaching, and mystique about how they walk among us. Heather's book opened up new dimensions, new perspectives, and new truths, gifting to me personally new understanding that I have not experienced before but clearly am now ready to receive.

The Core Four are powerful, multidimensional angels and guides that are the best friends we have, the best friends we wished for, longed for, miss. And now we get to know with absolute certainty they are always with us, guiding, nudging, poking, teaching, loving, helping us to remember who we are, helping us to embrace our inner strength, helping us to see through the illusions and lies we tell ourselves, healing our karma, and liberating our souls so we can live our best lives.

From personal experience, I know you are about to go on a unique and insightful journey of personal understanding. Some might say discovery, but the gifts in Heather's book reveal deeper truths for you to understand about you, truths for you to implement and make changes in your life, and truths for you to live a happier life.

My invitation to you is to be open to possibility, be curious about your reactions/responses to the stories, listen to the messages that rise up from within you, and ask yourself, "If this is my truth, how am I going to use this new blessed awareness?"

Heather is an exceptional writer and storyteller. Her psychic channel is one of the purest, cleanest, and most accurate I have come across in a long time. The Core Four trust her with their most precious teachings, and they trust her to share them with you directly, untainted, and unfiltered. This is why, as Heather has suggested, you must read this book from cover to cover and in order; otherwise, you may miss something important to you.

Heather's book came to me at a time when I felt disoriented and adrift in the wilderness of life, waiting, wondering, and treading water. The Core Four independently and collectively helped me to release unknown fears and resolve unconscious stories revealing the next phase in my life's adventure. The healing I have received is already having a positive impact on my life.

After reading this book, you *will* see the world differently. Everything looks brighter, clearer, sharper, and more colorful, and you will see the gifts the K9 spirit guides bring to us each and every day.

—Clayton John Ainger, spiritual guide and mentor, author of the award-winning book *The Ego's Code*

Preface

How This Book Came to Be

Coworkers, clients, family members, and friends found stories about my life incredible and somewhat unbelievable. The typical response was that I *needed* to write a book. Spiritual healers told me I was *going* to write a book. But I never took any of them seriously. I thought it was just something people said when they didn't know what else to say. In the spring of 2022, the message got undeniably stronger and louder. It was no longer about writing a book someday; it was to happen now! But I had no idea what I was to write about. There are so many events in my life that would make a great story. You will see what I mean by that as I share some of these with you. But how was I to narrow down the topic of my book? What exactly was I to write about?

After weeks of searching my heart and several false starts on a manuscript, a single dream answered my question. In this dream, I was discussing possible titles of the book with my spirit guides. Several options were mentioned, and they all contained the words *K9 spirit guides*. Without opening my eyes or fully waking up, I grabbed my journal that I kept next to my bed just for such occasions and scribbled down these words. Then I abruptly fell back to sleep. I was thankful I did that, because when I awoke, I could only vaguely remember this dream, much less what was said. Now, with a clear title in hand, I knew without a doubt what I was writing about. Or so I thought.

Initially I assumed I was to share some amazing stories about the special dogs in my life. This would be so easy to write! However, as events began to unfold and the veil began to lift, I realized this was not to be an endearing tale about how loving, special, and beautiful my dogs were. There are already many books like that in print. No, my book was to contain specific information channeled directly from angelic K9 guides that I wasn't even aware of yet! And channeling was not something I even knew that I could do! What I didn't realize was that I was about to embark on a journey of profound spiritual development, investigation, and healing just so I could receive the messages from these healing entities and deliver them to you!

Introduction

We're going to explore a reality where dogs serve a much larger purpose for humanity than mere unconditional love. We have always suspected that dogs were magical angels from God, but now I will give you proof! Our canine companions possess specific divine gifts that can facilitate our healing, elevate our awareness, and expand our consciousness as children of God. Man's best friends have their own spirit guides, which is why they appear in our lives just when we need them most. These unique guides connect with humanity through our treasured companions. They serve to assist in our enlightenment and our overall ascension. They share a powerful message of healing that can energetically propel us into the best version of ourselves. These guides lovingly provoke us into action, ultimately assisting us in becoming more connected to God, our true Source.

They refer to themselves as "K9 spirit guides."

Get ready to see your canine companions in a totally different light! Get ready to truly understand why they are with you and what they have to teach you. Even if you do not own a dog or like dogs, there will still be profound meaning for you in these pages. The content in this book may challenge your beliefs, your spirituality, or push you out of your comfort zone, and I hope that it does. Read it with an open mind, enjoy it as a story, embrace it as a magical journey, and accept it as your truth if it so resonates with you. If it does not speak to you, then just enjoy the story.

Please join me on a unique adventure that will warm your heart, tantalize your emotions, and liberate your consciousness like nothing you have ever experienced!

Prologue

I was at a dog show. It was a national championship *schutzhund* trial. I recognized the dog and handler teams that compete at such events, so that's how I knew where I was. I was there as a passive observer taking it all in since I did not yet have my own dog to compete. As the day drew to a close and the sun began to set, I found myself at the edge of the trial field adjacent to a big lake. I gazed out over this incredible body of water, fascinated by its size. It felt like the edge of the world, yet I could just barely visualize the bank on the far side.

On that far bank, a subtle movement caught my eye. I couldn't quite make out what it was. I could only see glimpses of something over there traveling through the trees. It seemed to be moving rapidly as it made its way along the outer edges of the lake, moving in my direction. Then for a moment, my attention wandered back to the trial field behind me. I was surprised to see that it was empty; everyone had gone back to the hotel.

Now, startled that I was all alone, I turned my focus back across the lake. The object of my fascination was now close enough that I could make out an animal of some sort. Seemingly in the blink of an eye, it closed the distance between us in one giant leap. And now I could see that it was a wolf! I wasn't sure whether to be excited or anxious, but I waited in anticipation. The wolf moved effortlessly, rounding the last corner of the lake's edge before it squared itself with my precise location. I was impressed with its diligence and efficiency. I wondered why it was in such a hurry and why it was coming this way. I could see no other wolves, no sign of a pack. This seemed to be a solitary creature on a solo mission.

When he was within five hundred feet, I got a little nervous. I held my position, uncertain of his intention. In the final one hundred feet, he slowed to a trot and quite deliberately looked into my eyes. A sense of relief poured over me as I realized it was a dog, not a wolf! Not just any dog but a Belgian Malinois! Many of the competitors here at this event had this breed. Maybe someone's dog had run off.

He came all the way up to me, wagging his tail as he solicited my affection. He was a friendly fellow. Not sure what to do with him, I took him to search for the competitors. Surely this dog belonged to one of them and they would be grateful that I had recovered it. I went around to all of them and asked, "Is this your dog?" But no one wanted to claim him. I was very puzzled and uncertain what to do next. And then someone suggested, "If no one claims him, he must be yours. He must be your dog." Well, I wasn't expecting to take a dog home today, but he seemed like a pretty cool dog. I wouldn't mind having such a dog.

At that moment, a great sense of honor and gratitude washed over me in a familiar tingling sensation. Instinctively I knew this dog had chosen me somehow; he had made a tremendous journey just to find me. I lovingly embraced him and decided to keep him.

And then I woke up.

Yes, that was a dream. But it wasn't just any dream, I would soon learn. This Belgian Malinois was my next competition dog calling to me from far, far away. He was way across the pond, just like in the dream. He was across the Atlantic Ocean in eastern Germany as it turned out! His owner was selling him, but he did not speak English. He did not have a computer or access to the internet. It would be difficult for me to find him. Nonetheless, I heeded his calling, connected the dots to all the clues I was given, and managed to do just that. Within the month, I imported him to the US. This amazing dog catapulted me into the world of schutzhund competition, quickly progressing to national events. I would soon be competing against all the dog and handler teams that I had noticed in my dream. He opened many doors for me and escorted me through them. The dream had been a message. He was calling me. He was telling me that he was coming and to prepare for our grand adventure together!

SECTION 1
The Basics

CHAPTER 1

What Is a K9 Spirit Guide?

K9 spirit guides are angelic support entities that connect with us through our canine friends. Essentially, our dogs have spirit guides much like each of us has our own spirit guides that helps us along our journey. Only the dogs' spirit guides are not present to support the dog; rather, they are here for us! They watch over us offering their unique wisdom and benevolent healing through man's best friend. They are *not* your dog's individual spirit, and they are *not* what psychics tap into when they tell you what your dog is thinking. These stealth guardians have never spoken out until now. This book serves as their debut, an unveiling of sorts, to enlighten humanity about their presence, their purpose, and their gifts. It is an invitation for humankind to use these gifts to empower expedited healing and enlightenment. These special guides have specific messages for all of us. When they have one for you, they can appear to you physically as an actual dog, which is clearly visible, or they can appear spiritually, invisible to the untrained mind, maybe as a dog from your past. They can visit you energetically even if you don't have a dog or don't like dogs. Their gifts and messages are for all of humanity and are designed to assist in expanding our consciousness and ultimate ascension process.

Each one of these spirit guides is a unique blend of an angel *and* a spirit guide, which makes them incredibly unique! Their images are blended to exemplify this uniqueness. Each guide identifies with a dog breed, representing the angel form, and an animal spirit, representing the spirit guide form. You will notice images of them in each section with their chosen blended identities. This unlikely collaboration makes them incredibly unique and even more powerful since they possess *two* almighty aspects of spirit conjoined! The angel half or dog breed side conveys a particular personality, temperament, and characteristic of that angel. Some of these traits may also reflect a part of ourselves that we need to look at and take action on for necessary healing and integration. The dog breed of the guide doesn't have any relation to the actual physical breed of your dog or the dog they appear with. So your dog may be a basset hound, but the angel associated with that dog may exemplify a basenji if it carries the Oeragon spirit guide. In this case, you might even notice characteristics of the basenji in your dog even though he is a basset hound. These angels, as we have come to understand and expect from angels in general, provide us with valuable direction, protection, unconditional love, compassion, and wisdom. And this is already how most of us perceive our canine companions.

Adding complexity to what we already assume to be true, each guide also resonates with an animal spirit. This is because these wild animals better reflect the actual *energy* of the guides. That is, the energy they wish to share with you whether it be courage, persistence, calmness, focus, etc. It could reflect the energy that resides within you, an energy source that you have yet to access, or one that escapes you and is necessary for you to embody. Spirit guides are generally accepted as advanced and more evolved entities that have agreed to assist in our soul's evolution. Having such robust coverage from specialized divinity, these K9 guides provide us with a unique opportunity for spiritual healing, growth, and expansion. And they have always been with us!

In addition to their specific dog-spirit identity, each guide also has their own spirit name precisely reflecting their essence. They have also provided the specific messages and teachings they wish to share when they appear in our lives. I am told there are over fifty K9 guides in total. This book will introduce you to the first four, the "Core Four" as they wish to be known. These four represent core tools and concepts crucial for steering humanity toward spiritual enlightenment.

We'll explore their messages and teachings and delight in their brilliant energy through stories of my own dogs they have instructed me to share! Through my dogs, you will also learn about my journey to enlightenment because they have been leading me my entire life. Enjoy these stories. Relish in the beauty of the messages. Embrace what speaks to you. If it resonates with you, then there is a definite divine message for you. If it seems way too far-fetched to be possible, then enjoy it as a fantasy. The divine energy in these pages will move you as you are ready and only when you are ready. So every human will have a different response to what they read. Every human will have a different interpretation of the message. And this is the beauty of *divine design*.

All I ask is that you read it with an open mind and allow the divine energy to flow as it sees fit with you. I also thank you for coming along on this very powerful, life-changing journey with me and the K9 spirit guides. Cuddle up with your best friend and enjoy the journey as I escort you through an adventure of expanding consciousness!

CHAPTER 2

Who Am I?

Who am I, and what makes me qualified to write such a book?

That's a great question and one that I certainly asked myself when I was given this task. I am just a girl with a dog-sharing a story. I have always been a physical therapist, an educator, a dog breeder, and a trainer. I now find myself thrust into the role of author and spirit channel. I have always had a unique connection with dogs that I did not fully understand. Add this ethereal connection with my life experience and the result is a lifelong, insatiable quest for enlightenment and understanding. And now, quite unexpectedly, I have been chosen as a translator for the K9 guides' messages—a voice through which they may reach you.

This realm was all new territory for me. I did not meditate, do yoga, go to church, or participate in any spiritual practices whatsoever when I began this journey at the beginning of 2022. Even so, I had always felt a deeply rooted connection to God in an indescribable way. I just knew in my heart and felt in my soul that we were intimately attached. There was no church or religion that could ever exemplify that for me. It was just who I was.

Still, this experience would require me to stretch, trust, learn, heal, and grow far beyond the limits of what I ever thought was possible. And all of this would be integrated at a dramatically rapid rate to boot. There was no time to stop, think, ponder, question, hesitate, or deliberate. Things happened very quickly and all in divine order. I had to abandon all resistance to the unknown and just *trust!* I anchored my faith in God, let go of the reins, and just let him work through me. It was a magical ride to say the least!

And now I have the tools to receive and deliver the important messages these guides have for humanity!

CHAPTER 3

How This Book Is Organized

First and foremost, much of the content for this book was provided directly by the K9 spirit guides themselves as they channeled their messages through me.

Each section of this book outlines one K9 spirit guide defining their unique message and energy. Their sections are further divided into parts consisting of each dog associated with that guide. Depending on the message, the rate of the learning, the degree of difficulty, and the level of support needed, each guide would return as much as necessary to share the learning. They have shown me which of my dogs embodied each guide and the stories about these dogs that serve as an illustration for their message. The stories give a real-life example of how these gifted entities may appear in your own life.

The guides were very specific about the order of their appearance. And they would like me to urge you to follow this order and not jump ahead. As the book advances, the messages and the gifts become more complex and powerful. And this is an example of the ever-so-present divine design that is frequently highlighted in these pages. For me, the further the book progresses, the deeper the teaching and healing reached into my soul. The experiences grow more magical and powerful as the book evolves. See how it works for you.

You might notice that this book does not follow my life in chronological order. That's because the priority is to discuss each guide in their specified order. So for the first guide, Anthea, I will share stories with you during three different visits, or three different dogs, in which she appeared. And the order of these three dogs is specific only to the instructions the guide provided. The messages of the Core Four are illustrated by ten of my own dogs, spanning from early childhood through present day. If you would like to meet the dogs mentioned in this book or see color photographs of any of the images, they are available to you on my webpage under their respective guides (www.k9spiritguides.com).

It is also worth mentioning that the guides heavily emphasize irony as a teaching tool. They have pointed out ironic foreshadowing events along my path, suggesting key significance in them, a bookmark of sorts, to communicate an important message. Encoded within the irony is the realization that there are truly no accidents or coincidences in our lives. I think you will see how they demonstrate this through the beautiful stories they have instructed me to share. I will point out these ironic messages and their meaning as we go along.

The only information that I have added in this book entails the beautiful stories of the adventures I had with my dogs while they were here. I have also included key content about my spiritual adventure and progression to illustrate how one may need to integrate the teachings. All other content, all other information, was channeled directly from these beautiful, powerful, and benevolent K9 spirit guides.

But before we begin, the Core Four wish to share a message with you.

Heather Leigh Strom

A Message from the Core Four

No matter what the circumstances,
they were willing to sacrifice their own comfort,
their own existence, to assist.
Angels without wings, angels without voice, angels in disguise
As a quiet, mute best friend who never judged.
Only quietly provoked my spirit into action, into direction, into myself.
In a direction I could not foretell, although it was written,
and they knew the way to show me, lighting my path along the way.
Secretly knowing what I needed to get there.
My pack of angels had a big job to get me back to my light.
So I needed an army, and so there were many.
They have been undercover until now.
Now they wish to be known, to be seen, to be heard, and to be loved.
We have always loved them, but now we know why.
We have always thought we could hear them, but now we know that we actually did.
We always thought they should have wings, and now we know they do!
We always thought they looked and seemed familiar, but now we know they are!
They are back! They are here for us!
Embrace your guardians, embrace your angels, embrace their message, and learn to hear them!

One thing my mother always used to tell
me when I was a stubborn teenager was
"The things you resist the most are
those that you need the most."
She had no idea how truly correct she was
at the time. But I have always used this as a
gauge for my own learning and acceptance.

SECTION 2

Anthea

(An-thee-uh)

"Anthea"

Anthea is the first of our Core Four spirit guides. Please take a moment to notice the beautiful, blended image of her wild animal and dog identities. These images are specifically detailed to capture the actual energy and personality of each guide. Her eyes are open and kind while ever watchful. Her expression is joyous, radiant, and infectious. The set of her ears is receptive and open. These specific qualities were considered when creating each image to precisely match the embodiment of the individual guide. These details are also part of their message. You will see it change with each guide. So I will point out these features as I introduce each one.

Anthea's spirit animal (her guide form) is the majestic *cheetah*. She has chosen the cheetah because this predator, the fastest of land mammals, is also skilled at conserving energy and practicing patience. She wisely sits thoughtfully watching and waiting until the appropriate time to act. The cheetah also works alone to obtain complete synergy with her purpose without distractions. These are the energies she wishes to share with you. She may be demonstrating your need to slow down in life and practice patience, not diving so quickly into projects that don't serve you. Rather, patiently waiting, observing, and weighing the pros and cons before deciding if a task fully resonates with you. Or perhaps it's time for you to break out on your own and follow your true individual path instead of doing what everyone else does or what others wish you to do. Exuberant energy could be what you need, reflecting your time to "go wild" and enjoy yourself or dive fully into your passion.

Her personality resonates with the *golden retriever* because this breed (her angel form) reeks of constant joy and happiness while donning a permanent smile! This breed is tremendously devoted to its human companion. But she is also affectionate toward and accepting of strangers because she has ample love and wisdom to share. Her energy is abundant and enduring while her heart is kind and patient. Keen and instinctive, the golden retriever adjusts her interactions with each human as appropriate, displaying her inherent understanding. Anthea has so many beautiful qualities to share here. She could be encouraging self-love, enabling you to tap into your own constant joy and happiness! It might be time for you to become more devoted to yourself, your spirituality, your family, or your education. Or maybe it is hard for you to adjust to or accept people who are not like you. These could all be parts of you that she wants to connect you with. Anthea will show you the way by displaying the gifts you require.

This engaging guide lovingly carries your divine joy and exemplifies your self-love because they are so vitally important to us as humans! Many of us have lost touch with these parts of ourselves through abundant hardship, pain, and loss in our lives. It can be so easy to toss the joy aside when buried under the illusion of survival. She is here to help us reconnect and permanently engage with it even at times when we are stretched beyond our perceived limits. The joy you see in her is the radiation of *your* divine joy. Her mission is to attract you to it and realign you with your essential self-love and abundant divine joy!

She appears when we have forgotten ourselves, when we are lost in our fears and buried under self-doubt. These confusing emotions lead us into a spiral of confusion where it is so easy for us to lose our way. Anthea normally shines like a bright beacon in the sky, but when she is blocked or stifled, she shows the shadow of her true nature. When the human self turns judgment inward, it is rearranged into an illusion of betrayal, persecution, self-doubt, and inadequacy. It can even feed into an unconscious fear of failure. These emotions drive all our experiences in life creating a cascade of unpleasantness. Each of them acts as a flare or a tag that alerts her as a summons. She will be drawn to you because you need to hear her message. She may appear as a direct reflection of these emotions to show them to you before being released into her natural self once you integrate her learning! The stories about her will exemplify how this works. She cleverly utilizes irony, illusion, and tags to demonstrate her message.

This beautiful guide has appeared in my life during three very critical periods and through some incredible canine experiences. Each time she was a different breed, but she always carried the same qualities, energy, and message. Anthea is undoubtedly a unique experience. She is easy to spot in all these dogs because her energy is consistently obvious. In each of them, her cheetah spirit zoomed effortlessly at great speed as if she herself were the wind. She was absolutely, ultimately, limitlessly joyful with an exquisite smile on her face! It was this joy that always drew me to her. I was completely fascinated by her. But what I did not realize was that the joy I admired so much in her was actually *my joy* that she was mirroring to me! Anthea carried my joy when I could not, guarded it for safe keeping. What also escaped me was that each time she appeared, I was struggling to love myself. I had fallen victim to unconscious self-hatred that obstructed my ability to fully experience joy. The spirit of Anthea within these dogs served as a guardian of my soul at critical times when I struggled to connect and carry it myself. Utilizing Anthea, receiving her gifts, and ultimately finding your way back to yourself can be one of the most beautiful spiritual transformations of a lifetime!

Each of these beautiful dogs I am about to share with you was not just your average dog. They were very special spiritual beings appearing in my life with specific messages and for specific purposes. I intend for the stories in this section to provide you with better clarity about the gifts of this guide and how she might appear in your life. As you read about them, ponder any similarities with your dog(s) and whether Anthea may be visiting you.

A Message from Anthea

Powerless, angry, terrified, lost,
wanting so badly to be connected to myself.
Chasing but never catching, loving but never loved.
Desperately seeking the freedom to be me, to know myself again,
to find myself, to be the pure joy that I really *am* inside!
The joy that's clawing under my skin, struggling to get out,
to break free, to leak through.
To emerge in its full version.
Each time she came, I was a little closer.
Each time she showed me the next piece, the next step,
the next evolution of myself.
She was unbounding, uncontainable, pure ecstatic joy!

She fiercely guarded her joy, just as she fiercely guarded my mission to find mine.
She drew me in with it, completely engulfing me, my path, my pain, my suffering, my darkness.
She absorbed all of it into her little body.
She sacrificed herself to hold it for me.
I had no idea how much she took in and how much it would consume her.
But she bravely embraced the challenge knowing the outcome, knowing the sacrifice she would have to endure, and never backing down.
Bravely taking it all on, taking it all in, consuming everything she could so that I didn't have to.
Our days were numbered as they always are.
It's only for a brief moment, a wrinkle in time, that I get to enjoy with her. Leaving me lonely and longing for more, my heart broken, my soul fractured.
I always want more of her so she comes back for just another taste before leaving again.
When it's over, I can feel it coming. I know there is nothing that I can do.
Here we go again!
(From Catori, May 3, 2022, thirteen years after her death)

PART 1

Catori

Catori was the best canine and teammate I have ever had the honor to work with. She seemed to embody all my ambitions, fierce competitiveness, as well as my OCD perfectionisms. She was incredibly talented, smart, and competitive. Our unique bond molded a magical experience when we competed together. Tori was one of the great loves of my life. I have had many, but she penetrated my heart and my soul in the deepest way. My time with her was some of the best, most fulfilling years of my life! I am so honored to be able to share her with you!

"Catori"

CHAPTER 4

My Little Indian Puppy

Catori is a Native American name that means "spirit." I had no idea how fitting this name was for her when I picked it before she was even born. I just knew her name was to be Catori, or Tori for short. And as you read our story, you will see how this name is absolutely perfect in every way! It even offers a preview into her true purpose in my life.

Even though I have always been deeply connected with my dogs, I knew Tori was something extremely special. I realized it when she was only six weeks old and I was suddenly intoxicated with her. The thing that fascinated me the most was her robust joy for life. She always ran full speed with pure joy and abandonment. Tori did not walk on a leash; she joyfully floated in circles around me. This was an expression of her core being. This was her true self even from a small puppy, and it never changed or waned. She wore a massive smile on her face that could not be erased! She was simply exuberantly joyful! She was in love with life! I so envied her naive zeal.

Anthea was truly shining through Tori. What is important to understand is *why* Anthea was here at this time in my life. What purpose she served and the message she was desperately trying to share. Those clues were not nearly as visible as the joy that radiated from her. So it will be critical that we dig deeper into these experiences to truly appreciate her gifts.

Tori was a Belgian Malinois from my own breeding program. She was born and raised here in my home. She knew me since the moment she came out of the womb. I warmly embraced her for the first time in 2004, catching her on her way out of the birth canal. As she took her first breath, I affectionately nuzzled her with my gentle lips on that soft spot at the top of the nose between the eyes. It's equivalent to the velvety soft nose of a horse. This is where I have always kissed my darling little puppies. It was like our secret greeting.

Since she was bred, born, and raised by me, I got to watch my little Indian spirit dog emerge piece by piece from this innocent round puppy loaf into the beautiful canine spirit that she eventually became. Her name was no coincidence as I would soon discover, and her free spirit would cradle me in ways I could not have imagined.

Our training began when she was six weeks old in a playful motivational manner. Teaching puppies was one of my favorite things to do because it was so natural for them to be inquisitive and willing. She performed on cue without realizing it and I delighted in watching the light bulb go on as she learned to read my mind. Tori loved it as well because her efforts always ended in a game with her favorite toy. It was a quick and effective way to bond. This puppy was also full of energy as most Malinois are. She never got tired or bored and delightfully worked with me as long as I wanted. But above all else, she had an insatiable desire to run as fast as she could whenever possible. This was the cheetah energy of Anthea shining through her spirit. She sought to share this freedom with me, allowing me to break out of my psychological chains and share in her exuberance to be myself!

When she was born, I was a professional dog trainer with my own company. I helped my clients train their pets. I did in-house obedience programs, group lessons, house calls, hosted training seminars with other professional trainers, and even coached a few aspiring competitive students. I also competed with my own dogs in many sports, such as schutzhund, French ring, and AKC obedience at the local, regional, and national levels. I was very successful with my business and in competition. The success I achieved with my own dogs in competition was attracting my customers. But despite my achievements, I struggled to accept my success and allow the business to grow and prosper. I doubted my full abilities even though my customers had complete faith in me. I struggled to slow it down and keep it under control. I needed to let it grow, but I was terrified to take a chance and risk everything. Instead of feeling joyful about my divine gift, I found myself terrified and reluctant to follow through. The irony of *self-doubt* weighed heavily on this one. And this was one reason that Anthea was here.

Nonetheless, Tori was in experienced, capable hands, and I couldn't have been more thrilled with the quality and potential that she possessed. When she was only ten weeks old, she accompanied me to a French ring trial where her half sister, Apachi, was competing. Tori pranced around the trial grounds quite boldly as if she knew she belonged. She was overtly inquisitive and engaging, yearning to experience everything. And when I took her for a stroll around the property, I accidently discovered she loved to swim! She literally jumped into a pond without hesitation and took a spin around! She was just as happy in the water as she was on land. She turned out to be rather insanely crazy for anything water: lake, pond, ocean, wading pool, or water hose. It was another passion of hers. And this was her retriever brightly shining through.

My lovely girl matured into a very beautiful female with a broad chest and an impressive head. She weighed only sixty pounds, but she looked much bigger. Her neck was thick like her father's, resembling an abbreviated mane. I used to love to take a gentle hold of it and bury my face. Her coat was so soft, velvety thick, and beautiful. I also remember a rather interesting feature about her tail. She had several kinks in the last half of it that made it almost form a subtle *S* shape. I noticed it because it reminded me of another dog I used to have, which you will meet next. Tori used to sit up on her tail end with her front paws crossed in front of her chest when she wanted to be adored. A cheesy, goofy grin on her face said, "Please touch me! Please adore me! Aren't I irresistible?" She was simply the light of my life! I was so proud that she was mine.

She was also endearing, friendly, and affectionate to everyone she met. I swear she did all she could to bring a smile to everyone's face. I found it so *ironic* because this was the polar opposite of my own personality! I didn't really enjoy being around other people. I liked to be alone more than not. I found most people annoying and would rather not hassle with them. Anthea's purpose and message was reaching for this part of me. She was here to show me a side of myself I was avoiding. The reason I was so attracted to Tori and so in love with her energy was because I needed to reconnect with *my* joy and self-love. Only when I did that would I feel the way she did.

Tori was a very focused dog in her training and around the house. Much like the cheetah, she didn't like to waste her energy. She saved all her passion for when she was free to run as fast as she could. Unlike her kennel mates that wasted a lot of nervous energy jumping, barking, and spinning around in their kennel, she sat silent and motionless. When I approached to let her out, she would sit and vibrate, saving all that precious energy for the moment she was released. Once freed, she erupted out of her pen and ran full speed round and round the yard. We had a huge yard, over an acre completely fenced. So there was plenty of space for her to joyfully run as fast as she wanted for as long as she wanted. And this, along with biting, brought her tremendous joy!

My darling Tori also seemed to be able to size people up. When visitors came during training or to the house, she was always very polite and submissive to them despite her powerful presence on the training field. She loved to invite guests to tug with her, which made me a little bit nervous. You see, she had a vicious thrash when she tugged. It was the same thrash that was designed to instantly kill small animals. One fast powerful shake and the prey was dead. It was the veracity of this thrashing that had cracked my neck on multiple occasions while I held the end of her toy. She was so powerful and quick that the force rippled all the way up my arm to the vertebrae in my neck ending with a *pop, pop, pop*.

But to my surprise, when she played with other people, she restrained herself and was very gentle. I was amazed! But if I snuck in to grab her toy while she was playing with the guest, she instantly reverted to her normal powerful thrash. And I swore she winked at me when she did it! At the very least, she seemed to smile. When the guest resumed playing, she settled back into the "gentle" play. I did not teach her this; it was just her. I had also never exposed Tori to children, but she instinctively knew to be very careful around them and gentle. Unlike her normal zippy self, she slowed way down and moved carefully when she was around them. It is a beautiful sight to observe when an animal recognizes the delicateness of a situation without having to be instructed, curtailed, or restrained. She just had a beautiful gift of innate understanding. Little did I know at the time just how much she really did understand.

CHAPTER 5

The Flare of Betrayal

As Tori matured, she became my favorite dog to train. We began her career by preparing for a working sport called French ring (FR). We traveled frequently to seminars with professional trainers in the sport and I even hosted seminars here on my own field to build her foundation. She was to be my first dog bred and trained specifically for this sport. I had cross-trained other dogs into French ring after they were successful in other sports. But Tori would be my first dog dedicated specifically to French ring.

I was delighted about her potential. She possessed all the qualities I had hoped for when I bred her mother. She was easy to train with abundant food and toy motivation. She had an insatiable desire to please no matter how many times I asked her to "do it again."

What is French ring? A French dog sport with obedience, agility, and protection tests specifically designed as a breed suitability test for the Belgian Malinois, but all breeds may compete. The dog must pass the brevet before moving on to level 1 (FR1), level 2 (FR2), and then level 3 (FR3) in consecutive order. Except for the brevet, all levels must be passed twice under two different judges to be awarded that level and be allowed to move up to the next level. The tests get progressively harder and longer as the levels increase.

The decoy is the man in the full-body bite suit who provides the opposition for the biting exercises.

Her speed and stamina were both extreme! She was my fastest dog on retrieves, send-aways, and even when running down the field to bite the man in the suit. She had a strong, full, powerful biting technique, which is critical for this sport. She even liked to wrap her front legs around the decoy while she bit his leg so she could cram as much bite suit in her mouth as possible. This girl could train for hours on end and never get tired or bored. She was full throttle and everything I wanted! To complete this perfect picture, she was also clear-headed and social, adoring all people. Life was good for us, and I was so excited about the future with her!

But when our first opportunity to compete presented itself in May 2006, I almost didn't go. I was reluctant because of a recent conflict with two terrific, talented dog trainers who were integral in our development as a team. I felt *betrayed* by both people for separate reasons. My coach had attempted to manipulate me over a business deal that didn't go his way. I never liked to be controlled and firmly stood my ground. After training with him for three years, valuing his wisdom and guidance, I was no longer willing to trust him. I did what I always do when my trust is violated: I completely broke ties with him. I wrote him out of my life. In my family, we call it "writing people off." My mother calls it "throwing the baby out with the bathwater."

My other friend, my decoy, was more of a brother to me. He used to live with us, and we worked closely together in training my dogs. I had hoped to include him in my dog business, but that opportunity never evolved. Nonetheless, we were together daily, training, traveling, and competing, and supported each other as we both learned the ropes of the sport. I literally could not have been so successful in dog sports without his help. Unfortunately, we had a falling out over the disagreement with my coach. He did not share my feelings about the situation and refused to break ties with him as I expected him to. He couldn't understand why I was so upset. In hindsight, he was totally correct. He was only doing what was best for himself and attempting to stay out of the feud between us. But his lack of commitment to how I felt really stung, and I was devastated by his lack of devotion to me. All my trust in him had disintegrated. So I wrote him off too.

My emotions over this incident seemed to come from down deep inside my soul. My reaction felt extreme over a simple disagreement and misunderstanding. Yet I was prisoner to its force. Could this be "old pain"? Based on what I know now, such deeply rooted dramatic eruptions are triggered to provoke me to take notice and heal something that is fundamentally broken. Although I had no way of understanding it, this event was orchestrated to draw my attention to lifetimes of *betrayal* that were waiting to heal. That's why it elicited such a big reaction in me!

Tags are beacons or flares in your energy field that attract lessons you need to learn to heal your soul. Once the lessons are learned, that part of your soul is complete, and the tag is removed. These learning experiences will no longer be drawn to you.

You see one cannot fully embrace joy in the presence of fear, doubt, or anger. In fact, these emotions attract negative experiences, such as *persecution* and *betrayal*. Anthea was bringing these situations to assist me in healing parts of myself that desperately needed it. These parts of me required attention before I would be able to fully experience joy. Each time I resisted healing these tags, the bigger and louder the experience would be the next time. The *betrayal tag* would have to be healed so that I did not have to experience this again. Tori sat quietly by, whispering answers and solutions that I could not hear. She feverously worked to illustrate the action I needed to take, but I could not see it. Her purpose was to absolve my deep-seated emotion that kept activating the tag and further separated me from my own joy.

When I was finally able to understand it in this light, it made a whole lot more sense. I was able to think of my friend with tremendous gratitude for the gift of healing that he appeared in my life to offer. He had willingly acted as a catalyst to brew the storm that got my attention. In fact, when I was writing this book, I had a dream about him. In this dream, we were both sitting on a star contemplating our life together. We were very close and knew each other well. I could tell we shared a kinship that was deeper than any friendship I have ever experienced in this life. In this dream, he told me that we were "star brothers." I awoke with complete understanding of our journey together and was eternally grateful. It only took me sixteen years to fully understand the meaning and purpose of our turmoil!

Hindsight gives us empowering clarity when we utilize it for understanding. Painful memories can be transmuted into magical gifts of overwhelming gratitude for those who have volunteered their service in our growth. My friend and I have grown apart since our "dog days" together. Our relationship had run its course and served its purpose. I still think of him fondly as our lives have moved in different directions, and I am so thankful for his willingness to help me grow. Even if I was so slow to "get" it!

> Star brothers are those born from the same soul (spiritual) family.

So here I was with my emotional wounds and bruised ego when the opportunity to compete with Tori arose. As a result of my petty conflict with my friends, we had not trained for the six months before the trial. I didn't feel fully prepared for this upcoming event and my anger provided more rationale to support skipping it. But it must have been Tori's silent psychic urging that motivated me out of my self-pity and out the door. I couldn't see any logical reason why I would voluntarily expose myself to those who had just violated my trust. Yet I felt a strong urge to push that ego and all those fears aside, experience terrifying vulnerability, and honor her. I was willing to do it for her, but only for her. I never would have done it just for me.

The memories of that first trial with her are still vivid in my mind. When I watch the video of our performance together, all the emotions I was experiencing come flooding back. I can still palpate the fear, the pain, and the negativity my body held onto that day on the field. Although now I *observe* it as an *outsider* rather than experiencing it as a participant. I was so incredibly grateful that I swallowed my pride and showed up.

Let's see what happened that day …

CHAPTER 6

Tori Emerges

Tori was just fifteen months old when we competed for the first time at the Cup of Americas Championship in Chicago. We were both a bit out of our comfort zone since this was my first French Ring Championship Trial and Tori's maiden competition. I never really know how my dog is going to react the first time on the trial field. Some of them are the same dog they are in training every day with no surprises. Which applies to most of the dogs that I have competed. However, there are those that seem to morph into a completely different animal when you're on that field without a leash or collar and no means of reinforcement in front of the judge. I had no idea which dog Tori would be, but I was about to find out.

We would be competing against dogs from all over the Americas. Tori was going for her brevet, an entry level test which is a temperament test to determine if the dog is suitable for the sport. It includes basic obedience, a food refusal, and two biting exercises with a decoy. As in all the levels, these exercises are to be completed on an open field and without a collar or leash. I knew Tori was reliable in a familiar environment, but I had not proofed her in new environments, with strange decoys, or without equipment. The combination of freedom and stimulation from the crowd and the decoy can sometimes provoke the dogs into disobedience or belligerence. I was about to discover how solid her nerves were and how reliable my training was!

It was a cold day as I checked in with the judge, Dominique Piton, from France. I could tell that Tori was nervous and excited based on her rapid panting and twitchy glances. I could feel her bottled-up energy radiating as she pranced next to me. She had no idea what was going on. This was all new to her and her adrenaline was building up like a bottle rocket ready to explode. If she could keep all this energy controlled, it would translate into a beautiful performance. But if the nerves got the best of her and fogged up her brain, it could be a disastrous event for both of us.

My ex-coach was assigned to be my deputy judge for the event. I would be accompanied by him as well as evaluated by him as he assisted Dominique throughout our test. It took a great deal of courage and vulnerability just to tolerate being near him, speaking to him, and relying on him. Luckily, he treated me impartially and professionally and I graciously welcomed it even though it was a bit less cordial than our usual interaction. I even found his presence a bit comforting. He knew me and my dog well because he had coached us from the beginning. He knew our strengths and our weaknesses. If he was hoping for anything less than our best, he certainly did not show it. I was equally professional to him but not nearly as "Southern" friendly as I usually am. I just could not bring myself to forgive and trust that easily yet. But it was not an unpleasant interaction, and I was thankful.

Our test began with a couple of heeling exercises. The French ring heeling test is the easiest heeling test of all the sports I have competed in, so we received full points. Next, she had to refuse food being thrown at her while in a down stay and with me out of sight. She certainly passed this test and refused to even look at the hot dog as it whirled by her face. But I was beginning to feel my nerves ramping up as adrenaline surged into my body. The obedience portion was now over, and we were transitioning into the protection portion of the test. The hardest part would be next as I noticed the decoy enter the field. And Tori saw him too!

There are two biting exercises at this entry level: a "defense of handler" and an exercise referred to as the "face attack." Don't worry; no one is bitten in the face! It just means that the dog runs downfield head-on at the decoy as he presents a frontal invitation. Both exercises are always favorites of the dogs and are a little bit tricky to execute correctly. Let me explain them so you understand the complexity of the training, the mindset of the dog, and the uniqueness of the judging and scoring in this sport.

First, in the "defense of handler," exercise the dog must heel with the handler (on the left side in my case) as the team approaches the decoy and the handler shakes his hand. This is tough for many dogs because all they see coming at them is a big bite toy. They must restrain themselves, remain under control, and keep clear heads as the decoy is only inches from them and sometimes teasing them. Remember the dogs have no collar or leash on at any point in this test. It is so tempting for them to just take a bite! These dogs love to bite the suit. And most of them, Tori included, are bred specifically for biting this type of material. I'm quite certain it is what they dream about when they sleep!

"Backward Heeling"

I taught Tori that as I greet the decoy by saying hello, she is to automatically move from heel position to in between my legs. In this position, her head is sticking out the front of my crotch as I speak with the decoy. This is what we refer to as a guarding position. Once the decoy and the handler shake hands, I say goodbye and the decoy walks in the opposite direction of the dog and handler team. When Tori hears me say goodbye, I taught her to automatically swing from in between my legs to the outside of my right leg facing behind me and watching the decoy. That's right; she moves from her initial heeling position on my left side to in between my legs, and then finally to my right side all *automatically* at specific points during the exercise. And she executed this flawlessly! As I began to walk forward, Tori is to heel in this new position, facing behind me and walking backward! The decoy begins to follow the team from behind at a distance but gaining.

She maintains this backward heeling as she watches the decoy behind us begin to approach. She is only allowed to watch him and must not engage or bite him no matter how close he gets until he strikes me on the shoulder with his hand. This is a tremendous tease for the dogs. Since she's not looking at me, she's keeping her eye on the decoy; she has to lean into me as I move forward so she can maintain contact with my right leg. If she should move away from me, she would be penalized. If she should bite the decoy before he strikes me, she is penalized.

Part of the training is to teach the dogs the rules. This means that the dogs are taught every possible scenario that they may see within a competition so that they always know the answer to any situation if they are thinking clearly. And this is one characteristic of this sport that makes it so much more difficult than other sports. The dogs must be very well trained and educated yet still have tremendous desire to perform and fight within the rules.

Another thing that sets this sport apart from other dog sports is that the decoy's job is to find weaknesses in the dog's training and to exploit those weaknesses during the competition. This will cost the dog points or in some cases cause it to fail the test. In other biting dog sports, the decoys are to follow a set script so that all the dogs are tested the same. In French ring, that is not true, which makes it a more rigorous test of the dog's nerves, innate character, obedience, and training.

Tori performed this exercise beautifully and waited to bite as she was supposed to, even though I could tell she was conflicted with her own desires. She outed (let go) on command immediately and returned to me on my whistle recall. We got full points for this exercise, and I was relieved. One down and just one more to go. I must have been holding my breath because my mouth was totally dry from the freely flowing adrenaline!

> The line of departure is a chalk line on the grass. The handler must leave their dog in a stay position behind this line and step behind the dog. The dog is not to cross this line and go after the decoy until commanded to do so by the handler. The decoy will attempt to tease the dog and get her to be disobedient and leave the line before commanded. So the dog must be well trained and compliant.

Next was the "face attack." So we took our position at the line of departure. I instructed Tori to *coucher* (French for "lie down") and took my position behind her. She was already trembling with anticipation. I hoped that she would hold her position amid such temptation. The dog's ability to override instinct here requires a lot of practice and discipline. It also helps to have a strong bond between the dog and handler, which creates a sense of obligation. As Tori matured and her training progressed, she developed her own strategy for maintaining control at the line of departure. I noticed that she very deliberately learned to kept one ear pointing forward on the decoy and one ear flipped back on me. This meant her focus was equally divided between me and the object of her desire (the decoy). I could see it in all her videos. It was quite ingenious! This became her tell that she was tuned in, she knew her job, and she was 100 percent committed to the rules. On this day, however, she had not developed that keen sense yet so it was still uncertain whether she would honor my instructions.

But there she was, lying in front of me, trembling with excitement as the decoy shook his clatter stick at her then ran farther away to the sixty-meter line. This was her utmost ecstasy; she was so ready to go bite him that she was drooling! I held my breath as the milliseconds ticked by. I had to wait for the judge to signal me to send her. *Hold on, girl,* I thought. *Just stay with me.* I tried to energetically hold her in place with my mind. Then I heard the judge's horn and told her to go and bite. *Good girl!* I thought. But I was still holding my breath because the hardest part was yet to come.

With her being so far away once she engaged the decoy, it would prove to be a challenge to maintain control of her. I had to remain behind the line of departure, and I was now trembling in anticipation as I stood my post. With the decoy pretending to fight with her, tapping her with his clatter stick and pretending to try to get away, it amped up her desire to fight and her conviction to holding on. These dogs enjoy the fight even more than the biting itself. So anything that revs up this fighting instinct also makes it harder to control them. With Tori being so young and inexperienced, I was not sure if she would be able to fight those desires when it came time to relinquish control.

After agonizing seconds of Tori joyously enjoying this game with the decoy, the judge finally signaled for me to recall her. I blew my whistle as loudly as I could with my dry mouth, her signal to let go and come back to me. She did let go and thought about coming back. Then I saw a familiar look on her face. The one of pure ecstasy. This was the moment I had feared! In just milliseconds, she decided she liked the fighting better and took another bite of the decoy! I quickly blew my whistle again and she let go. For a second, she hesitated again. I could feel the wheels turning in her head and see her weighing her options! But before she could make the wrong choice again, I blew my whistle as loudly and hard as I could with the Sahara Desert in my mouth!

Oh no, you don't! I thought. I wasn't really sure what to do in this situation, but my instincts took over. And this time, she did end up returning to me on her third recall.

It was because of my quick thinking that we did not fail this exercise. Had she not returned to me within the allotted thirty seconds, we would not have even passed our test, much less the exercise. My instincts saved us. And I was so very proud of my little Indian dog! She had come through for us even after I had *betrayed* myself. We managed to earn a first place in her maiden trial at the Cup of Americas. I got a cute picture of Tori and me on the podium and a double cheek kiss from Dominique. I was pretty happy with our performance considering we were not fully prepared. But I also knew we had a lot more work to do. And my commitment to train and work toward the next level was reinstated.

This experience required me to step out of my comfort zone, out of my self-pity, stretch into a hidden part of me and trust. Everything came out OK. Nothing bad happened, and I did not get hurt. This did not change my feelings about the people who betrayed me. But then again, I was not willing for it to. I was not yet willing to be vulnerable enough for that growth to happen. But it would, and I would see this message again!

CHAPTER 7

The Flare of Persecution

Despite our success at our first trial together, I was not feeling that elated or joyous. The world of dog sports can be very cruel. Compliments are often tongue in cheek and when your back is turned the catty, snarky, derogatory comments begin to fly. There is often very little sincere admiration shared between competitors in dog sports. The more successful you are, the more people don't like you. I was accustomed to the cycling world where my victory alone proved my merit. If I crossed the finish line before my competitor, I was the obvious winner and no one could dispute that. But in dog sports, rather than acknowledging my skills that brought me success, fellow competitors or spectators would intentionally set out to discredit my character and abilities. I only knew about the backstabbing because of the videographers who were recording my performance on the sidelines. My videos recorded the conversations these naysayers were having about me while I was on the field. I was also cyber attacked in internet chat groups in the same manner and for the same reasons. This was heartbreaking to me, and I did not understand it. Why weren't people complimenting me on my success and acknowledging all my hard work? The more I felt attacked, the more I retreated into myself. It didn't feel safe to be me, so I unconsciously decided that I would hide from the world!

It was unfortunate because I actually worked diligently to achieve my success. My dedication far exceeded the necessary limits for my goal. I was extremely fastidious with my commitment, perfecting my technique, my training, my handling, and even in my selection of dogs. I had the will, the desire, and the ability to travel to gain the knowledge and coaching that I needed to achieve my success. The attempts to diminish my worthiness were only because they themselves were lacking in their own dedication and commitment. Consciously I knew and understood this. Subconsciously their criticism had a profound negative effect on my confidence no matter how I tried to rationally override it. That's because I was unaware of the *persecution* tag that beckoned these experiences.

This dynamic plagued me my entire career as a professional handler and competitor. The more success I achieved, the more I was ridiculed or discredited. It would be many decades and only after I began working with the K9 guides that I understood why this happened. It had nothing to do with how mean people were. And I know that's the knee-jerk reaction—to blame the persecutor. But *ironically* it was just another example of my subconscious illusion at work. My own deeply buried belief that I was not *worthy* was attracting the *persecution*. It was another opportunity, just like my previous example, for me to discover what needed to be healed. This was Anthea's work, drawing my attention to another part of me that needed to be completed. Highlighting this experience as another example of why my own joy was blocked. And why others were not reflecting joy at me. I was seeing my own angry negativity in the face of my persecutors triggered by my own unconscious beliefs. She was showing me this tag that needed to be recovered.

I would also like to mention here that if this type of scenario does not have the same deep-seated effect on you as it did on me, then you do not have an issue. If you can just laugh off the ridicule and not be affected by it, if you don't resent those who sling it at you, then there is no message for you. If you don't continue to stew over the event many days or months later, then there is no message for you. But only if you have absolutely zero reaction to it emotionally. If that is you, then there is no learning in this experience for you. It is the other person's experience. Your response is your barometer.

CHAPTER 8

We Find Our Stride

That first trial opened doors for our future. Despite my unwillingness to grow spiritually, I did manage to make new friends who would see us through our journey in the sport. Tori and I were invited to train with a club in Michigan, just four hours north of us. These folks provided the camaraderie, motivation, and support we needed to push us all the way through the levels in ring sport. For the next two years, we enjoyed frequent weekends in Michigan making some terrific memories with our clubmates. This reliable group was no accident and was critical for our journey.

And fortunately, it would also provide another chance for me to heal my broken friendship because my star brother would also join us. With an obvious second chance, I took full advantage of the opportunity. My friend and I were able to resume a great friendship, which did bring me joy. Anthea had succeeded in one of her missions! *Ironically*, this repaired friendship was with one of Tori's favorite people and her favorite decoy! I guess she did not want this one to get away!

The next couple years buzzed by quickly with abundant travel and adventure as we spent much of it away from home. Our training progressed as we meticulously worked through the levels of difficulty. Our lengthy practice sessions also helped solidify our bond as a team. Tori was such a willing and enthusiastic teammate that she made the long hours of travel and training so worth it. I enjoyed every minute with her.

Early in her career, Tori was already competing on world-class decoys, and these guys were like World Cup soccer players! They were fast! They excelled in physical agility and lightning-fast reflexes to fully test the dogs' courage and dedication. Just when I thought we had shown her all the possible techniques she might see, Tori would fall victim to a new one at the next trial. She was an excellent tactician and devoted to the rules I taught her, but she did not like to miss or mess up! If the decoy fooled her, she would attempt revenge and cost us points. Sassy girl she was, I admired her spirit. So I did my best to make sure she thoroughly knew what to expect. This required diligent hours of practice teaching her every possible scenario. I guess you could say that mutual passion for perfection dwelled in us both!

This was a magical, fun time for us. After earning her brevet, she was free to progress through the higher levels from FR 1 to FR 3. All the exercises at these levels are randomly drawn for order just before beginning the test. So it is not possible to pattern train your dog into knowing what is coming. You are also not permitted to coach your dog or rev her up in any way. The deputy judge walks next to you during your test to make sure you are complying with the rules.

I built in discreet signals to tell Tori what was coming next. A flick of my wrist meant we were doing a send-away instead of a heeling exercise and she would instantly stop looking at me and focus her attention one hundred meters ahead. If I left her in a sit position at the line of departure instead of a down, this signaled she would be jumping back into heel position for the defense of handler exercise instead of bolting down the field after the decoy. Our communication was finely tuned. She was in my head, and I was in hers. The level 3 test can take one hour to complete, requiring tremendous endurance and focus especially in the heat of the summer. Of all the dog sports that I have competed in, this one was the most challenging for the dogs and the most difficult to prepare for. Because of this, it was always my favorite sport to play in. I loved the challenge and so did Tori!

We managed to achieve the highest level, French ring 3, without failing any of her trials and with all first places! This is not an easy feat as most dogs struggled just to pass. Each time we competed, we got better and better and our scores got higher and higher, which is unusual. Most dogs get trial smart and realize they can disobey without consequence. So you will commonly see the scores decline with each competition. Fortunately, this was not an issue with my beloved Tori. The more that she understood what I expected of her, the more precise she was with her execution. I was always proud to walk next to her on the trial field. I knew I had a reliable teammate that would not let me down. Watching other handlers train and compete with their dogs showed me that our relationship was sacred and not to be taken for granted.

CHAPTER 9

Flare of Inadequacy

As much as I loved the thrill of competition with Catori, the grueling pace was exhausting. By the end of 2007, all the hard work, time, and travel we had invested in competing and completing her titles had taken its toll on us both. But my clubmates were urging me to enter Tori in the Cup of Americas again in Chicago. This time we would compete at the highest level (ring 3) against teams from around the world for the championship title. I knew in my heart that she was a true competitor and would do well. I knew that we were completely prepared for such a test. But emotionally the pressure under the expectation for an incredible performance at such an important event was too great for me. And subconsciously I was succumbing to those familiar insecurities. An invisible undercurrent of *inadequacy* was back to play. Anthea presented these tags again to see if I was ready. But it was a hard pass for me on this one.

So instead of entering her and giving her a chance to prove what a great dog and competitor she was, I avoided it. I know my clubmates were very disappointed. Our success was in large part due to their commitment to our training. And I know they were looking forward to displaying our work at such a prestigious event. But I just could not do it, so I feel like I let them and Tori down. I do regret that I let my fear stop me this time. Had I known then that we would never have another chance later, I might have swallowed my exhaustion and insecurity and done it anyway.

One thing I've noticed about myself is that the more I was expected to perform or produce an outcome, the harder it was for me to make it happen. It was like the pressure caused me to freeze for fear of failing. This also plagued me in my cycling days. I preferred to come from behind and succeed when no one expected me to. I rather enjoy the underdog persona. That way there was no external pressure, only my own internal expectations. It was much safer to not have to live up to other people's expectations. This was also something that Tori would reflect back to me. The more pressure I put on her to get her exercises perfect, the more stifled she became. Her true joy could not shine if I overpowered it with fear-based control techniques. The more driven I was to be perfect, the more her light blew out. This innate desire to succeed or to obtain perfection was activated by my *fear of failure*, a close cousin to inadequacy. My negativity caused Tori to become rigid and nervous, afraid to move. Her brain froze and she couldn't figure out what I wanted her to do. I could see *her* fear of failing, of getting it wrong, and being corrected. This is the *shadow* of Anthea's true being. This reflected how I was showing up in the world at that moment. If I changed my approach, my energy, or my intention, she changed. She was the perfect reflection of me and would change her expression as soon as I changed mine! It was remarkable, except I could not see it fully; I only saw the tip of this dynamic at the time. The irony of *inadequacy* is quite insightful, and we will go into greater discussion about it at the end of her story.

Even so, Tori kept providing these opportunities in hopes that I would finally hear her messages, understand the purpose of the lesson, and find my way to her immediate solution. Unfortunately, until the day that I could recover my missing pieces, this tag would continue to obstruct the view of my own joy. It continuously caused me to avoid any opportunity that invited me to prove my worth such as with the Cup of Americas. Sadly, I would not find the solution until I began to write this book and long after Tori's visit.

CHAPTER 10

A Welcome Change of Pace

I don't know about Tori, but I was a bit burned out after spending almost two years on the road. The sport was difficult and required arduous dedication. It was time for a break. We set out to enjoy a couple months of rest. I spent some time training and competing another dog in a different sport that required less effort on my part. And Tori got to just be a dog.

One of her favorite things to do was to follow me around the yard. When I mowed on the tractor, she would grab a Kong toy and prance along behind me. Every turn or circle I made, she was right there, step for step, toy in mouth, tail wagging, and a smile on her face. I had to be careful if I needed to back up, because she was always right behind me. It was precious. None of the other dogs did this. Just her. We played fetch in the yard, or I took her to a nearby lake and we fetched in the water to her heart's content. All these things brought her tremendous joy. The time we got to spend together brought me tremendous joy.

During our rest break, I took Tori in for an annual health check. She had a couple of sebaceous cysts on her neck that I wanted removed. Because of their location, they became irritated when we trained. I also noticed that Tori had a sore toe that was quite painful if she accidentally got stepped on. There seemed to be a tiny bump, some sort of hardening on this toe. It was probably nothing, but it wouldn't hurt to have it checked out. So while she was sedated for the cyst removal, I also had the vet examine this toe more closely.

The cyst extraction was quite extensive because these types of cysts tend to grow very deeply under the skin. She had a couple of pretty big holes in her neck from the extraction and would need to wear an Elizabethan collar for a while to keep her from scratching them open. The preliminary testing on her toe showed a possible tumor growth. So the vet biopsied it and sent the sample off to the laboratory. A couple of weeks later none of the tests clearly identified what type of tumor this might be and only recommended further testing. It did not seem like a huge priority since she was not complaining of pain unless she got stepped on. So I tabled any further action for a later date if needed. I did not want to put her through more stress of painful testing if it really wasn't necessary.

But shortly after the biopsy, I did notice that Tori just didn't seem to have her normal fire or intensity that she usually did. She was beginning to sleep a little bit more and she wasn't as obsessed about playing. She seemed to be content with napping for the first time in her life. I also remember that if one of the other dogs bumped into her, she would viciously attack them. She had never liked other females, but this new aggression was nondiscriminatory. I vaguely noticed these little details, not really understanding their significance at the time. I brushed these things aside thinking they were probably irrelevant. I just figured I was overthinking things as usual.

At the end of 2007, I had pretty much closed the chapter on my French ring days. The training and traveling were just too demanding. I had accomplished everything I wanted with Tori in this sport. But she and I were not finished competing just yet. We had to find something else to do, something to sink our teeth into and obsess over. It's hilarious to realize, but she was just as obsessed about competing as I was. She was a technician once she knew her exercises, once she knew what was expected. How could I stop competing with such a master? She was now four years old so we turned our attention to something a little bit tamer and less time consuming. AKC (American Kennel Club) obedience would be our next focus.

I have competed in AKC obedience many times in the past, with a few of my dogs and different breeds. It was like putting on an old pair of jeans. I was impressed that the knowledge and technique in this sport had changed since I last competed. The AKC world was now on the forefront of training theories and strategies whereas it used to lag quite severely behind the biting sports. The AKC world had finally embraced techniques capitalizing on the dogs' true drive systems or natural instincts. I used to be shunned when I showed up to train with my dogs because I rewarded them with a tug on a bite toy. These trainers used to erroneously believe that a dog who bit a toy was aggressive and dangerous. I was thrilled to learn that the obedience world had changed its tune. This was going to be a lot more fun, and I would no longer be outcast just for the reward system that I chose!

We just had to adjust our thinking slightly because the competition space was so much smaller, more crowded, and more distracting than what we were used to on an outdoor field. And instead of one dog competing at a time, in AKC there are multiple rings, multiple dog and handler teams, and multiple judges calling instructions all simultaneously often in an indoor space. So it was considerably more hectic than what we were accustomed to. I wasn't sure how Tori was going to react to the busy, noisy, and chaotic environment. But she really surprised me and made the transition quite easily. She didn't seem to be bothered by any of this at all. I even marveled at how she would sleep in her crate quietly when we weren't working despite all the frenzied activity around her. I thought maybe she was settling into her age a little bit and calming down. (*Here it comes.*) I was very proud of her for taking this all in stride, nonetheless.

> The French ring field size is 100 feet x 230 feet whereas the AKC ring size is 40 feet x 50 feet.

There were some distinct differences in the exercises for us. The basic level was pretty easy and consisted of individual heeling exercises, a stand-stay for examination by the judge, and a recall (come when called).

The class finished up in group exercises with a one minute sit-stay and a three minute down-stay with the handler in sight on the other side of the small ring. It was pretty easy stuff for us. As with her previous sport, Tori quickly assimilated knowledge and understanding with each trial and managed to get better and better. Her scores just kept improving as we progressed. I do believe she was undefeated in all three of her companion dog legs (three trials). We ended up having a lot of fun with

---

In American Kennel Club (AKC) obedience you must have three qualifying scores under three different judges to achieve a title and before moving on to the next level. This sport is considerably more difficult than others since you may not pass your trial if you do not pass all the exercises in the test. Whereas other sports allow you to pass your level even if you don't pass all exercises.

---

it with significantly little stress, training, and travel than we were used to. These competitions were a lot more relaxing and enjoyable for us. It was an opportunity to take things a little less serious and be a little more laid-back without sacrificing too much of our competitive edge. It was a welcome change of pace.

We also tested our skills in a new class called rally obedience, which is a lot less formal than the traditional obedience classes. In rally you can talk to your dog throughout the exercises to encourage and reassure them, so it's just more fun for everybody. I thought this would be a terrific switch for Tori after all the years of formal competition and pressure to perform. She seemed to have a good time with my more relaxed demeanor, and she managed to win all three of her classes for her rally novice title. In a pretty quick period of time, we managed to add two new titles to her name, giving her "FR3, CD, RN" after her name.

Since Tori had demonstrated her keen workability, drive, and clearheadedness on the competition field and she had passed all her health and joint checks, I decided it was time for her to be a mom. In 2008, she gave birth to her one and only litter of puppies. She was an incredible momma. She gave me eight bundles of joy with their own unique personalities. She was a natural mother and doted over her babies. It was so rewarding to see her relaxed and enjoying life as God intended her to. I thoroughly enjoyed watching her raise her babies, seeing them grow, develop, and show little pieces of her.

The hard part for me was choosing which one I wanted to keep. I liked so many of the puppies and could see parts of Tori in each one of them. But none of them *were* her. Each of these puppies would go to sport or competition homes with very important jobs to do. I had big plans for my puppy as well. But as the time drew near for me to make the selections, I really struggled with parting with any of them. For some reason with this litter, I was reluctant to let them go, unlike any of my past litters. I did individual training sessions and temperament testing with these babies so I could get a better feel for their personality. This was a process that I had always used with my litters. Typically, I found both positive and negative traits present in all puppies. It is rare to find a perfectly balanced puppy containing all the traits I seek. So it is a matter of weighing the pros and cons in each individual specimen when choosing puppies.

Despite all the testing I did searching for objective evidence to support my process, I relied more heavily on my instincts for matching these little puppy souls with the customers who had reserved them. Over the years, I was able to develop my keen abilities for matchmaking when it came to placing dogs. I seemed to have a knack for placing the right puppy with the right buyer. Or sometimes the appropriate buyer would appear as soon as I had an adult dog available to sell. I can't really explain how all that worked. I just learned to trust the process and to trust my intuition. I sensed this might be a gift I possessed, so I began to rely on it more and more. I quietly listened for that voice in my head to tell me each puppy's future story. I would later learn this was an early expression of my innate clairsentience (a form of psychic ability) that I so frequently relied on.

In the end, I decided to keep a somewhat petite female, Janaki. She would later play an extremely important role in my life so you will eventually meet her. I was going to also keep a male, but he had a more urgent position in a different home so I released him to complete his duties. I also later reclaimed another female from this litter after it was obvious that I was supposed to have kept her. She kept calling to me from her new home, and when the opportunity presented itself, I requested her back. I was so thankful that I followed through on those instincts too! You will hear from her in future books because her message is very important as well. So after all the other puppies were gone, Janaki was left to become the newest member of our family. I called her Nikki for short. Her story is in section 4.

CHAPTER 11

A Surge of Inadequacy

Even though our life together was full of adventure, joy, and delight, in the spring of 2009 I began to have a nagging feeling that something was about to happen, that something was about to change. It brought me sadness and a bit of trepidation. I didn't know what any of it meant. I could feel an end, a closure approaching. Maybe I was just getting burned out after such an intense decade of training, traveling, and competing with the dogs. I felt like I wasn't enjoying it as much anymore. My passion for training and competing was dwindling. Maybe it was time to retire. This was only a vague sense, almost an echo, that was hard to hear. So I wasn't sure how serious I should take it. And instead of focusing on it, I decided to ignore it. Maybe I was wrong.

Around this time, I also closed my dog training business and resumed my career as a physical therapist. The closure I felt around the dogs had also crept into my dog training company. My passion dwindled and so did my customers! More irony here as my lack of self-worth was being reflected by the dwindling business. I felt like I needed a change. I reverted to the safety of my physical therapy license, and I took a part-time job at a rehab facility. I would still have enough free time to continue to train and travel if I wanted so it seemed to make sense. But this career change presented its own challenges. I had spent the last five years working alone as a dog trainer and now suddenly found myself thrust back into a very interactive and hectic environment. Being completely out of my element gave my insecure undertones a huge leg up! I had been at the top of my profession as a dog trainer and competitor and now I was back at the bottom as an employee. My therapy skills were a little rusty, and it was overwhelming to keep my head above water in a very fast-paced setting.

I felt very uncomfortable, in over my head, and vulnerable to being judged by my peers. I was slightly terrified even. I got through my day as quickly as I could and went back home. I did not enjoy what I was doing, where I was working, and felt totally out of place. They say you will find all your answers amid discomfort, that such discomfort provides a tremendous growth opportunity. Well, I had half the equation but didn't see any answers. My discomfort seemed to escalate uncontrollably. The unaddressed tag of *inadequacy* had attracted paranoia in spades! Anytime someone needed to discuss a patient with me, I thought for sure that I was getting in trouble for something, anything. I felt like I was always looking over my shoulder. The stress markers were all there: elevated heart rate, sweating, dry mouth, and lack of appetite during my lunch break. I avoided working directly with other therapists because I was so afraid my insecurities would show through. Why was this so hard? I used to be so good at it. I envied Tori's natural abilities to readily accept her work and do it so happily. Why couldn't I do that? (Because my self was chained and my joy was blocked!)

Anthea was giving me yet another run at my tag of inadequacy, and it was a much larger dose this time! I had not acted on my previous opportunities to address it, so now the message and emotions were much stronger. The signals were easier to see but harder to ignore. I found these insecurities to be incredibly overwhelming and I feared they would cost me my job. So yup, you probably guessed it. The *fear of failure* tag jumped on the band wagon. Misery loves company, as they say. So instead of getting to the bottom of it and healing what was broken, I did what everyone else does. I drowned my emotions with pharmaceuticals. I made it all go away with antidepressants and sleeping pills. What a marvelous invention!

But Anthea was desperately trying to get my attention. She was giving me one last chance before she had to go. One last chance to see her message and allow her to help me with it. But I could not see it, especially in my medicated fog. How could I pull a trigger when I could not find it? So I squandered yet another opportunity to heal and reclaim my power. When would I learn?

CHAPTER 12

A Bunch of Rocks

One evening in May 2009, I came home from work, fed the dogs, and noticed that Tori refused to eat her food. This was not normal for her. She usually ate her food as fast as she could. So for her to not want to eat meant that there was something very wrong. I instantly became alarmed and asked her to jump up on the bed so I could take a closer look at her. When she tried to jump up, she yelped out in pain and my alarm heightened. This was not a good sign. I quickly retrieved my dog thermometer and discovered she had a low-grade fever. Now I was really concerned. I felt a clenching in my gut as my head raced with all the unfavorable possibilities of what might be wrong.

    I am not one to rush my dogs to the vet. But this felt serious. So I loaded Tori up in the back seat of my Ford Escape and headed to the closest emergency hospital. The pit in my stomach would just not go away and I had a *terrible* feeling that something very big was wrong! In the car, I was overcome with emotion. Tears streamed down my face, and I began pleading with Tori as I drove. I was hysterical with grief for whatever reason. I don't know how I drove that car without wrecking it. Tori lay there looking at me as I spoke to her. I could see her in the rearview mirror. I pleaded with her to please not let this be something long and dragged out. My heart was ripping in two now, and I just knew I could not endure seeing her in pain for any length of time. I am a strong woman, but there are some things that I can't bear. I have never been able to tolerate watching any of my dogs suffer.

I remember thinking how odd it was that I had immediately jumped to some horrific outcome. In my mind, there was great clarity that something significant was about to happen. But when we arrived at the ER, Tori jumped out of the car and seemed to be OK. My heart skipped a beat. Was it my imagination or did she look better now? She greeted the vet with a tail wag and a smile, and she seemed totally normal! I told the doctor what had happened. He checked her out and took an x-ray. Her temperature was now normal. The vet concluded that there was nothing imminently wrong with her. I was shocked! Here I was prepared for the worst.

However, he did say something that didn't make any sense. Her x-ray showed a "bunch of rocks" in her stomach like she had eaten some gravel. My dogs don't eat rocks and their kennels are paved. She wouldn't have had any access to gravel. So I thought that was very strange. But he assured me she was "fine" and told me to take her home. I was relieved to be wrong and that I still had my beautiful Tori! I took her home in a much better state of mind than when we left. She happily ate her food and was back to her typical cheery self.

I followed up with my regular vet and had him run an extensive battery of blood tests to see if there was something that had been missed. Could it be Lyme disease? Cancer? I still couldn't shut out that little voice in my head. But nothing showed up. For the next few months, she acted totally normal. *Can you feel it?*

CHAPTER 13

I Just Knew

We busied ourselves over the next few months with training for Tori's next AKC title. Nikki was learning the basic puppy stuff and Tori had moved up to the Companion Dog Excellent (CDX) level. I expected her to breeze right through these competitions much like she had the first three. But we hit a very unexpected speed bump.

In September 2009, Tori, Nikki, and I attended a trial in Louisville, Kentucky. Tori was going to be attempting her first two legs of her CDX, and Nikki was attempting her maiden competition in rally novice. Tori's open class was pretty straightforward. All the exercises were off leash and included two retrieves and two jumping tests. The group stays were with the handler out of the room. All of this was easy stuff for Tori, and I didn't anticipate any problems. She had performed beautifully in all the fun matches we entered to prepare.

The French ring high jump is 47 inches whereas
the AKC high jump is 28 inches.
The French ring broad jump is 118 inches whereas
the AKC broad jump is 56 inches.

But things got strange. Tori's individual exercises were flawless and beautiful! She was sitting in first place as we prepared to complete the group stay exercises. This was another exercise that Tori was very familiar with from French ring and had never messed up. She was to remain in a sitting position for three minutes while I was out of sight and then again in the down position for five minutes. During both days (the trail was Saturday and Sunday), Tori lay down on the sit! This instantly failed us in the class! I was so disappointed and so perplexed. This was an exercise she's always been reliable on and she's never had a problem with. Why was it suddenly an issue? I just couldn't figure it out.

Of course, I was also disappointed because she had never failed a class at an AKC show. But even more so I was concerned about my dog. This just was not like her. I thought maybe we needed more training, so I planned to bring her home and work on it. Unfortunately, Tori would never get to redeem herself as this would be our final competition together. It would also be the one and only time that her daughter, Nikki, would ever compete. And she did so well by winning her first competition ever! She was such a superstar just like her mom!

After several weeks of struggling with Tori's training, I finally decided to give her a break. Nothing seemed to be working, and the more frustrated I got, the more inhibited she got. So I decided to just give it a rest and let her be a dog for a while. But a couple of months later, as I came home from work, I suddenly noticed that her chest wall was protruded on one side. Once again, I got this awful feeling in the pit of my stomach. My mouth dropped open, I stopped breathing, and I dropped to my knees to get a better look at what I thought I saw. My head was spinning, my heart was racing, and none of my thoughts made any sense. But it was immediately apparent that I wasn't imagining things. The left side of her chest was quite a bit larger than the right side! Not by a little bit. It was significant! Panic struck, and without even thinking about what it could mean, I started crying. My husband couldn't figure out why I was crying. When I pointed it out to him, he didn't really seem to understand the significance of what he was looking at. But I *knew*. Deep down inside, I just *knew*.

CHAPTER 14

The Beast Inside Her

The next three days went quickly. Tori endured a series of tests the next morning by her regular vet, and the preliminary findings were not very good. But I didn't need anyone to tell me that. I had been feeling this coming on ever since he biopsied that toe. With her mysterious fever event in May, her sudden onset of fatigue, and her need to lie down on her sit-stay, everything was making perfect sense now. All the signs had been there, and my instincts had picked up on them. I just didn't want to believe them.

Tori had honored my request back in May and she had kept her pain from me until the very last minute. She had heard my desperate plea in the car that day. She had concealed her symptoms as much as she could to protect me from the pain of knowing. Even at this moment, she was not complaining. She just looked exhausted and wanted to go home. For the first time during all the years I had known him, my vet was speechless. He did not want to have to tell me the bad news. I just hugged him and told him it was OK. I didn't need to hear it. I already knew. I had known for some time now. I broke into tears as I took my baby home.

After all the testing (x-rays, ultrasounds, blood tests) and repeated palpation and handling, Tori's mass in her chest had tripled in size at an alarming rate. I could see what was happening. I painfully stood by as everything we had built together was about to come crumbling down. Her tumor was biopsied, and as we waited for the results, I focused on keeping her comfortable. Since it was a Friday, we did not expect to hear anything back until Monday or Tuesday. But I didn't need a biopsy to tell me she had cancer. I already knew it.

Tori had waited until the last possible minute to reveal her fate to me. Time was not in our favor. She could not wait any longer. For the first time ever, she allowed me to see her pain. We never got the results of the biopsy. Over the next forty-eight hours, her symptoms progressed rapidly. This type of cancer thrives on heat and vibration. So all the testing at the hospital had expediated the proliferation of the beast inside her. It became very difficult for her to breathe. The cancer created edema around her lungs, limiting their ability to expand. It was obviously difficult for her to move around, and she was unable to get up and down the steps to the yard. Within just two days, she was no longer able to get herself down on the floor to rest because it hurt too bad. She stopped eating and stopped sleeping. She would just stand like a statue, softly whining and trembling. I could see her pain clearly now and I couldn't stand it. She was my love, my light, my pure joy. Watching her struggle and suffer was more than I could bare. It ripped my heart in two and I wanted to die.

I reached out to her vet again, desperate for her pain to stop, but there was nothing he could do. The time was nearing for me to make a difficult choice. One that I had felt coming from a distance but hoped I would never have to make. We had shared a lifetime together in only five years. It was not long enough. I was not ready for her to leave. But my love for her was greater than my desire to postpone my own agony. It took every ounce of strength I had to be strong enough to make the call.

The vet came to the house just three days after we found the cancer. She died in my arms very peacefully. We cuddled under a tree on her private field where we had spent so much time together, so many hours working and playing. Where all our dreams had come together and become reality. Where she ran after her toys like the speed of the wind. Where she played in the snow with pure delight. Where she followed my every turn behind the mower. Now she could run free as much as she wanted as fast as she wanted. She could finally be the wind that she always imagined she was and fully embrace her cheetah! We laid her to rest on her sacred training field on November 9, 2009.

The pain was unbearable for me. My husband dug her grave himself. I brought Nikki out to say goodbye to her mother. But I could not watch him put her in the ground. I just wanted to sweep her up, to hold her forever. So I fled into the house while he covered her with dirt. I bawled my eyes out!

It was after my husband came in from completing his task that Tori came to say goodbye. Amid all my crying, I suddenly smelled this dirty nose in my face, and I could vaguely see her cheesy grin as she licked me on the nose for one final time! That just made me cry even harder! I had never experienced anything like this. It was simultaneously beautiful and overwhelming! But it made her loss even more unbearable, and I asked her to please go away. Knowing she was there in spirit just made me hurt more for some reason. Really, I just wanted to hold her close and never let her go. I just wanted to bury my face in that gorgeous mane of hers, to softly nuzzle that magical spot between her eyes one more time!

For several days, I fought the urge to dig her back up. It just didn't seem real. One moment she was totally fine, and the next moment she was gone! Of all the dogs I had raised and trained, she was the only one that I wanted to grow old with. I had sent all my other dogs away so I could fully focus only on her! And now she was gone. I desperately clung to everything about her, trying to memorize her smile, the sound of her bark, and her smell. I tried to remember the feel of her mane, that thick, velvety fur of hers, and the click of her nails on the floor. I clung to all the memories I could, reviewing them over and over to burn them into my brain. I knew that these memories would fade quickly. I wanted to keep them fresh on my mind as long as I could and keep her alive! The house was so lonely and quiet without her.

I cried every day for the next year. Nikki could not possibly fill the huge void that her mother had left. Losing Tori broke me. It broke me deep down inside in a way I have never experienced before. I suddenly understood that my days of training, competing, and breeding dogs were over. This was the big change that I had felt coming. The big closing of a chapter. All my instincts had been so right, so true. I knew it was going to be something big, but I could never have imagined this. It was all over. My life would never be the same again. For the next eleven years, I didn't pick up another leash. I didn't train another dog. I didn't even finish the training on her daughter.

Interestingly, nearly eleven years after she died, I finally understood what Tori had been dealing with and why she got so sick so fast. In October 2020, we learned that our home and the dog kennel were riddled with mold! Mold sickness is very serious as I would soon find out in my own body. And the type of mycotoxins in our home was specifically carcinogenic. Dogs, having a smaller body than people, can succumb much more quickly to mold exposure. Poor Tori had silently been dealing with mold sickness her whole life and I had no idea. What she told me in her poem was that she was trying to absorb all the mold so that it didn't get to me, so that she could save me from it. But her body had specific limits that she could not breach without severe consequences. She had offered herself as the ultimate sacrifice for me. It's almost like a romantic love story only you don't realize you're in it until it's over. I can't even tell you the gratitude that poured over me when I heard her message. I had no idea and she never complained.

Tori's death in and of itself seemed an ironic expression of betrayal. Or was it? Let's discuss all the beautiful irony in her story.

CHAPTER 15

The Irony of Tori

There are so many beautiful lessons I have shared here with you in Tori's stories. We also see some key ironic messages, and irony, as I have already explained, is an important teaching tool of the guides. So let's examine them a little further for those who are interested or curious.

Early on, you might notice the expression of *self-doubt* in my own abilities as a trainer and a business owner to actually develop my business into what it needed to be. We saw that betrayal appeared frequently, and persecution showed up every time I attempted to be myself. And then there was the big one: fear of inadequacy. Logically you could see in these stories how I might feel the way I did. But the irony of these emotions is that they were all twisted *illusions* of deep unconscious *self-judgment* and *rejection* that Anthea was alerting me to. The *double ironic twist,* if we peek even deeper, is that the destructive self-image was birthed from a lack of *deservability* and *fear of punishment*. Anthea was here to show it to me and then help me to heal from it. In the next section, you will learn how these deep-seated beliefs became part of me. But for now, we will focus on the outcome of their presence, *unconscious judgment,* and *self-rejection*.

The *irony of betrayal, persecution, self-doubt,* and the *feeling of inadequacy* is that they all serve as a defense for my own doubts around *self-value and safety*! I didn't truly feel that I deserved what I had achieved or earned, not deep down inside. And I had a program running unconsciously that fed my terror of being punished somehow if I did it wrong. These tags provided the insatiable drive to always get it right and succeed. They consequently fed the need to be overly prepared and fully ready. Don't get me wrong. These core values served a purpose for me by creating the ability to always provide for myself and achieve in the face of despair. But no matter how much I did achieve or succeed, it was never enough. I never truly believed that I deserved it because of this underlying irony. And that's where all the lessons of betrayal and persecution inserted themselves.

Until Anthea helped me to locate and terminate this deep, faulty, recurring program, nothing I did with my conscious mind turned it off. No amount of success or appreciation proved it wrong. These emotions and programs were very deep, completely unknown, and unreachable with any self-help technique I tried. It would take a very special angel to help find it and heal it.

Anthea's message is all about self and joy. Her joy is amazing, contagious, and addictive! But I could not experience my own until I uncaged my *self*. Her name means "Guardian of Souls" because she helps us to find our true selves again. And until we are able, she stands guard over our souls. That was a *huge* piece of my awakening! For me it was not about trying to talk myself into being happy or joyful. It wasn't about plastering a fake smile on my face and showing the world that I was happy, even when my soul was not. That fire and light had to come from within myself radiating passively and abundantly. Only then was I able to drop all these tags and stop attracting all these lessons. Because then I was finally whole and connected to my soul! Tori only seemed to be the polar opposite of me because she was showing me parts of me I could not reach yet. The irony was that she was the mirror of the person I was supposed to be. And that "me" was struggling to come out and play in the world! I know this is deep. These guides don't mess around; their messages are complex and complete. So hang with me here.

Unfortunately, I was not able to take advantage of the gifts Anthea had to offer me because I did not understand what was happening. But I share the K9 guides' gifts with you now so that you will not miss your own opportunity. Let my experience be your enlightenment and your gain. If you know to look out for these signs, it can be so much easier to see them and act on them. So whether you identify with the beautiful pieces of her (love of self and joy) or even the shadow pieces (fear of commitment, freezing amid a challenge, nervousness, fear of being yourself fully, or inability to make a decision), she has a message for you! Even just being drawn to or moved by her image could be an indication that she wishes to work with you!

Another important message that Anthea was illustrating through Tori was that the events in my life were all perfectly aligned to provide opportunities for healing and growth. The events, the people, the traumatic experiences were all opportunities for me to release pain from this life and beyond and the option to heal and grow from it. If I had accepted the invitation, I would have easily been able to reclaim the missing pieces of myself and experience her joy. But when Anthea could see that I was not ready, that it was not time for me yet, she would step out of my life like she has here with Tori and return at the next opportunity. These K9 guides are present in our lives when the opportunities for growth are ripe for cultivating. So they commonly return repeatedly until you finally see the invitation and accept their gifts of healing.

Tori was the longest of all of Anthea's embodiments at just five years. Her other visits were much shorter. Anthea tends to get in and get out especially if the time is not right for the healing. So if you have had dogs that remind you of Tori's energy yet they did not stay with you for very long, chances are they may be coming back when the opportunity for growth presents itself again.

Next we'll turn our attention to Anthea's first visit.

PART 2

Sally

1973

Anthea came to me three times as different dogs. All these dogs had identical energies, and when I looked into their eyes, I saw the same soul looking back at me. I always recognized her by the eyes. But Anthea's energy was also so unique and distinct that I recognized her spirit in them as well. The energy, the joy, and the free spirit of the dogs were undeniably the same each time. Along with that goofy, cheesy grin of hers! Her first and shortest of all visits was when I was four years old.

I will now share some of my very first memories as a child with you. There's not as much to tell here of course, because I was so young, and this is Anthea's shortest visit at just six months. This part of my story is critical for you to understand because it seemed to set the stage and foreshadow the events of my future. It also seemed to serve as an introduction to Anthea's energy making it easier to recognize later.

CHAPTER 16

Living at Church

When I was four, we lived in northern New Jersey in a wooded forest. Our home was on the grounds of Shiloh, a Church of Christ summer camp for underprivileged children. My father was one of the preachers and the executive director of the camp. The setting reminded me of your typical summer church camp property. I remember a mansion that served as the main headquarters with meeting rooms, worship chapel, and dining hall. The group cabins were scattered in the surrounding woods. I remember a pond where all the kids liked to swim with a rope swing, paddleboats, and canoes. My father sometimes took me fishing there, and I remember thinking how ridiculously boring *that* was. I also vividly remember getting leeches the one time I tried to swim in that pond! So now I avoid water that I can't see into.

Our house was down the hill from the mansion. I had a dog that looked like a smaller bobtailed German shepherd. She could have been an Austrian shepherd. She was nearly all black with the typical shepherd brown "edging" around her ears, nose, and eyes. The lower part of her legs was brown with a little white chrome on her feet. I'm not sure what happened to her tail. I just never remember her having one. No one could tell me where she came from or how old she was when she joined us. I only remember bits and pieces of our time together because it was so long ago. Sally stayed in an outdoor pen behind our house. We were surrounded by private forest land, so there wasn't much need to have her on a leash. I also specifically remember how she loved to run and explore when she was loose!

Living here was like living in the wilderness. It was remote, quiet, and isolated. There were not many kids my age for me to play with so my vivid imagination and my dog kept me company. I spent a lot of time in my head with my own thoughts and didn't speak much. Exploring the surrounding forest was also a favorite, but for some reason, the trees really creeped me out. When I was in the woods, I often felt like I was being watched. I remember catching vague movements out of the corner of my eye yet nothing was there when I turned my head to look. Sometimes I even thought I could hear faint whispering. This didn't help me feel all that safe and a general sense of insecurity began to creep in. I got the feeling that there were things happening around me that I couldn't necessarily see or understand. And it was hard to tell what was *real*.

Even at this age I did what I always do: put it out of my mind and ignored it. I have imaginary blinders that I put on so I can only see what I want to see. We all do this. Ironically, when researching for this book, I discovered that the camp property was located near a Civil War battleground. This certainly helped me to understand what I was perceiving. I really was "seeing" things, people, ghosts, spirits out in those woods. Young children are still deeply connected to the divine and the spirit world. Psychic abilities are very natural and easy until they are told "it's not real." At that point, children learn to ignore what they perceive, making it easier to fit in and not be different. Even so, these experiences only served to rev up my sense of insecurity, causing me to become painfully shy. I barely spoke to anyone, adults or even kids my age. It was like I was afraid to open my mouth, afraid of what might come out and being judged for what I might say. I was literally terrified to interact with other people. The lengthy time that I spent caged within my own imagination could have also contributed to this anxiety. I felt so out of place around other people. My reality was internal, and I had not developed any skills yet to focus it outward. So I kept to myself and stayed hidden as much as I could. I didn't want to show myself; people might realize I was different!

Anthea tells me (now) that her message for me at that time was "Lighten up a little and enjoy life." The irony here being that I finally got this message during Tori's story when we took a step back from competing. She also told me that I was safe even though I felt the opposite. "You are a joyful soul, but you can't feel it behind all that fear," she told me. In fact, the only thing that I remember feeling joyful about was the time I got to spend with her. Oddly, I still remember her smell. Even as a young child, I liked to bury my nose in her fur as I studied her scents. I noticed that the different-colored fur had different smells. She smelled differently, too, when she was hot and panting. Sort of like a sweaty smell, except dogs don't sweat. I also remember what an incredible free spirit she was. She ran as fast as she could whenever she had a chance to be free of her pen. On occasions she would run loose for days before returning home. This always made me mad as a child. I wanted so much to tame her wildness, to get her to bend to my will, to have her be responsive to me. Unfortunately, she didn't seem to notice me much.

One day she especially broke my heart. I was playing with her in the yard and the neighbor boys rode by on their motorbikes. Sally got very excited. Her ears instantly perked up as the sound of the bikes approached. This always made her bark and go crazy. I tried desperately, but I could not hold on to her. She easily overpowered me, broke free, and ran after the boys as fast as she could. This was her passion; her mouth wide-open, tongue hanging out, swinging in rhythm with her body. A big cheesy grin on her face! This was the look of pure joy and excitement. Something I could not yet relate to. I cried after her and tried to get her to come back. I was terribly unsuccessful, defeated, and devastated. I had no hope of being as fun to her as chasing those motorbikes. I pleaded with my father to get her back, but he only shrugged his shoulders and said, "She'll eventually come back." She did eventually come back on her own terms.

My mother used to tell a story about Sally and me. She says that I began training dogs at four years old. I would put Sally on a leash in front of an obstacle that I had set up all on my own. I would then run with her at the obstacle and tell her to jump! Sally's only options were to jump as I instructed, run around it, or refuse and pull me over. Normally she chose to jump and just make me happy! I delighted in the one thing that I could get her to do on command. I chuckle now because I do remember doing this. And it is something I have always done with all my dogs since. It certainly came in handy as I competed in sports that required such incredible feats of agility as did French ring. It was just the beginning for me, a premonition into my future.

CHAPTER 17

Sally as a Mother

During one of Sally's lengthy excursions exploring the surrounding wilderness, she must have gotten pregnant. She ended up having ten puppies, which I don't think my parents were thrilled about. I, on the other hand, as any child would be, was ecstatic! What four-year-old would not be thrilled about having ten puppies?

I remember spending hours out in the pen with Sally and her babies. These puppies were all different colors and so beautiful. I used my lips to nuzzle them in the soft spot between the eyes just like I did later with Tori's puppies. I noticed all the different smells of each color. I memorized them much like Sally would have. I had big plans for all these puppies. I wondered how many I could keep. I wanted to teach them so many things. This experience contained abundant foreshadowing of the future I was destined for.

As they got older and weaned, bigger and feistier, people came to visit them. I was very protective and didn't like other people playing with them. I felt they were my pack, my babies. One day I came home from school, excited to go out back and see all the puppies. But I arrived to find the pen empty! Sally and her puppies were nowhere to be found. Had Sally gotten out? Was she coming back? Did she take her puppies with her? My young and imaginative mind was racing. I was heartbroken! Sally and her puppies were my world! What could have happened to them? I desperately ran to the house and told my parents what I found. I expected them to launch a search party. I was so disappointed when they seemed unconcerned. "Oh, I'm sure she's fine" was all I got. But Sally never came back, and neither did any of her puppies.

The pen stood there empty with the door open wide never to contain another dog. I searched for her on my own, walking through the woods that surrounded our home. I had no luck. I called for her and called for her. She never came. My heart sank. I wasn't sure what had happened, but I just knew that she was gone. I was so sad, so unbelievably sad. The only thing that brought me joy was gone! My joy was gone. The world was back to being a scary, sad place. And now my trust was totally shattered. Did I not deserve to have her? Did I not deserve to be happy? Did I not deserve to be loved? These beliefs began to creep in, began to take hold as pieces of my soul crumbled. What else could I have possibly gleamed from such a painful loss at this age? Many of my tags began to light up.

My parents never told me what happened to Sally and her puppies. To this day, my mother can't remember. I can only imagine what might have happened.

I had kept these distant memories in a vault all this time. Riffling through some old photographs, I found a couple of Sally. Seeing a single picture of her brought all these deep memories back. I had forgotten what she looked like. But I was able to see enough in the picture to remember the feel of her personality and energy. To realize how familiar it now was. I recognized all the foreshadowing events that occurred in the brief time we had together. My root in dog training as well as whelping and raising puppies that would become my life just thirty years later.

The photo allowed me to recognize Sally's likeness to two other dogs in my life. And that's when I realized that she, Tori, and a dog named Trixie were all the same. They all shared the same eyes, expression, and energy! But I did not realize it until all of them had passed on. I initially thought that this book was to be about my dogs who had all reincarnated multiple times. But this book is about so much more!

PART 3

Trixie

Sally only had six months with me during my first decade. Trixie arrived in my second decade at a volatile time as I charged into my teens. My life was very different, and I had an even more significant need for her help. The story about Trixie also involves another K9 spirit guide, so I will tell their story together as they appeared in my life. They both had different purposes and different messages. I will first introduce the next K9 spirit guide and then Trixie will merge in to finish our learning from Anthea.

At the end of the next section, we will discuss the messages of both Anthea and Öskar and take a deeper look into the ironic twists for those who are interested.

Hindsight gives us empowering clarity when we utilize it for understanding. Painful memories can be transmuted into magical gifts of overwhelming gratitude for those who have volunteered their service in our growth.

SECTION 3

Öskar

(Oss-Car)

"Öskar"

Öskar is the second of our Core Four spirit guides. This masculine guide chose the mighty lion as his spirit animal (his guide form). The lion is well-known as a dominant beast exuding tremendous confidence and power within his calmness. He carries his head high among his peers and cowers to no one. He inherently understands that his abilities are his God-given right that no one can take from him. The voice of the lion is strong and loud and can be head for miles. This is your voice he wishes to give back to you. Öskar has chosen the powerful lion because this king of the prairie represents your courage and strength in overcoming deep-seated anger. Especially anger associated with someone who wishes to overpower or control you. He wishes to share his powerful and courageous energy with you. He may appear to you when you need to find your voice again and defend yourself or speak your truth. Or it might be time to dig deep into your core being and stand confident no matter how others may try to make you feel. It might be time to overcome those who wish to isolate you from your own inner strength. He will show you the way back to your own energy source and reintroduce you to your inherent confidence.

This angelic creature also resonates with the black and tan coonhound (his angel form) because this breed definitely has a voice! Your voice is needed to protect you against your oppressors, and Öskar can be called upon to help you regain your own power through your voice. The hound is incredibly loyal and loving and has no desire to fight or show aggression. But he is no pushover and will stand his ground with appropriate means. Though the hound is a pack-loving canine, he is keenly aware that certain situations call for following his own nose and intuition. He is prepared to break free from the crowd to do what is necessary to sustain his own divine truth. With his decisive angelic traits, Öskar may be showing you how to use your voice commandingly, express yourself, or to spread your important message. He may be encouraging you to focus on your loyalty to yourself or others, but in a strategic and meaningful way that resonates with your soul. It may be time for you to take your own path and deviate from that of your friends and family; your journey is unique to theirs. He is all about being strong and confident within yourself and doing what is best for you, despite what others think or need.

Notice how his image perfectly reflects his calm, all-knowing energy with a relaxed eye and ear. His lightly closed jaw lends a calmer vibration and a subdued "vital" rhythm with a slower heart rate and breath. This carefully crafted image perfectly portrays his accepting yet observant demeanor as he filters your emotions through his energy field allowing him to keenly understand where you need his assistance. It was always this stoic appearance that gave him away. He simply understood much more than I ever could!

Öskar's presence serves to lead you to your inner strength, your divine power, which is required to muster through this part of your life. He will carry you when you are unable. He lovingly substitutes his courage until you can reclaim your own. He also stands guard over your wounded intuition. He sees that you have appropriate instincts about who or what to trust but that your emotions suffocate them. He is especially present when you feel powerless against those who wish to wrongfully control you and when you feel powerless to speak up for yourself.

Öskar is also very patient, gentle, and kind. These characteristics along with his courage and confidence are really your traits he mirrors to you. It can be especially difficult to see these parts of yourself while under the weight of psychological strain. So he carries them for you, waiting for you to be ready to take them back. He will continue to support and protect you until you are able to fully embrace your own power and are no longer verbally suffocated. He serves to lift the delusional veil that holds you captive and prevents you from seeing your unique power.

When Öskar arrived, I did not realize I needed him. I was suffering through my life, accepting the cards I was dealt the best that I could. I felt like life so far was definitely not easy, but I felt I had no control over that. Events in my life gradually caused more and more oppression until I could no longer find myself. But I was completely unconscious of this. It is easier to become oblivious than to feel the overwhelming emotional strain. Without warning, I woke up one day to feel trapped without an emergency exit. And this is where I was for all Öskar's visits.

A Message from Öskar

I was a child merely twelve years old.
I stood as tall as I could, proudly next to my dog, my big German shepherd dog, Nick.
My voice was weak, muted, mummified, and stifled.
I was expected to be quiet, to comply without free will, and not allowed to have a voice.
Paralyzed with anger, petrified with frustration, powerless to express myself.
Unable to connect my soul to my throat and express my truth.
But the lion sat quietly next to me, guarding and protecting.
He held the fragmented pieces of my soul so they would not get lost.
He would keep them in a vault until I was ready to reclaim them many decades later.
My angel, my protector, my lion, my Nick.
Pieces of me that I have struggled to find, to reconnect, to complete.
And now the lion has returned them to me! God bless you, Nick!
(Delivered by Zozzo, April 12, 2022)

PART 1
The Prequel to the King

CHAPTER 18

The Day Care Center

I was twelve years old when Öskar first came to me. Since I was without a dog for nearly eight years, I want to catch you up on a few things. It is important that you fully appreciate why Öskar needed to come.

When I was six years old, we moved from New Jersey down to Memphis, Tennessee. I didn't feel any safer in Memphis than I had in the spooky forest. For one thing, our house had bars on all the windows and doors, and I felt like I lived in a cage. I spent my weekdays at a nearby church day care center while my parents worked full time. I have several distinct and terrifying memories from my time at this day care.

The first one occurred while all the children were out playing in the fenced play yard with the teachers watching over us. A black sedan with tinted windows suddenly pulled up next to the fence and two big guys jumped out, jumped over our three-foot chain-link fence, and without a word, grabbed one of the girls in my class. In a split second, they leapt back over the fence, shoved her into their car kicking and screaming, and sped away! It all happened so fast! I was stunned and had no idea what was going on. The play yard erupted into chaos as the teachers were screaming for the kids to run inside. I was frozen but somehow managed to follow the others in total shock. There was so much confusion with everyone screaming or crying. *Are they coming back to take more of us?*

I wondered. Most of the other kids were crying and clinging to each other. I was scared but could not cry. I was just numb.

When my parents picked me up that day, there was no discussion about the incident. I remember stopping for dinner at a fast-food restaurant and wondering why my parents were acting so normal. I still felt like those guys were out there waiting to snatch someone else, maybe even me! Why weren't they taking this seriously? I was terrified! My father was now a licensed family therapist. But there was never any discussion regarding what I had witnessed that day. I was not comforted or reassured in any way. I was traumatized but had no tools for dealing with what I had experienced. So I just tried to put it out of my mind and go on. I buried it deep into my subconscious so it wouldn't scare me anymore.

Not too long after that snatching, my best friend was abducted from our classroom at the same day care center! Our teacher left the room during nap time and a man walked in off the street. He was a scruffy-looking stranger and asked my friend to come with him. None of us recognized him, but he said that her mother (who happened to be the administrator of this day care) had sent him. So she followed him out. He escorted her down into the basement of the building and instructed her to take her clothes off. Luckily, she realized he was not a safe stranger and was able to get away. But the man was never found. Again, there was no discussion with my parents about the incident. I was not removed from the day care. They continued to force me to spend time there. I got more and more uncomfortable about being there. I didn't feel safe.

To make matters worse, I was bullied for years by a boy at that same day care. I was so terrified that I often spent my day hiding. Nobody came to my rescue or made him stop. I was given the "sticks and stones" speech by my teachers. Yeah, like that phrase was magic and somehow prevented emotional trauma. Just ignore it; it can't hurt you. Of course, now bullying is taken much more seriously. I never understood why my parents left me at such a horrible place. My mother always told me that we moved from New Jersey to Tennessee because it was a safer place to raise children. I didn't believe that, and I wasn't sure what her idea of "safe" was. She obviously wasn't the one in day care!

Understandably I began to have night terrors and quit sleeping through the night around this time. All I knew was that I was not safe. Every night I thought I saw someone at my window. I called for my parents to come, but they stopped responding after the second or third time. Most nights I just went and got in bed with them. That was the only way I got any sleep. My parents blamed it on the shows I was watching on TV. But I knew better.

CHAPTER 19

Church Camp

The final event that really locked my power and my trust in a vault was during my first and only summer church camp experience. By now I was eleven years old. Church camp was not my idea of fun, especially since I used to live on one. This was yet another *ironic* twist of fate. I tried every argument I could think of to get out of going, but none of them worked. My parents forced me to go, thinking it would be good for me. This camp was in Indiana where my grandparents lived, and I didn't know anybody there.

A couple of days into the five-day camp, I was playing in the pool with some of the girls in my group. I was tall for my age and had begun puberty early. The girls began making fun of me because I had body hair way ahead of everyone else. My parents would not let me shave yet so I was very self-conscious of how differently I looked. When I raised my arms to catch a ball, the girls visibly recoiled at my pit hair and didn't want to play with me anymore. Girls at that age could be so vicious. I tried to be strong and not show how rejected I felt. But my confidence was absolutely shredded. I already didn't have any friends here and now the girls in my group were shunning me. No one wanted to play with me.

There was a group counselor nearby who seemed to be paying attention to our squabble. After the other girls ran off, he appeared

Öskar

out of nowhere, swam up, and scooped me up in his arms. This total stranger cradled me against him as he squatted in hip-deep water. I was not sure what to think about this. I was a bit big to be held like a baby. But before I had time to react, he said, "Are you ready to get dunked?"

Finally, someone was going to play with me, I thought! Great. "Sure!" I said as I pinched my nose with my fingers. I was expecting him to toss me up in the air like the other kids were doing. Instead, he lowered both of us down and under the water. For a split second, I almost panicked and broke free because that was not what I was expecting. But then I got an even bigger shock.

While we were both underwater and my face was close to his, I felt him plant a kiss on my cheek. For half a second, I was perplexed. Did I feel that right? But then my instincts exploded into panic as my nervous system screamed, "Danger! Danger!" I frantically wiggled to get free from his grasp. I consciously tried not to inhale a bunch of water in case I needed my lungs for running! Once on my feet, I quickly wiped the water from my face gasping for air and turned to face the counselor. He had a mischievous grin on his face as he said, "Did you like that?" I moved through the thick water as quickly as I could to get away from him and out of the pool. I wanted to get as far away from this guy as I could. All my internal alarms were going off! Had anyone else seen that? Hopefully, someone would come to my rescue.

I was not sure who that guy was. He was not my group counselor, thank goodness. I ran to the girls' bathroom and stayed there the rest of the swim session. I frequently peeked out to see if he was still out there. I remembered his face in exquisite detail: his predator half-rimmed glasses, mustache, and five o'clock stubble that had brushed up against my face when he pressed in for the kiss. It gave me chills just thinking about it. I quickly scanned the crowd while maintaining my cover to prevent giving up my location. But I didn't see him out there.

When my group returned to our cabin, I told my girls group leader what had happened, and her reaction was astounding. She did not believe me! When I got upset and threatened to go to the camp administrator myself, she called me a "b*tch." I had never heard such language from an authority figure. But if she did not believe me, was he going to? What if he didn't? I was paralyzed with fear the rest of the week. I did not know what to do. I refused to go back to the pool so I stayed in our cabin while the rest of our group went. Whenever we ventured to the camp clubhouse for big group activities, *he* would be there. He would stalk me standing ten to twenty feet away just staring at me with his hard, cold gaze. I assumed this was intended to scare me out of telling anyone what he had done. But I refused to look at him. I didn't want to give him any more power over me so I just ignored him. I avoided all possible activities where he might have been. So much for a fun week at church camp! I hated my parents for forcing me to go there!

On the last day when all the parents were coming to pick up the kids, my parents did not come. I was to ride home with the camp administrator. He was the preacher at my grandmother's church. But this meant I had to stand around for hours while everyone else left. It was added torture while that man stared at me with his heavy gaze the whole time! It took all my will power to not look back at him. When the preacher finally drove us home, I half expected to see that counselor following us. I never said anything to the preacher because I had no idea how he would respond. What if he was like my counselor? I just wanted to get home. I had no idea who I could trust.

I did make it home, but the experience laid a strong foundation for distrust, anger, and fear. I became very suspicious of all people and their possible intentions in my life. At only eleven years of age, I realized that I could only trust myself. Everything in my life up to this point also taught me that *I didn't matter*. I also decided to stop speaking up for myself because *no one cared*. I was literally scared silent. My voice box was now sealed behind lock and key. I had learned the hard way that my voice was powerless in this world. I was *powerless*. I pretty much shut down emotionally, but in a way that I could keep it hidden from others. My father had taught me it wasn't safe to show my emotions. So I kept it all to myself.

I never told an adult about what happened. I just didn't think anyone would truly care. Besides, now that I was home, I just wanted to put it behind me and forget.

CHAPTER 20

The Scoop on My Father

In addition to all the extrinsic psychological stress in my life, there was also the ongoing intrinsic stress of my relationship with my father. He had his own psychological issues that were invisible to me, but I could sense them. I was acutely aware of what a miserable person he was. My only memories of him were of his anger. When he got angry, he got vicious. He would explode with snarky personal attacks or criticisms that hit their mark as intended. I don't remember him showing any kind of love, affection, or kindness to anyone. I did my best to avoid him when I could. When he lashed out at me, I felt totally powerless, speechless, and lost. I did not have the social maturity to understand it or the communicative skills to deflect it. So I just absorbed it unknowingly while I stuffed my own feelings down deep where they wouldn't show.

Ironically, his rage became my rage! I seethed in anger anytime I was subjected to his. But I had no outlet for my emotions; they brewed quietly inside me. My rare attempts to stand my ground resulted in ridicule and passive-aggressive threats. I attempted to throw it back at him once when I threatened to call the police on him. He just laughed at me and made me feel powerless and insignificant. Oh, how I wished I could have! *Ironically*, he would end up in prison fourteen years later without my help.

I also witnessed the same snarky, manipulative rage at my mother.

I never saw them loving each other. I kind of felt sorry for her when she simply cowered under his fake power. I pitied her but was also angry for her. I didn't understand why she allowed him to treat her that way, to treat us that way. Why didn't she stand up to him or at least stand up for me? Aren't mothers supposed to protect their children? I did not understand it at all. Neither one of them made logical sense to me. So I kept my distance from them both and walled off my emotions to protect myself the only way I knew how.

Thankfully, my father did not have enough courage to strike either of us. All his abuse was verbal, but his words and actions caused plenty of psychological damage. I learned to hide my emotions because if he sensed my fear or weakness, he would use it against me. I adopted a stiff upper lip and solid "game face" from a young age. This unfortunately stifled my ability to feel and express emotions, such as joy and happiness.

My astrologer, forty years later, would describe him with astounding accuracy.

> He was obsessive-compulsive, a control freak. He had no touchy-feely at all. Emotionally unavailable, manipulative, verging on psychological cruelty. He projected his inadequacies onto you. A father energy that was bipolar, a schizophrenic of conflicted identity. His profound rejection of you caused you to feel unseen, unloved, devalued. And this would have put into place a very deep insecurity that you've been working your whole life to heal.

She absolutely hit the nail on the head with incredible precision, painting the most vivid picture of who my father was! And through her words, I finally felt accepted, seen, and valued. What I came to realize as I wrote this story was that my father was just a giant-size bully, a bigger version of that kid in day care. Only my dad carried much more authority over me than a little boy. His brutal parenting style kept me prisoner for so long that I lost track of who I was. My true self was buried somewhere beneath the rubble of the fear and anger he had instilled in me. Silently cowering beneath the towering cruelty that kept my mouth shut kept me from speaking out and defending myself. I am sharing these intimate details about my life with you so that you understand my state of mind and the reason that I needed two very potent spirit guides (Öskar and Anthea) to come into my life at this exact moment.

Have you been able to identify any tags in these events? There will certainly be more opportunity to see them in the coming chapters. Now let's look at the two dogs that Öskar came through with: Nick and Zozzo. We will begin with Nick's story, which will be shared with Trixie, allowing us to finish our exploration of Anthea.

PART 2
Nick

CHAPTER 21

My Big German Shepherd Dog

Nick was a blessing to me on many levels and in many ways. He had a very important job to do in looking after me on two separate occasions. I think you will find his story is very interesting. There were things about myself I didn't clearly understand until I started to receive his message in 2022. And the words in his poem completely blew me away as they clearly outlined his purpose. Even as a fifty-year-old adult, I had never truly understood the amount of oppression I was under as a child at the hands of my own father. I was not able to see it until Nick showed it to me. Only then could I set out to heal it.

Sometimes it's hard for us to appreciate the impact of childhood situations and how they shape us as a human and as an adult. To me the greatest gift about receiving the messages from the K9 guides is being able to finally see clearly where my soul needed to heal, where the pieces were missing that needed to be returned. Had it not been for their messages, I may not have found my pieces and been able to finally become whole again. With that being said, let's begin our exploration of Öskar's blessings and the message that he has to share with you.

Nick was a big German shepherd dog that I had as a child. I

purchased him with my own money when I was twelve years old. I saved my money from babysitting, dog sitting, yard work, and my allowance. For weeks I browsed the newspaper ads and the color ads in the AKC magazine. I finally settled on a breeder about forty-five minutes from our house. My mom took me out one Saturday to see their puppies.

I had no idea what I was looking at when I sat down with a litter of puppies. They all looked so cute, and the puppy breath was irresistible. For some reason, I decided I wanted a male puppy so I picked one out that day. We were to return in a couple of weeks when he would be old enough to take home. The breeders were a nice couple that lived in the country and the parents of the pups seemed to be good dogs. Other than that, I wasn't sure what I was looking at or for. One thing I did know was I was beside myself with excitement! I had trouble sleeping until the day arrived when I could go and pick up my new puppy. I am sure I drove my mother crazy with my anticipation!

When we brought him home, the first thing I had to decide on was a name. Since he came with a five-generation pedigree, I was able to familiarize myself with his heritage. I noticed that one of the dogs in his pedigree was a dog called Nikolaus von Lockenheim. This dog had many titles including a schutzhund 3 (Sch 3) and he was in my puppy's pedigree twice. This made him seem like a pretty important dog. I wanted my dog to be like that so I decided to name him Nikolaus. I called him "Nick" for short. *Ironically*, I would get my first experience in schutzhund with this puppy!

The only thing in my life that I could enjoy or that I had any control over was this new puppy. He was a cute little thing, and I thoroughly relished in all the puppy training. Leash training, potty training, and crate training were all very fun to me. I kept him with me all the time when I was at home, closely following the monks of New Skete principles. When I was at school, I daydreamed about our future life together. We had a big, fenced yard that gave us plenty of space to run and play.

Training methods back in those days were more barbaric than the methods of today. Most of the obedience schools followed the teachings of Bill Koehler. His method was known as "yank and crank" by his followers and critics. Basically, the dog wore a choke collar attached to a six-foot leash. The handler would intentionally set the dog up for failure just to make a negative correction. The theory was that by yanking on his collar harshly and saying, "No!" you effectively communicated he had made the wrong choice. I know it was brutal. But that's all we had back in the early 1980s. It was hardly what I considered fun. These compulsive techniques intentionally set the dog up for failure as a teaching tool. This was a very clumsy method, and the timing was significantly delayed compared to today's standards. It wasn't quite as effective as we thought it was back then. Nor did it clearly convey a message to the dog; it was just plumb mean. There was very little positive reinforcement for our companions, no happy experiences to motivate them to please us. It's hard to understand why the dogs tolerated it, but for some reason they did.

Case in point is a memory that haunted me and seemed to create a shift in my relationship with my puppy. When Nick was about three months old, I was giving him a bath in the tub. I wanted him to lie down in the water so I could rinse his belly, but he was refusing. He was just being a little bit defiant and challenging my authority. As an impatient soon-to-be teenager, I didn't react well to the dispute. I immediately donned his choke chain and leash, thinking, *I'll show him!* and I repeatedly forced him to lie down in the water at my will. I didn't stop until my *rage* was over and we were both soaking wet from all the splashing water.

This memory tormented me throughout my entire life because I did not like the "me" that I saw in it. I was the perfect reflection of my father. I was guilty of the very behavior in him that I despised so much. Looking back on it from a more mature view, it is easy to see how I was mirroring what I experienced, my observations of my parents, and my father's approach with me. I felt so guilty that I subjected this poor puppy to such cruelty. Not because he deserved it but because I could not control my anger toward my father, and it would periodically leak out as rage toward others. It would be four decades before I truly understood how to remove this *rage tag* in my personality. And it was a gift that Öskar delivered me.

I suspect that some of my readers may identify with this experience, either within themselves or someone else in their life. It is important to recognize what a valuable teaching opportunity this presents. Nick was providing this experience for me so that I could learn from it. Even though I did not immediately understand the message, I did eventually. The other caveat is that sometimes we recognize what's happening, like I did, but we have no idea what to do about it or how to change it. I spent decades trying to remove or expunge this part of me that I despised so much. But that is not the answer either. This tag is not wrong; it just needs to be healed. Part of Öskar's message is to explain this.

Nonetheless our relationship changed after this encounter. Nick seemed a lot more subdued. He was no longer that frisky, happy, little puppy. It was like things just got real for him and he knew it. He had challenged my authority and I made him regret it. So he decided to never do that again. However, from that point forward, he was never joyful about complying with my commands. He did as he was told out of fear of my reaction if he did not. Nick became more reserved and quieter and tried his best to stay on my good side. He was perfectly mirroring my reaction to my father! It was a sad shift and weighed deeply on my heart, which is a clear indicator that my actions were not congruent with my soul's core being.

Despite our hiccup, Nick and I breezed through his puppy obedience class, and then he graduated with high honors from his adult novice obedience class at the kennel. I was so proud! His maturity gave way to a big-boned adult dog of significant stature. He had a quiet, thoughtful presence about him, like he was always observing. He was very devoted to me, and we were nearly always together when I wasn't doing school stuff. We also spent a lot of time at the kennel together. Now that we had graduated class, we volunteered to assist the instructor with new students. Ironic, isn't it? At only twelve years of age, I was assisting with group obedience classes. Yet more foreshadowing into my future.

It was also around this time that I was talked into entering an obedience fun match which is a practice show where people prepare for real competitions in AKC shows. We did a baby class, sub-novice, where all the exercises are on leash. Nick and I did well, had a good time together, and earned a ribbon. This experience marked a new beginning for me. Competition would be my next focus and a huge passion during my early teens! Öskar had successfully delivered me to the next integral chapter of my path. This new hobby of mine would set the stage and prepare me for the epic experiences that were necessary for the contents of this book! How beautiful is that?

> Ironically it was at one of these fun matches where I first encountered a man that I would compete against two decades later in a national championship on the other side of the country!

Nick and I got more serious about our training as we both got older. The subconscious desire to please my father had instilled in me a need to be overly prepared for all my ventures. So we practiced a lot. I wanted to get our performance perfect. I don't think Nick shared the same OCD interest as I did. He was not overly excited about his new vocation and all this work. Lazy days in the yard or long walks around the neighborhood were more his speed. It was difficult to get any pep out of him when we practiced. He was compliant but did the bare minimum requirements of his job as my loyal companion. And in the end, we managed to earn our first obedience title, AKC Companion Dog (CD), with three consecutive shows. His work proved to be predictably reliable and devoted, even though he did not seem happy about it.

CHAPTER 22

Flares of Worthiness

Since I was only twelve years old, we were also competing for "Highest Scoring Junior Handler" awards. Except I routinely ran into a problem with this at each show. Even though I registered myself as a junior competitor, I was often overlooked when the scores were tallied. The award was frequently issued to another child with a lower score. This was devastating to me since I had clearly earned a higher score and the distinction. My parents would have to raise an objection with the judge to rectify the mistake. This meant the trophy would then have to be taken from another child and reissued to me, understandably provoking tearful, angry responses from them in the process. This just didn't seem fair to either one of us, and it made me feel like the bad guy even though I had clearly earned the award.

I even had a little girl's father file a complaint with the American Kennel Club against me. He claimed that I had not trained my own dog and therefore didn't qualify for the award. As you can imagine, this promptly lit a fuse for my internal *rage*. I mean come on! All I did was train my dog. I'm sure that father was trying to look out for his child. It was an honorable defensive, protective maneuver; I give him that. But why were people trying so hard to take my well-earned credit from me?

This theme followed me into adulthood as we have already discussed during Tori's story. The very deeply rooted insecurity I developed as a result of my father's treatment of me placed a couple of "tags" in my energy field. One tag read, "I'm not worthy," and was attracting these experiences like a magnet. Later Anthea would continue to light it up for me to see, examine, and provide me more opportunities to clear it. But for now, Öskar was highlighting a different tag with this same experience. His tag read, "I have no voice" or "My voice is powerless." Both exemplified the necessity for me to speak up and defend myself. When I shut down from my father's treatment, I stopped attempting to verbally defend myself feeling like it would do no good. As if doing so would only expose me to more mistreatment. Öskar was illustrating how critical it was for me to learn to use my voice. It was not adequate for me to just be quiet and silently stew when angered. This *internal rage* would only serve to boil over inside me with nowhere to go and create turmoil for my physical body. I needed to learn how to speak up for myself tactfully and rightfully. Suffering in silence only resulted in loss of my own God-given power. I was willingly, but not knowingly, giving my *power* away.

This was the ultimate point of this experience. Öskar and then Anthea wanted me to see it. If I had accepted the learning and completed it, I would then have a quick and easy solution for my issues with my father. Öskar was lovingly and skillfully attempting to show me this. But I couldn't see that by any stretch of the imagination. I was just angry that I was not receiving the just recognition that I deserved. It was because other people were rude and selfish. I was the victim. It had nothing to do with me. Oh, the *irony* of it all!

CHAPTER 23

A Peek into My Destiny

Around this time an interesting turn of events happened at our training kennel. We had a visitor who wanted to start a club. He was looking for a group of people interested in training and possibly competing in schutzhund. Our group members seemed very excited about this possibility. *Ironically*, this visitor was the very man I referred to as someone I would compete against at a future schutzhund championship!

> Schutzhund is a German dog sport that was traditionally a German shepherd temperament and breed suitability test. It is now an all-breed dog sport practiced around the world. The sport begins with a basic temperament test (BH) that includes obedience exercises to determine if the dog is suitable to compete in the sport. Once this initial test is passed, the dogs then compete through the ascending levels of difficulty from level 1 (Sch 1) to level 2 (Sch 2) and finally level 3 (Sch 3). Each test contains scent tracking, obedience, and then protection tests all in one day and all outdoors on an open field. The teams are required to pass each level only once before progressing to the next level.
>
> This is contrary to French ring and AKC obedience, which both require multiple passing scores under different judges.

Öskar

Our group decided to form a club that is still intact to this day. We were shifting our focus to a multidiscipline sport that would now include tracking and protection. But I was not very interested in tracking at that age. This scent test seemed so boring to my young mind, and I did not understand its vague precision. The protection portion, however, was thoroughly enjoyed by both Nick and me. This was where he came to life. It seemed to allow him to free up from the restrictive expectations placed on him in obedience. He got to express himself with his *voice* and his *power* and be rewarded for it! Hmmm, maybe yet another illustration of Öskar's teaching? This is probably what I would feel like if I finally addressed those tags and collected my missing pieces!

I remember feeling immense power and energy holding onto my big German shepherd dog as he strained at the end of the leash. Here he got to do what came naturally when confronted by a decoy shaking a rag in his face. He got to bark as loudly as he wanted, answering the challenge, and voicing his willingness to engage. He reveled in his reward, sinking his teeth into it and thrashing fiercely. Head held high, tail wagging proudly, he paraded around the field with his prize for all the other dogs to notice. His thick coat and domineering voice reminded me a lot of a lion, my lion.

Our training did eventually carry over into everyday life with Nick. He blossomed into a very reliable partner that I grew to trust. I was amazed at how quickly he could read a situation and react appropriately. One day I was walking in our neighborhood with him on a six-foot leash as usual. Some of the neighborhood kids were out riding their bicycles. They noticed us and came over to chat. Since they were on their bikes and didn't want to stop moving, they just started riding in a circle around me as we spoke. Nick perceived this as a threatening gesture and naturally assumed a defensive posture without me saying anything. He moved to the end of his leash and just started barking at the kids as they circled us, a verbal warning to not come any closer. I was so surprised that I didn't see what was happening at first. He usually wasn't interactive with other people and tended to be aloof to strangers. I had never seen him bark at anybody before.

Then I realized how similar this event was to an exercise in our protection training class. All I had to do was to tell him to "leave it" and he settled down at my side again. It was like he said, "OK, Mom. I'm just looking out for you." It made me smile, and I felt a sense of pride wash over me. I had a guardian looking after me after all!

There were other times that Nick made his presence known, especially when my father and I would argue. He seemed to pick up on the tension between us, motivating him to come and sit next to me. When my father offered his typical snarky "bitterisms," Nick would utter a low growl. It was quiet and I could hear it, just a gentle warning. But I don't think my father ever heard it. Because if he had, he most certainly would have killed my dog. His ego would have never allowed such a rightful warning.

One particular evening, my father was supposed to be home with me when my mother was out of town on a work trip. As usual, he was not there; no one was home when it was time to go to bed. This had happened before when I was only seven. But then I did not have my own German shepherd guardian. Irritated with him for once again falling short of his agreement, I decided to bring Nick inside and put his training to the test. I placed my true guardian in the living room on a down stay and told him to "watch." This was his alert command when we did protection exercises. It means to keep an eye out for the bad guy. And my father was the epitome of "bad guy." I then went to bed satisfied that Nick was watching over me in the other room.

I'm not sure how much time passed because I fall asleep, but I was awakened by a commotion in the other room followed by Nick barking. I heard my father calling for me as I struggled to clear my sleepy head and figure out what was happening. I leapt out of bed and into the living room only to see that Nick had my father cornered at the front door. He was not about to let him into the house. I chuckled because I knew that Nick was a good judge of character! It served my dad right for coming home so late and not being here at bedtime.

But my father was not amused. So rather than risk the safety of my dog, I pulled him off before he decided to take a bite out of my dad. I relieved Nick of his duties and sent him outside with lots of praise for a job well done! Nick's training had certainly paid off if it served to teach my father a lesson!

Nick and I continued our path with AKC obedience progressing to more difficult classes. I never actually competed in schutzhund at that age. It was just fun doing all the training, and *ironically*, it laid the valuable foundation for the pivotal role it would play later in my life. It seems our entire experience together was a bit ironic in a way. With the references to teaching obedience classes, meeting a man that I would later compete against as an adult, and my first experience in a sport that I would later be successful in were all quite incredible. These experiences seemed to foretell the specific path I would journey twenty years later! But he had much more to teach me than just dog training and competition. And he would prove to be such a great mentor and protector.

We also notice in this part the emergence of the tags around *rage* and *powerlessness* that Öskar is here to help me with. In the prequel, you could see how these overwhelming emotions crept in, expanding over several incidents before Öskar arrived. You could also see how I learned that my voice was not important and that I decided to smother it to protect myself. You witnessed how I had totally lost my own power, given it away, at such a young age. Öskar was lending me his power until I could reclaim mine. He urged me to resurrect my voice and use it to protect and express myself reclaiming my own power. I was never meant to be scared silent, and it would not serve me to surrender to that fearfulness. He also urged me to stand my ground and follow my instincts that were incredibly accurate even though I did not realize it at the time. I already knew I needed to break from the family path and follow my own. I knew that I did not want to fall into the same illusions my father suffered from, but I had no idea how to avoid them.

Öskar would continue to be there for me, but he was calling in reinforcements. Our life would shift just a little as another spirit guide was arriving. Let's meet Anthea's new body.

PART 3
Anthea and Öskar

CHAPTER 24

Anthea Returns

The fact that these two guides felt such urgency to warrant simultaneous intervention is significant to the importance of the message. Anthea chose me and came into my life totally unexpectedly as Trixie. We will shift our focus now to how Öskar and Anthea interacted to create a crucial opportunity for my soul's development.

Trixie was a gift that I was not expecting. Anthea made sure to insert herself into my life at this precise moment. She was quite a surprise since I had no intention of getting another dog. Just like all of Anthea's other incarnations, Trixie was something very special. She was given to me by a woman in my training club who bred German shepherds. This darling little puppy was the last one from her litter. She exuded the undeniable spirit that I would come to recognize as that of Anthea.

When Trixie came into my life, I had a part-time job at the local boarding kennel where I did all my training. It was only three miles from my house so I rode my bike to and from. I cleaned out dog runs, bathed dogs for the groomers, and did other odds and ends. I also volunteered with the group obedience classes on Saturdays. On Sundays I trained with our schutzhund club group. So I was at the dog kennel nearly every waking moment during the summers.

Trixie was a very positive addition to my life, and she was also quite sassy! Her solid black coat was gorgeous and offered beautiful contrast to her amber eyes. She had a funny little kink at the end of her tail that I noticed when she was just a baby (a smaller version of what Tori had). I often fondled it trying to figure out what might have caused it. With her smaller size, she was extremely agile and fast for a German shepherd. We had a blast working and playing together. She was very brave and much more outgoing than Nick ever was. She seemed really smart and whizzed through all the puppy training.

Nick appeared to enjoy his new company as well. He finally had another dog to play with! As Trixie matured, they became a pair. I took them for walks in the neighborhood together. I taught them to run next to me on my bicycle. We went for hikes in the state park, and we played in the abandoned ditches that surrounded our neighborhood. On special occasions, we went to the park and played fetch in the lake. Trixie loved to swim! They were very loyal to me and never offered to run away. Even so, Trixie could be a little testy at times, pushing the limits to see exactly what she could get away with. All the while feigning her innocence. She figured it was better to grovel later than to obey so easily. She was not as sensitive as Nick and didn't seem to be as easily affected by any type of punishment. She was always smiling and looking for something fun to do, even if it meant getting into trouble for it. She loved to run and play in the backyard as Nick struggled to keep up with her.

Hanging out with my two dogs really gave me a sense of belonging. I now had my own family or pack if you will. And when I was with them, no one was yelling at me, criticizing me, or demoralizing me. I was in charge, and I got to control the experience. Working with my dogs was a fulfilling hobby that kept me busy and engaged. It also got me out of the house. It provided me with a sense of community among the training group, even though they were all much older than me. They didn't bully me like my dad or the kids at school. They just allowed me to be me, accepting me as a full member of the group. My days at the kennel provided a healthy escape from my home life that I so desperately needed. The older I got, the more tense things got at home. I managed to stay out of my father's path, avoiding his wrath most of the time. So it was good to have a safe space to just be me.

Just like when I was four years old, I still loved to teach the dogs fun things to do. I was constantly trying to come up with new stunts to teach them. These shepherds were easy to work with and liked to learn. Trixie was a bit quicker and snappier than her older and bigger brother so she tended to catch on a lot faster. One day I thought it would be fun to teach them to climb a ladder. Only Nick didn't find this fun at all. His larger body was not as agile and made it difficult for him to keep his feet on the narrow, skinny ladder steps. Trixie, on the other hand, was thrilled about having a new challenge! Her petite size and agile body took to it easily. She zipped right up the ladder and onto the folding table I had it perched against. Getting down the ladder was a little trickier, but Trixie discovered it was easier to just leap from the top! She was so clever. She landed it easily and confidently on her short springy legs. I thought about teaching her to climb the ladder to the roof of the house. That would be so cool! But I figured my parents wouldn't appreciate it.

Let's just take a beat and consider the *irony* here. Anthea as Tori would repeatedly climb a seven-foot wall from a standstill in French ring competition. Trixie was demonstrating the same abilities that I would rely on with Tori. This experience provides yet another premonition into my adulthood. However, teaching Trixie this skill would soon come back to haunt me!

I rode a school bus every day to and from school. This meant I was gone all day until about 3 p.m. When it was time for me to come home, the school bus could be heard making its way through the subdivision. Apparently, the dogs understood this and knew it meant I was home. It took me a while to catch on that *they* had figured this out.

Our large, one-acre backyard was fully enclosed with a wooden six-foot privacy fence. Behind the house was a ditch and then a railroad track. The ditch was some sort of drainage system through the neighborhood that continued into other neighborhoods. It was a place I had explored with the dogs on many occasions when it wasn't overgrown or flooded. There were also lots of wild animals and snakes back there.

One day I came home from school and ran out into the backyard excited to see my dogs. When I entered the yard, Nick was at the back fence pacing and whining. Out of the corner of my eye, I saw a shadow drop down from the top of the fence. *What was that?* I wondered. Then I notice Nick disciplining Trixie by grabbing her by the scruff with his teeth and growling. And that's when I realized that Trixie had just climbed *back* into the yard! Apparently, she had been leaving the yard to go explore while I was at school during the day. When she heard the school bus coming down the road, she then knew to climb back in so she wasn't caught! Only on this day, she was running a little bit late! I had no idea how long she had been doing this. But it was brilliant!

I'm sure there were so many fun things for her to get into out there! So many scents to check out, so many animals to hunt down, and so many places to adventure through the never-ending network of ditches. Why did I never think of that? Nick was too big to get himself over the fence so he couldn't go with her. Trixie was the perfect size, weight, and agility. I guess I shouldn't have taught her how to climb a ladder!

CHAPTER 25

Their Shadow Sides

Once I got focused with Trixie's training, I began to prepare her for competition. She was a little spunkier than Nick and somewhat flashier. The compulsive training certainly didn't showcase her spirited attitude in her work. So it was not the fulfilling experience I would later enjoy with Tori. Trixie just looked like she was trying not to get into trouble. There was no fire in her eyes or spring in her step that I would later become accustomed to with Tori.

Before I began competing with Trixie, I had never failed a class in AKC obedience competition. Nick was always very reliable and did his job dutifully. Trixie of course was a little bit sassier and was about to deliver a valuable lesson about the feminine psyche. Anthea prepared to cleverly shove a learning opportunity right in my face!

In the novice level AKC class, you have on-leash and off-leash heeling, a stand for examination by the judge, then a sit-stay with a recall (to come when called). For some reason, Trixie was not happy with me during that show and I can't remember why. I vaguely recall some type of battle of wills between us that day. She was not making me happy, and I was complaining to my parents about what a b*tch she was! (Poor dog.)

When we got to the recall exercise where she was to come to me when I called her, things took a drastic turn. I think Trixie could tell by the look on my face that I was annoyed at her. Instead of coming to me, she creeped halfway and stopped. Her head hung low, her eyes locked with mine, and she said, "Take that!" as she lay down in the ring. I couldn't tell if she was "giving me the finger" or if she was afraid to get close to me. My expression instantly transformed into pure *rage*; daggers shot out of my eyes at her! How dare she defy me and fail me! I had never failed a class before, and I felt so humiliated. I felt so *betrayed* by my own dog. My teenage brain saw it as a personal attack that required vindication. *Ironically,* the only times I would ever fail any competition were with Anthea, once as Tori and once as Trixie. I guess Anthea knew this was a good way to get my attention!

I stormed out of the ring with my sassy little dog in tow. I sent her to her crate and began to tell my parents what a terrible dog she was. I was furious with Trixie. I threatened to spay her and never show her again. Anger and resentment boiled up inside me.

What I did not realize, and wouldn't for many decades yet to come, was that the insecurities my father had instilled within me spawned a ruthless standard for perfection. I unconsciously attempted to gain his approval with everything I did. I assumed that the more perfect or successful I was, the more likely I was to earn his approval and accolades. This was an "impossible standard," as my mother informed me repeatedly throughout life. But this was a core part of me that I felt I could not change. I didn't realize it stemmed from so many years of emotional conflict around my father. I thought it was just who I was. Nevertheless, this level of dedication and commitment carried me through life and served me well. It provided me with a diligent work ethic and rigorous ethical standards that allowed me to succeed in life. I was always able to provide for myself no matter the difficulty because of it. The only thing it did not do for me was to acquire the one thing I so desperately wanted. I never gained the recognition, respect, or admiration of my father. Never. This is a huge *ironic twist* that we will thoroughly explore at the end of this story.

It was this ruthless quest for perfect performance that Trixie was reacting to. She was crumbling under the pressure, but I couldn't see it. This experience brings up many messages from both Öskar and Anthea!

Can you guess what they might be? It was a teaching from the "shadow side" of both. Let's take a look.

We know Öskar's teaching is about identifying and overcoming oppression as well as finding your voice and learning to express it. There is a shadow side to his teaching too, and that is when the oppressed unknowingly becomes the *oppressor*. Subconsciously we mirror what we see, especially as children. Unknowingly I was mirroring the intense need for control I saw in my father and displaying that back onto my dogs. I was using my father's energy to fuel my quest for ultimate perfection while preparing for this show. This created an oppressive situation for the dogs. The pressure I placed on them in my quest of perfection was tremendous for them to endure. They were feeling just as I often did under my father's reign. This suffocating pressure had snuffed Trixie's joy right out of her! She could see what was happening, and she was trying to send me a message. Nick was a bit more stoic and not as easy to read so I didn't see his message. Ahh, just like me—stiff upper lip and solid game face. Nick was mirroring my response to my father literally once again. Are you beginning to see the pattern?

Anthea's shadow side is the opposite expression of her normal joyful self. When she is stifled, she appears hesitant, reluctant, and fearful. Instead of her captivating joy, she expresses self-doubt and insecurity, frozen in place and unable to move or make decisions. These powerful negative emotions blocked her joy and shoved it out of reach. Her light was inhibited and can no longer shine. She reflects this shadow side when you are blocking her message. Anthea was also illustrating for me that I needed to lighten up a little and not take life so seriously just like she had been as "Sally."

This event definitely provoked me by angering me, but I couldn't see past that. Once again, I did not heed the invitation for healing and missed out on another opportunity. I did finally forgive Trixie and continued to compete with her. We managed to complete her Companion Dog (CD) title without any more hiccups.

CHAPTER 26

Like Father, Like Son

During these years, the divide between my father and me continued to grow. He struggled to find ways to relate to me because fatherhood did not come natural to him. He did not have a happy childhood, and this left him clueless about providing one for me. Spending time with him was often awkward at best. But it was during my research for writing this book that I truly appreciated why this was. I finally understood the deep level of cruelty he had suffered from his own father. I got a glimpse of the brutality my grandfather afflicted on my father with his judgment, anger, and absolute psychological suffocation. Unfortunately, this style of parenting was acceptable in rural Texas in his day.

You see my grandfather was an oil worker, a tough man with a heavy hand. As a teenager, he and his brothers wreaked havoc in his small Texas town, controlling it with their violence. Even the local law was afraid of these redneck gangsters. I learned of many instances where my grandfather forcefully struck my father for minor things. I can only imagine the fear my father must have grown up with. Fear of his own father, the inner rage it created, the same rage I saw in him now. Gaining this knowledge made my dad seem harmless in comparison. He acted like any child of a bully, and I could now see that fatherhood terrified him. Perhaps the potential of becoming his own father was

Öskar

enough to paralyze him. I will never know for sure because I never got to ask him.

This knowledge gave me tremendous clarity about why my father had been who he was to me. This is what he had learned from his own father. And just that little bit of knowledge led to understanding that created a shift in my anger toward him. That cemented anger began to slowly transmute and crumble as echoes of compassion appeared on the horizon. I wasn't quite capable of loving him yet, but I had a newfound sense of understanding. Of course, all of this occurred forty years too late. But later is always better than never.

One very sad story I heard about my father's childhood was that of his unrealized musical prowess. Apparently, he played the base cello in high school. My uncle surprisingly reported that when his brother played, it was like angels singing! By all accounts he was incredibly talented! My father's music instructor wanted to send him to Juilliard in NYC. But my grandfather would hear none of it and threw the instructor out of the house. "No son of mine is going to be a sissy!" he reportedly proclaimed. My father never played again after that day. I never even knew he could play. Can you imagine how painful that must have been? I can palpate his anguish even now! This must have been why he appeared to obstruct anything I wanted to do. This was his programing. Children didn't get to do what they wanted to.

> One very special irony for my father was that after my grandfather died, my grandmother remarried. The man she married in her sixties played the base cello in a band!

This story provided so much clarity for me. My father battled his own insecurities around feeling worthy, having his own voice, being lovable, and feeling safe to be himself. He never got to experience love, kindness, compassion, or genuine interest from his own father. No wonder he could not provide it for me! Furthermore, he had passed these insecurities, "tags," or ancestral burdens onto me quite literally as if they had been written into my hardwire. This explained why I felt like I was swimming against the current my whole life!

Despite all his damage, he tried his best even if it was awkward and often too little, too late. One such occasion was when he randomly decided to teach me about running a business when I was only thirteen years old. Maybe he knew this would be the last opportunity he would get with me. Surprisingly, this topic proved to be of great interest. He gave me valuable insight on forming and running a proprietorship and some of these points I still remember to this day. It must have made an impression on me because I was never more fulfilled in life than when I was self-employed. The *irony* is that I would spend more than 50 percent of my career self-employed. And much of that was with my dog business that would emerge in my thirties, the one I mentioned in Tori's story. It was like he had seen into my future and decided he'd better make sure I was ready!

We really tried to come together, but we were like oil and water. I think I reminded him of himself and that brought back painful memories of his childhood along with deeply rooted subconscious self-hatred instilled by his own father. He just could not seem to find his way out of it. He did not have the help of the K9 spirit guides like I have, and it certainly curtailed his ability to transmute all that pain into love. I really regret that our relationship never stood a chance and that we could never find our way back to each other before he died.

Fortunately, the dogs served as surrogate family and friends for me. I still found it very difficult to make friends. My stifled confidence was not a billboard of attraction for other kids. Most kids my age had no interest in me or the things I liked. I also continued to be ridiculed by my peers through middle school. I felt so out of place, uncomfortable, and unwelcome at school. I couldn't find a way to fit in. Consequently, I could not wait until it was time to go home. The dogs filled this painful social gap for me and provided me with a sense of belonging. I don't know what I would have done without them! But because of this isolation, I lacked basic communication skills. Feeling very self-conscious about this, I became even more afraid to speak. Öskar could see my struggle and his messages were for me to learn to use my voice. But until I was able, he would stand by me holding my energy, my confidence, and my voice until I was able to take my power back.

By the end of my thirteenth year, my parents announced they were separating. I was thrilled that my father would be moving out! It was a giant exhale of relief as I realized I would no longer be forced to endure his toxicity. I didn't really like him, and I couldn't wait to expunge everything about him from my life. Only then could I move on and be free to be myself. Or so I thought.

Once my father moved out, I didn't see him much because I realized I had a choice. I was supposed to spend every other weekend with him, but I decided that I would just rather not. He was understandably upset with my defiant decision to stand my ground and immediately blamed my mother for my desire to avoid him. He just couldn't admit that my disdain for him was only as a direct result of his own treatment of me.

CHAPTER 27

The Closing of a Chapter

I think it was a Sunday morning when I woke up and found Nick to be in distress. He couldn't stand up straight and kept walking in a circle to the right. His head also tilted to the right while his eyes darted back and forth. He didn't seem coherent, didn't respond when I called his name. I was horrified! Something was wrong, and it didn't look good.

I convinced my father to take us to the doggie ER. This was no easy feat because he was stingy with his money and especially resented spending it on my dogs. But I promised to pay for it out of my allowance. The vet who was on duty was very kind and compassionate. He had children of his own and could see how frightened I was. In the 1980s, they did not yet have MRI technology available for pets. It would be difficult if not impossible to fully assess and diagnose Nick's condition without it. He did, however, offer two probable scenarios. First, and the most favorable possibility, was an inner ear infection. This could certainly cause the lack of balance and coordination as well as the head tilt. But the more likely explanation was that Nick had suffered a stroke! This would better correlate to his rapid eye movement and diminished cognition. There were not very many solutions available for him, unfortunately. We could treat him for an ear infection and see if he improved. But all we could do was wait and hope. I was hysterical with concern for my dog, and all this just made my head spin!

I took Nick home and kept him as comfortable as I could. He seemed stressed and nervous like he knew something was wrong. I was worried about my guardian. I could not imagine my life without him! I think Trixie would be heartbroken without him, too. The next few days were filled with angst. I could only hope that he would pull out of this somehow. All the training stopped while I focused on taking care of my Nick.

The vet did call to see how Nick was doing a couple of days later. But there was not much change. It would become a waiting game, something I was not good at. When events in my life tend to run amuck, I find myself bailing. I inherently avoid instability and uncertainty. This is another core value that would take me decades to understand. The pain, heart ache, and betrayal I was beginning to experience from this scenario were more than I wanted to deal with. It would be easier to just walk away from it than to feel it. Unconsciously I began to erect a wall around my heart. A wall that poor Nick could not scale. I was not willing to allow him to hurt me by leaving me. And if I emotionally left him first, I could prevent it.

Nick gradually improved in small bits, but never completely. He was able to walk a little straighter, his eyes normalized, his head was closer to midline, and he got some of his strength and endurance back. But we never resumed our training. This whole experience had initiated a big *shift* in me. On some level, I felt *betrayed* by Nick, and that I could no longer trust him. I was angry that he was now broken. This was just my bruised childish ego trying to protect me. Unconsciously I began to detach myself from him and Trixie. It would be safer this way. I could throw all my energy toward my dream of having a horse instead. That would replace the pain with joy! I had not yet learned that joy could not be implanted, that the block for receiving joy must first be removed. So as I mindlessly went through the motions of caring for Nick and spending time with Trixie, my heart had already left.

In my eagerness to find something safe to sink my passion into, I reverted to an older flame. Ever since I could remember, I had obsessed over everything horses: books, movies, riding, shows, and racing. What teenage girl doesn't? I constantly begged my parents for a horse, but their response was always the same. "No!" In a way, the dogs had been my substitute for a horse. But if given the choice, I would give them up in a heartbeat. As far as I was concerned, there was no limit to what I would do to get a horse.

My father grew up on a ranch in Texas where he used horses to work the cattle. For some reason, he did not care for horses, or at least not in the romantic way that I did. His typical retort to my pleading cited how expensive and dumb horses were. Claiming it would be money absolutely wasted, money that we did not have. But I was willing to work for it, save my money up, and get a job at the barn to pay for all the expenses. Still, he said, "No!" I just didn't get a sense that he wanted me to be happy.

With my heartbreak over Nick's disability, it seemed now was a good time to switch gears. So I started pushing my father even harder. I tried to negotiate. I proposed, "If I got rid of my dogs, could I have a horse then?" Being the ruthlessly deceptive and manipulative man that he was, my father replied, "Sure, you sell your dogs, and if you can afford it, you can buy a horse." But I don't think my father ever expected me to go through with that. He knew how much I loved my dogs, and he didn't believe that I had the guts to part with them. But I was determined to prove that I did, no matter what the cost. I was fully committed to reaching my lifelong goal.

Once I had been given the green light, I set my sights on selling my dogs. Initially I didn't give much thought to what this would mean to me. I was only focused on the outcome. I had no idea what impact it would have on all of us. But once I make a decision, I am fully committed to it and won't back down. This is yet another core value that I adopted because of my father's lack of such. He rarely kept his promises; I *never* broke mine, no matter what it cost me. So I put an ad in the paper to sell Nick and Trixie. And in that moment, they were suddenly transformed from my loving companions to assets to be traded.

There was quite a bit of interest in the dogs, especially since they were already trained, AKC registered, and obedience titled. Most of the inquiries were only interested in Nick but not Trixie. I had a few people come to the house to test Nick in his training. But his subtle head tilt and lingering diminished endurance deterred any sales. It was painful for me to watch these prospective buyers test Nick. I felt a sense of deep regret creep in and a vague sense of shame for my cowardice in running away. I shoved these emotions down as deep as I could. I knew no other way to cope with my situation at this age. Nick and Trixie continued to trust me. They faithfully worked for the strangers who showed up to meet them. I didn't give any thought to the fact that I was about to part with them forever. I couldn't bear to think about it. I felt like I was wrenched between my greed to have a horse and the pain of the *betrayal* of Nick's health issue. And I was angry that my father was forcing me into this position. He was playing with my emotions; I think he thought I would back down when it got hard.

After a couple months, I finally got a call from a man in Mississippi who was interested in both dogs. He drove up on a Saturday to see them. Mr. Sample was exactly sixty-six years old I remember. He was very kind, polite, wore a big hat, and arrived in a great big Cadillac. He was very impressed by Nick and didn't seem to be bothered by his physical imperfections. He simply wanted a dog, a manly dog, as his constant companion. Since I would only sell them as a pair, he felt Trixie would be great for his girlfriend. I remember thinking, *This old man has a girlfriend?*

Mr. Sample seemed like a really good fit for my precious dogs. And before I knew it, I was accepting full payment. Things were happening very fast now, and my brain couldn't keep up. I heard my mouth speaking words that my heart struggled to understand. "But wait," it kept saying. "Do you really want to do this?" But the questions fell on deaf ears because the ego wanted the horse and was not about to back down. So just like that, Mr. Sample took possession of my best friends and loaded them up in the back seat of his Cadillac. They looked so confused.

> My heart was beating so fast, trying desperately to get my attention! I was trying not to cry. I was trying to be brave, to be an adult about this. I wanted to stand fast on my mark without wavering or showing any weakness. My father would be so proud that I was like him!

Mr. Sample said his goodbyes and backed out of the driveway. In slow motion, I watched while he drove down the street. A big knot had formed in my throat, making it hard to breathe or swallow. I could see both dogs staring out the back window at me for as long as they could see me. And as the Cadillac left the neighborhood, I collapsed in tears. What had I done?

CHAPTER 28

Consequences

Sadly, on October 23,1983, I watched my best friends in this whole world drive out of my life. The pain of my choice was agonizing! At only fourteen years of age, I had not yet experienced anything like it. What had I done? They were my best and only friends in this world, and I rejected them!

    I wanted to be strong. I had set out to prove to my father that I was willing to do whatever it took to achieve my goal of owning a horse. I had hoped to earn his respect, and then he would allow me to have what I really wanted and what he promised. But my father never let me have that horse. He showed his true colors and ultimately *betrayed* me. I was totally devastated and heartbroken. I had granted him temporary trust, extending my vulnerability to him just this once. But this was unforgivable. Subconsciously it was on this day that I decided to never trust him again. He had only proven what I had learned when I was eleven; adults aren't to be trusted.

    My parents' divorce was brutal for both my mother and for me. And now I had nothing to distract me from it. I longed for the company of my dogs to comfort me. I cried every day as I realized I had truly made a grave mistake. I would never go back on my conviction unlike my father, but I would suffer because of my dedication to it. For the next year, I often dreamed about Nick and Trixie, about desperately trying to find them again and bring them home. And sometimes in my dreams, I did find them and we had a joyous reunion! Unfortunately, our most painful experiences in life have the most valuable lessons to teach us. And losing Nick and Trixie was a huge lesson from Öskar and Anthea.

Nick did eventually find his way back, and you will hear about it next. But I never saw my beautiful Trixie again, and I never found out what happened to her. I had to live with the choice I made that day as a desperate teenager.

CHAPTER 29

The Ultimate Truth

Although this is an incredibly sad story, it is important to realize the true message here. There is abundant irony in the choices I made. My father didn't really *betray* me. That was just an illusion my mind conjured up. The irony is that I betrayed myself when I did the unthinkable and sold my best friends. Not only did I betray my own soul by going against what I instinctively knew to be correct, but I also betrayed my dogs and their trust in me! My core being has always been steadfast committed and protective of those I love. By rejecting my dogs, I rejected myself and betrayed my own core values. And this is what creates guilt! This is a perfect example of how it can be difficult at times to see through the illusions of our human mind and perceive the actual truth and the lesson to be learned.

There were many *ironic twists* in the beautiful story of Nick and Trixie. Trixie gave us a cute tale when she used the skill I taught her to expand her own joy and explore all day. It was like she was trying to draw attention to the fact that she could do it and how important it would be in my future. She also seemed to fail me in an obedience competition when, in reality, I actually failed her and myself. But there were also three more lessons in irony involving my father. My lifelong subconscious desire to gain his approval and love was really a lesson in accepting myself and acknowledging my own power. I had the power to fill those voids, yet I spent my whole life trying to get him to do it for me. I unknowingly gave my power away to him in many ways, and Öskar was showing this to me. If I only loved myself the way Anthea was showing me, I could reclaim my own power the way Öskar was presenting me.

We also visited the painful irony of my father's life that revolved around self-value, voice, and power. He was dealing with the same issues I was. I mirrored him much like the dogs mirrored me. As a result, he was unable to love himself, much less me. We could not *be* for each other until we were healed and whole. The guides, although devoted to me at this point, were actually speaking to both of us. As you can see, we had some of the same lessons. And this is, as they say, "the sins of the father." If these important tags are not addressed, they just keep getting passed down the line. And yet, we saw such a loving irony when my father taught me how to run a business as a teenager. How could he have known I would need such a skill?

Part of the guides' teachings is to illustrate our own role in what we experience. The people in our lives are no accident, and they play a critical part in our growth much like actors do in a play. Our costars have agreed to be present and to facilitate certain experiences that are an opportunity for our souls to heal and become whole again. My father agreed to show me the betrayal tag in such a vivid way so that I would realize how much I needed to repair that part of myself. He used himself as an example to motivate me to get the work done. He knew I would not want to end up like him! So ultimately, he was not my enemy; he was my gift!

We also saw many tags in the powerful coupling of Öskar and Anthea. Anthea continued to push her ever-important messages around *betrayal*. She showed it to me when she failed me in the show ring. We saw it concealed as regret and shame when I was selling my dogs. We clearly see the illusion of betrayal when my father backed out of our deal. (This, by the way, was one of the reasons I reacted so passionately about my coach's betrayal over our deal in Tori's story.) And then the ultimate betrayal of myself occurred when I sold part of me, my dogs. We have already discussed the irony of betrayal and what it really means. So you might already recognize the significance of these emotions, including how I didn't feel I deserved to be happy. I just kept punishing myself to prove it! No one else was doing it *to* me. Until I understood this, the K9 guides would keep bringing it to me.

Öskar's message is all about using your voice and owning your own God-given power. No one can really *take* these from you, but you can sure *give* them away! Öskar is also the "guardian of intuition" because you already know these things; you have just forgotten how to connect with that part of yourself. He is your source to reconnect with your own intuition.

PART 4

Nick Returns

The guardian would not leave his post.

CHAPTER 30

Nick Comes Home

1985

By now my parents' divorce was final and the psychological strain had taken its toll on my mother. My father was not a gracious person, and he set out to make the experience as miserable as he could for both of us. He intentionally caused financial devastation for my mother, which had its downstream effect on me. The overwhelming strain of the emotions and the residual financial woes proved much too great at times. She struggled with her motivation to establish her emotional independence and her ability to summon financial means. I could sense the turmoil and the deep-rooted pain even though I did not know specific details. My telepathic mind was in overdrive, picking up on the vibrations between them. And this created even more unease within me. This provided more fuel for my resentment of my father. Why did he insist on being such a miserable person?

It was now a year and a half after Nick and Trixie left and we found ourselves moving back to the house I grew up in. I was yanked from the comfortable, safe suburbs and returned to the house in Midtown with the bars on the windows. A house that stored tremendously painful memories for me. I was not happy to be back there. I was now fifteen years old, deep into the throws of adolescence, and busy with high school.

My mother's health was beginning to suffer under all the strain. She spent a lot of time in bed and invisible from my world. I was learning to get along without her. I knew she was going through a tough time, but so was I. Only I did not allow myself to curl up and surrender to it. I had learned from my father to hold my head high and never show my pain. It was in my best interest to never allow my opposition to see me struggle. So I kept moving forward, not allowing time to feel my emotions or dwell on them. I just did what needed to be done. I went to school, worked hard, and only permitted thoughts about my future, a future that did not include my father.

It was around this time that I got a phone call from the executor of Mr. Sample's estate. It seemed he had passed away and they were looking for someone to claim his dog. Nick was being cared for by a veterinarian about two hours away in Mississippi. I asked about Trixie, but she didn't know anything about her. All she could tell me was that Nick needed to be picked up or else he would be sent to the shelter. Of course, I would come get him; I was elated over the moon to have this opportunity to get him back! So a couple of days later, I found a ride and made the trip to Mississippi.

All I could think about was how excited I was so to see Nick again! But my heart sank when I first laid eyes on him after so much time apart. He was not the dog I remembered. He was not the dog I had taken meticulous care of. He didn't seem to recognize me at all! He couldn't even look me in the eye. He looked very sad and very old. He appeared to have aged tremendously in a very short period. I wondered what he had been through, how his life had been. I was heartbroken, but I loaded him up in the car and hoped for the best.

At our current house, we had a very small fenced-in yard. It was an older house with hardwood floors and window air conditioning. The floors creaked when you walked on them, and the rooms were echoey. Other things had changed since Nick left. I was now well into my teenage years, running track at high school, and staying busy. I wasn't home as much as I was when I had him the first time. There wouldn't be as much time for us to share together this round.

I tried to make him comfortable as he settled in to be a family pet.

He never really seemed to understand who we were, and this really rattled me. There was no recognition in his eyes when I said his name. There seemed to be a vacancy about him. Like part of his soul had been vacuumed out! He was still the kind and patient dog I remembered, but he was not nearly as confident. He just hung out in the yard and stuck to himself. What I couldn't see was that he was forming a bond with my mother. She needed him this time. She was at home alone while I was busy being a teenager and keeping my distance. She took care of him, and he took care of her. He had come back for her this time. Nick provided the emotional support and unconditional love she required during such a heartbreaking time in her life. He now held her pieces as well and was silently showing her the way she needed to go.

The life of a teenager is constantly evolving, and in a flash, it was time for me to go to college and move out of the house. I didn't want to burden my mother with the financial responsibility of caring for Nick when I was gone. So I put an ad in the paper once again. A family in search of a new pet came to look at him. The fact that he was already trained and grew up with children (me) was a definite plus for them. They really liked him and decided to take him home. So I found myself once again saying goodbye to Nick. This time it was not due to my own selfish reasons, and it was not nearly as traumatic. It was the best option for him and my mother, or so I thought.

But the new arrangements did not last long. I got a call at college from his new family. A vet check had found heartworms. He would need to be treated and they wanted to return him. I was overwhelmed with this news adding onto the new stress of college. But my mother took him back and paid for his treatment even though she couldn't afford it. She wanted to do right by him, so she found a way to take care of our guardian angel.

Nick was apparently not to leave the family. But this time, he was there to watch over my mother, helping her to heal her broken heart and wrecked ego. He brought her comfort and kept her safe. He was her angel now, providing the same lessons of voice and power for her that he had for me.

CHAPTER 31

The Rage That Lies Beneath

Still struggling financially from the divorce, my mother sought refuge in a property that a friend of hers owned. She rented his house for significantly less than the mortgage on our home. This older house in Midtown Memphis was in a nicer neighborhood, had a negligible yard that was mostly pavement, and was located on a very busy street. This house was a massive, old, three-story on Peabody Ave. It was also haunted. You could hear the ghost walking on the third floor as well as going up and down the old, wooden staircase. Nick would frequently watch this ghost tracking her movements with his eyes. This gave me the creeps but didn't seem to bother him one bit. He had fully recovered from his parasite invasion but was beginning to show his eight years now with his graying muzzle and diminishing mobility. But he was a trooper and never complained. He was just there for Mom.

By the end of 1988, I was making plans to move to Nashville. I was now a very competitive cyclist, a sophomore in college, and wanted to join my new team in the Music City. I got accepted into Middle Tennessee State University, where I would continue my education allowing me to be much closer to my team. I was excited about all the upcoming changes, especially that I was finally leaving Memphis! This move was long overdue, and I was ready to leave all these painful memories behind. I wanted to strike out on my own and start a new beginning. However, Memphis wasn't gonna let me go without getting the last word!

I was out on a training ride just before Christmas when the unthinkable happened. I had ridden for a few hours in the cold and was anxious to get home and warmed up again. I needed to cross a busy four-lane road. I checked the traffic to the left and there was a car coming toward me, moving very slowly with the right turn signal on, planning to turn on my road. Then I turned my attention to the right and saw that the traffic was clear after the next vehicle passed so I began to move slowly into the intersection, preparing to cross. While I still had my head turned to the right, inching forward into the road, I felt this external force sweep me up with tremendous power. Instantly I knew what was happening, and I uttered one single word. "No!"

I knew, even though I couldn't see it, that I had been hit by a car! The car that was supposed to turn right did not and headed straight into me! I was instantly filled with *rage!* I was also suddenly conscious of another presence. Three angels had arrived at my rescue. One of them, ever so slightly, waved her hand in front of my face and everything went black as the lights went out. I felt them lift me up. They carried my limp body and guided it through a precise trajectory to ensure that I would land accurately, preventing permanent, devastating damage. In the blink of an eye, the vehicle struck me from the left, swept me up over the hood, and as the driver began to brake, I was thrown into the air like a ragdoll. My body landed where the angels meticulously placed me, in front of the car precisely on my left butt cheek. The rest of my body followed and collapsed down to the pavement, landing supine as if I had just lain down for a nap in the middle of the road.

As soon as I hit the ground, I returned to the here and now with a snap of the fingers like I had never been out. I suppose this was *divine design* to spare me the pain of hitting the ground. Survival instincts kicked in strongly as I tried to right myself and spring off the pavement. But I couldn't move! I noticed a car to my left, not realizing it was the car that had struck me. I cried out for help. I was beginning to feel the pain in my back. A passenger was getting out of the vehicle and moving in my direction. I reached out for him, begging for help, noticing an elderly man as he staggered closer. Even as the back pain was beginning to roar, I was acutely aware that I had been hit and did not want the guilty driver to flee the scene. My nervous system was in overdrive; all my defenses were screaming! He reached out attempting to comfort me, but as the agonizing pain began to tighten its grip, I blurted out, "Did you see the m****r f****r that hit me?"

Cycling certainly had its predictable dangers. I had rehearsed this moment numerous times in my head just in case such a thing happened. I already knew exactly how I was going to react and how angry I was going to be. All the *rage* that had been hiding inside was more than willing to make an appearance. This poor fellow was so surprised by my outburst that he turned around and went back to the car. I had no idea that it was his wife who had run into me.

A crowd began to form around me as the traffic stopped to take a look. I continued to scream out in pain because my back was killing me, and I could not move. I could only hope that I was not paralyzed. It was the week before Christmas, and all I wanted was a peaceful bike ride in the cold. Someone in the crowd called the ambulance, and I could hear the sirens approaching in the distance. Others were volunteering to call my family. I began to blurt out phone numbers of my mother and my ex-boyfriend. But for whatever reason, none of the phone calls could get through. They couldn't reach *anybody!* No one answered. *Divine chaos* ensued!

The EMTs arrived and loaded me into the ambulance. There was a nice lady there who offered to ride with me to the hospital. She held my hand, providing me with the comfort that my mother would have had she been there. She knew; she had a son my age who also rode bicycles. She would not want him alone in this situation. Her husband took my bicycle home with him. I was terrified, but I didn't want to admit it or show it. The ambulance ride was rough and only served to create more pain for me. The adrenaline was coursing through my veins, and I was helplessly hyperventilating. I struggled to catch my breath and assert any level of control.

More chaos ensued at the hospital as I became bombarded with massive confusion and disarray. The police arrived and slapped a traffic violation in my lap. They told me I had been found at fault even though they never interviewed me about the incident. This further enraged me. I was then wheeled into radiology still wearing my sweaty cycling clothes, and the male technician asked me to remove my bra before testing. "Are you kidding me? I can't move!" I said to him through chattering teeth as I trembled uncontrollably. I would need maximum assistance to do so. Without saying a word, he left me there in the freezing cold radiology department for about thirty minutes. I was all alone, trembling, and terrified. *Rage* continued to boil without an outlet. I had no call light or means to obtain assistance. Where was everybody? I screamed out for help, but there was no answer, and no one came. All I could do was cry and shiver.

After what seemed an eternity, the radiation tech finally returned with help to get me out of my sweaty clothes and into a gown. I was thankful they did not have to cut off my newly acquired 7-Eleven team jacket that Tom Schuler himself had given me at a recent training camp!

In that day, the 7-Eeven professional cycling team was quite popular and a very strong team here nationally as well as on the world circuit. As a teenager, I had posters on my wall of professional cyclists instead of rock bands! So this jacket meant a lot to me and twenty years later I was still wearing it on training rides!

It was a relief to finally be provided with a warm blanket. The ER nurses continued their efforts to reach my mother but had yet to find her. I don't know how long I was there before my mother finally showed up, but I was relieved to see her when she did. The preliminary radiographs showed a possible spinal fracture, but there was too much swelling to make a conclusive diagnosis. They were going to admit me and do further testing after the edema subsided. Thankfully, they administered some pain medication and I was finally able to relax a little. But I still could not move and had not yet attempted to stand. I had no idea if I could.

My mother stayed with me that night in the hospital. I hadn't been in one since I was a young child. During the night, I finally needed to urinate. Realizing that I had not done so since 8:00 the previous morning, I figured it was about time. I refused to use a bedpan as the nurse instructed and instead persuaded my mother to help me to the bathroom. Leaning on her heavily, she helped me get from my bed to the toilet and left me standing there holding the rail. I convinced her that I was OK to potty on my own. My legs were a little shaky but felt OK. I just couldn't bend my back. So I gently lowered myself onto the toilet using the rail and did my business. I then stood back up, pulling my undergarments with me as I rose. But as soon as I got fully erect, the lights went out!

My mother was horrified as she heard me hit the floor. She came running in, worried that I had hurt myself even more. But my body had naturally protected itself, and even though I collapsed and was on the floor, my back was still completely straight! I had neatly collapsed into side sitting while keeping my back rigid. The beauty of the body's protective mechanisms at work! I was too weak to help my mother stand me up so she had to call for help. This huge orderly came in, scooped me up off the floor, and carried me to my bed. He then scolded me for getting up by myself and told me to never to do it again. That time I agreed.

The next day the swelling had subsided enough to perform an MRI. Back in the eighties, they transferred you from your room to testing using a transport gurney. This meant that I had to endure a very painful transfer from my bed to the gurney. No matter how the four nurses attempted to move me, it caused tremendous pain in my back. By the time I got to radiology, I was beside myself in agony. Having never felt this kind of physical pain coupled with no possible way of running away from it, I became agitated. The *rage* finding no exit was finally turning on *me!* I had always run from my pain in the past, and here I was trapped! I began to shake all over, and a sense of claustrophobia crept in. I was claustrophobic because I could not get out of my body or run away from the source of my pain! I could not run from myself!

All this was before I even got into the MRI! I remember feeling a tidal wave of *belligerent rage* flare up inside me like twisted, dark evil. I wanted so badly to get out of that bed and run! This was the only way I had ever learned to cope with such intense emotion before, and now I couldn't. I had no skills for dealing with what I was feeling. I was backed into a corner with no way out: *divine internal chaos!* I became hysterical, inconsolably crying and fighting with the nurses who tried to help. I felt like punching someone. The rage tag was getting louder! I guess Öskar wasn't entirely done with me after all. I was embarrassed that I was losing control in front of everyone. I usually keep such a tight rein on my emotions. Thankfully I was sedated, and I welcomed the heavenly bliss the artificial calm gifted me. It offered a temporary "hall pass" for the homework I had yet to complete.

The MRI confirmed a complex burst fracture of my first lumbar vertebrae (L1) in the middle of my back. The attending physician defiantly announced that I would not ride my bike for six months, much less sit upright for three months. As a college student and a cyclist, this was devastating news. *You've got to be kidding,* I thought. To twist the dagger even more, he added, "If you crash or fall again, you could possibly become paralyzed." I'm not sure if this was his attempt to intimidate me or what, but somehow, I doubted and rejected the information he provided.

As I was preparing to discharge home, a complication developed. I found that I couldn't keep anything in my stomach. The location of the fracture had traumatized the vagus nerve creating extreme nausea. Every time I tried to eat, I vomited it back up. Every time I tried to stand, I vomited bile. This also meant that I could not tolerate oral medications. The hospital could administer intravenous meds to get around this, but it would prove problematic when I got home. Even so, I was anxious to get out of the hospital. I would just have to find a way to make it all work. So my mother borrowed a van to get me home according to the doctor's instructions and we decided to take our chances on our own.

CHAPTER 32

The Power of Energy Healing

I was glad to be out of that hospital, but I would soon learn that caring for myself would prove to be more challenging than I anticipated. First, none of the bedrooms in my mother's house were on the first floor. Since I still needed maximum assistance just to walk, and definitely could not get up all those steps, I ended up sleeping on the couch in the den. The main-floor bathroom was on the other side of the house so it was a process just to get me there. Each time I stood up, I invariably puked. I had not bathed since the day before the accident, because I couldn't stand up long enough to tolerate one, and I couldn't sit in a tub. I was miserable and at this moment had no idea what my future held. Things were looking a little bit bleak. Christmas was next week and a couple of days after New Year's, I was planning on moving four hours away. I had no idea if my move or school change was even going to happen. Would I miss out on school or racing this year? I was depressed, angry, and sad but powerless to do anything about it. Öskar was revving up my agitation again. Here was yet another chance to heal my tags around *powerlessness and rage*.

Nick kept me company while I was confined to the first floor. He was just a quiet presence watching over me. He was waiting for me to accept the opportunity to expel all the toxic anger that kept attracting these tags. Each time I ignored the message, it came back with a louder version. This was the loudest one I had ever experienced by far. I can't imagine how much worse it would get if I continued to ignore it.

My father called from Texas, where he now lived with his new wife. He voiced his concerns about my continued participation in such a dangerous sport. He wanted me to quit. But cycling was the one thing that brought me joy. So of course I wasn't going to give it up. He desperately offered a trade. He suggested that if I quit cycling, he would set me up in any other hobby I chose. "How about that horse you always wanted?" he suggested. I was flabbergasted! Now he wanted to get me a horse? There was no way I was falling for that again! No, thank you.

The only comfort he had to offer was to "take care" of the woman who hit me. I had no idea what he actually meant by this, but I also did not want to know. The geriatric driver was in her eighties and probably should not have been driving. But I didn't wish any ill will on her over our dreadful encounter! I just shook my head at his willful lack of compassion for either of us. As usual, the conversation with him left me feeling even worse than I already did, and I regretted even answering his call.

My mother had a friend, a very nice man that I also befriended many years later. He happened to be a Reiki master and volunteered to come over and work on me. I had no idea what Reiki was and didn't really care. I agreed to accept the healing just to get my mother off my back about it. Tony came over that evening and silently worked on me as I lay on the couch. He didn't even have to touch me. His hands quietly hovered above my body with his eyes closed. I had no idea what he was doing as I drifted off into a peaceful sleep. An astounding irony here was that my mother and I both became Reiki practitioners a few years later. My mother even went on to become a Reiki master.

Reiki is an ancient Japanese form of energy
healing transferred through the palms
of the practitioner restoring balance and
function within the energetic body.

When I awoke, he was gone and it was morning. For the first time, I had slept all night and without any pain. I also noticed that I was hungry. Without even thinking, I stood from the couch and walked to the kitchen. I made myself a sandwich, relishing in how good it tasted. I had no problems keeping it down. Finally realizing how rank I smelled, I decided to take a shower. So I walked into the bathroom, took off my clothes, and took my first shower in a week. I did not make the connection between the Reiki and my sudden improvement for more than two decades!

Tony would be someone I swapped father stories with in the future as we became closer friends. He shared his own traumatic history with his father. Tony was a talented healer yet humble and gracious. He was always ready to be of service to a soul in need. He was a welcoming positive male figure in my life. I am honored to have met and shared time with him. The crossing of our paths was no coincidence; it never is. He carried a heavy burden of his own that was easy for me to see on his face. His emotional pain spoke volumes in his body. He struggled to be loved and appreciated by his father the same way I did. Nevertheless, he was a divine gift from God, and because of him, I was able to physically heal and get back to my life in rather short order!

After my session with Tony, I was able to move as planned the next week and returned to cycling with my new team three weeks later. It turns out that crabby hospital doctor had it all wrong! Five months after being hit by a car and breaking my back, I won my very first road race (cycling)! Interestingly, a year later, I would also achieve my goal of racing professionally! I was so glad I did not fall for my father's trickery this time.

There was a light at the end of that very dark tunnel after all! Even though I still had not addressed my issues with rage, I was allowed to move on into more opportunities.

CHAPTER 33

A Painful Parting

My mother hosted a family reunion at her house on Peabody Avenue in the summer of 1989. Her whole family came from Indiana, California, and South Africa. I was away at college so I didn't attend. This festive weekend of celebration would prove to have significant meaning for multiple reasons.

With everyone coming and going to and from the house, no one paid close attention to closing the gate from the yard to the driveway. Couple that with the house being directly on a very busy boulevard, and you get a bad scenario. At some point, by the end of the weekend, it was discovered that Nick was gone! The gate had been left open and he was just gone. My mom launched a search party, posted flyers, and called the humane societies in the area. I worried from my college dorm room, frustrated that I couldn't be there.

I don't know how much time passed, maybe a week, maybe two. Nick was finally located at an animal shelter on the other side of town in need of urgent medical attention. He had been struck by a car and his pelvis was crushed. Mom rushed to him. Our dedicated guardian needed to be released from his duties once and for all. He had used all his eternal nine lives and his journey with us had finally come to a hard stop. He had held steady through many tough times and refused to leave us when we needed him the most. He had been an angel to my mother and me, a guardian of our souls, a protector of our emotions, a carrier of our voice, and it was time to say goodbye. It was time for his chapter to come to an end. It didn't appear there was going to be any resurrecting his story this time. My mother shared a very painful and difficult goodbye with him that day at the hospital. I silently grieved from my dorm room at college. Life would be so different without him.

What we did not know until later was that we were going to be moving to California later that summer. Soon after Nick's passing, my mother experienced a devastating blow when she suddenly lost her job. Her older sister in California offered to hire her as an assistant in her holistic health practice. She even had an apartment for her to live in. Since the two of them were more than ten years apart in age and had never really gotten to spend much quality time together, it seemed like a wonderful chance to rectify that.

So Nick had to leave to free her up for this big opportunity. It was certainly easier to contemplate such a big change when there were no pets to consider. He wanted to be sure she took this option by stepping out of the way. His timely exit created a doorway of opportunity that would send both our lives in another direction!

In Nick's second visit, we see more opportunities for me to address my own rage and feelings of powerlessness and for my mother to begin her healing process. It became more apparent that he was not just there for me. We also begin to see more clearly how everything was designed so precisely. The guides show us evidence of divine design, chaos, and even internal chaos suggesting that everything is as it should be even though if feels and appears random and out of our control.

There was a rather ironic twist when my father offered to buy that horse I had always wanted. But now it wasn't because I wanted it. Again, he was offering to control me, my emotions, and my choices. Only this time, I saw it for what it was and did not fall for his poor intentions. It almost felt like a test, but I was watching for it this time. And in this part, we see yet another foreshadow with the Reiki experience and the direction our lives were to take once we made that move to California. It was so critical for us to get to California so that we both received the training we would need for the next part of our lives. There my mother and I would both become massage therapists and Reiki practitioners. This benchmark would steer me toward my eventual profession and provide a means for my mother to care for herself financially. Nick made sure this opportunity happened so that everything else fell into place. There are so many clues in all of our lives if we look closely.

Let's continue our discovery of Öskar with his final appearance in Zozzo. Would I finally accept the challenge to dissolve my rage?

PART 5

Zozzo

"Zozzo"

CHAPTER 34

The Power within You

Zozzo was a huge Belgian Malinois that I imported from Belgium as a two-year-old. He was to become my new schutzhund competition partner, and he arrived in 2003. I was looking for a dog that I could compete successfully at the national level. My current dog did not have the necessary character for competitive scores at the upper echelon. I was hoping that Zozzo would possess the needed qualities to carry us into that distinction.

But first, I want you to realize the irony here. Nick was my first schutzhund dog when I was twelve years old. Zozzo would be my final schutzhund dog at thirty-five years old. Both were expressions of Öskar. Zozzo would effectively assist me in closing my chapter on this sport. And by the completion of our time together, I would have moved on to something that fulfilled me even more.

But let's take a moment to understand why Öskar had returned to me as Zozzo. In 2002 I had initiated my own Belgian Malinois breeding program totally by accident. You have already heard about Tori from my 2004 litter. You will hear in a bit about Apachi from my first litter in 2002. Simultaneously I was just beginning my transition as a physical therapist into a professional dog trainer. I did not *plan* any of it; it just happened. Doors opened and I walked through. I followed my instincts unknowingly following the guidance of my spirit guides.

I had many successes and reasons to celebrate throughout this process, yet something was holding me back from achieving all that I could and kept me from fully moving forward. Öskar was coming to help me with this, and for a brief moment, he and Anthea would be reunited during an overlap with Zozzo and Tori.

Even in 2003, I continued to harbor resentment and anger toward my father. He had not been in my life since 1994, but I continued to dwell on our relationship or lack thereof. I thought that the more I mulled it over, the more I might understand it. But it only served to keep me a prisoner in this toxic space. Do you ever feel that if you can just figure out *why* something happened, you can finally understand it then forgive it? Well, this is certainly what I thought. But two decades later, I learned this assumption is incorrect and only served to hinder my ability to heal. This is where I was at this point in my life: stuck. I just could not move forward even though some great things were happening for me.

As I mentioned before, the anger I felt toward my father and the lack of his acceptance was the subconscious motivating factor that drove my need to succeed. This is why I was never satisfied even when I was successful. My objective could never be achieved emotionally because it didn't erase the anger or the emptiness. Unfortunately, the acceptance I yearned for from my father would never come from him. It had to come from within me. But this is much easier said than done since most people, me included, have no idea what this actually means.

Zozzo wanted to show me this to remind me that I still had work to do before I could be free. Just trying to ignore the pain doesn't work. It must be acknowledged and transmuted into love before it can be removed fully from the core being: the soul. Otherwise, the soul continues to "tag" it and attract experiences to show it to you. So Zozzo was a gentle reminder of the work I still needed to do. I needed to reclaim my power and my confidence. But as with the others, I could not see or hear the message. Therefore, this book is so important for you! With the knowledge and awareness that you will gain from the messages of the Core Four, you have the opportunity to be much more aware than

I was. You will be able to act on their messages and the gifts of healing instead of missing out on opportunity after opportunity like I did.

Unfortunately, Zozzo's visit was quite short. He was only with me a year and a half before he moved on again to help someone else. Let's look at his special story, however brief it may have been.

CHAPTER 35

Waiting for Me

Finding Zozzo was much like my search to find the dog in my prologue. But to get to my short list quickly, this time I hired a dog broker in Belgium. It's better to have some boots on the ground in the territory you are shopping. This broker successfully located a few prospects in rather quick order. He had access to dogs that were not yet listed on the internet and served as a great multilingual liaison. After about six months of reviewing everything he showed me, I saw a dog that really caught my eye. He was impressive to watch on video. He was quick in his retrieves and recalls. And based on the small, low-quality mpegs I viewed, his protection work with the decoy was equally impressive. It was difficult to get a good feel for his actual size because I didn't speak metric and couldn't tell the size of his handler. Back in that day, we did not have the advanced video capabilities for instant streaming. Most people were still sending VHS videos for final determination. And sometimes I had to convert that from European PAL just to view it.

Regardless, I was able to glean that there was a special quality about him, but I could not put my finger on what it was exactly. I decided to follow my instincts and not let this one get away. I placed a deposit on him and awaited the health testing I required before proceeding. Once all his tests were completed with satisfactory results, I finalized the purchase transaction and made plans to ship him to the US.

Öskar

He arrived on a Lufthansa airline direct flight into Chicago. I was so excited to meet him, but I was totally shocked when he came out of the crate! He was *huge!* This was a massive dog at one hundred pounds, and he stood roughly twenty-seven inches at the shoulder. He certainly did not look that big in the little videos I had seen. I was hoping he would not be too strong for me to handle. We took a little walk so he could stretch his legs, and I was relieved to notice how well-mannered he was for his size. Thankfully, he tolerated the long flight over remarkably well. So I gave him some food and water and then we headed home.

Next I would have to assess his temperament and working instincts to see if all my other requirements were met. Over the next few weeks, I tested his tracking abilities and was ecstatic with his olfactory skills! He had a beautiful, deep nose and was very methodical and calm throughout the entire exercise. He didn't miss anything and was impressively dialed in to his job. His obedience was a little flat: no flash, no tail wag, no sign whatsoever that he was having fun. Ironically, I found it very reminiscent of Nick. But even though it wasn't pretty to watch, it was absolutely correct! He also leaped like a gazelle over the jumps, proving to be surprisingly light on his feet despite his larger size.

His wow factor, however, was the switch that flipped when it was time to do protection. Yeah, also reminiscent of Nick. He used his size and power appropriately and showed that special presence I was looking for! He was so tall that he met most decoys at the beltline. He had a massive head and a superb deep commanding bark. His passive quiet nature took a back seat when it came to his favorite phase of the sport, the bite work. In addition, this big boy was superfast! He charged down the field and hit the decoy like a freight train! I felt sorry for the poor guys not knowing what was coming at them.

As commanding as he was on the field, he was very calm and patient all other times. His overall energy was quieter than most Malinois. I couldn't see Nick in him until I was writing this book and Öskar explained it to me. But as I look back, the energy of these two dogs was identical. Zozzo had such a kind heart that when it came time to breed to a female, he did not want to hurt her. This was the only place where this personality was a disadvantage. It took him a long time to learn how to breed, and I truly thought he would never get it.

Just like Nick, he was not flashy, and obedience was not his favorite thing. But he had enough devotion to me to want to please me. He excelled where most dogs were weak in the sport, tracking and protection. And he was always consistent. You could set your watch by his performance because he never threw any surprises or deviated from his typical performance. He was absolutely perfect for what I wanted, and we would have many incredible trial experiences together!

Let's just pause here and recognize the beauty in how all this came together. It can be a little nerve-wracking and risky buying a dog from overseas sight unseen. I had to rely heavily on my instincts. I looked at many dogs, relying on video clips and testimonials from sellers with broken English. This forced me to read between the lines, listen carefully to what wasn't being said, and pay attention to my inner voice. I had to decipher through the muck to determine if this dog was the right fit and energy for me without ever being near him.

Instincts and intuition must be exercised much like any muscle. You must learn to hear them and to trust them. There is certainly a learning curve and with practice I have learned to perfect it throughout my life. It started out as a gut feeling or a hunch and grew to become reliable clairsentience (an instinctual feeling). Now finally as my consciousness has expanded through this journey, my skills have blossomed into reliable gifts of knowledge. Everyone has these abilities; they are *in* you. It is already part of your blueprint. But you must expand your awareness so that you can access it.

So it was no accident that Zozzo ended up in my hands. He was waiting for me. Most men would have loved to have such a masculine dog like him, yet he waited for me. There was a specific intended purpose that he had only for me so no one else could purchase him, and that's how *divine design* works. That's how I was able to find him from so far away. He was looking for me as much as I was looking for him. Remember there are no accidents or coincidences in this world.

CHAPTER 36

Dialing In

The more time we spent together training, trialing, and hanging out, the more I recognized that Zozzo was everything I was promised and everything I paid for! He was a magnificent dog, and he carried a presence that impressed anyone who saw him. I wish I had known that we had been together before. I would have cherished the reunion. But I am never allowed to know this while I have them. I don't think they ever intend for us to know. Even if I specifically ask, I am not told. It's only after they leave that I connect those dots. Sometimes I stumble upon a picture and realize that the look in the eyes is the same as another dog. So then I start comparing all the pictures I can find and finally realize, "It's the same dog!" Or I'll suddenly remember the feeling or energy of a dog while I look over old photographs and realize they are identical in that way.

None of that happened with Zozzo even after he was gone. It wasn't until I started channeling Öskar and was told that Nick was also Zozzo that I finally saw it and felt it. Their energy was identical, even their eyes were identical now that I look back on pictures of them.

One of the most beautiful experiences Zozzo brought me was my understanding and appreciation for tracking. Do you remember how I didn't appreciate it when Nick and I tried it when I was young? I just didn't see the point in it.

Well, Zozzo changed all that because he was a tracking master! He loved to put his nose to the ground and follow the scent. He taught me many valuable things about the lessons tracking had to offer. Because of him, I became skilled at laying and reading a track. I learned to use my spiritual senses (clairvoyance) to perceive where I had laid a track an hour or more earlier. Because by then, you could no longer "see" it with your eyes. Instead, I focused on the energy trail of the track so that I could predict the path of my dog thirty feet in front of me. This work was also additional practice in trusting my instincts and in trusting my dog!

> Tracking refers to the dog's ability to detect, recognize, and follow a specific scent or smell. In schutzhund, the dog's tracking abilities are tested on grass and the dog must follow the footpath of the tracklayer up to three hours old. The dog must also be able to identify articles that the tracklayer leaves on the track by lying down and "indicating" them.

Following from thirty feet behind my dog, I also had to learn to read his body language. I could tell by speed or jerkiness on the line how confident he was. And if my dog ever circled, it was a reliable indicator that he was lost because I always taught him to only proceed if he was sure, if he had proof to support his theory. Zozzo was so serious and intent on his track that there was no tail wagging. He was all business, focusing all his energy through the nose. It was exhilarating to have such an intimate connection from so far away.

Tracking became a form of meditation for me. It was something we practiced at dawn before the world was awake. I handled my dogs very quietly and calmly using very few spoken words to exemplify how I wanted them to work. A calm, focused mind is accurate, but a frantic, excited mind misses things. I taught them to read my mind based on what I didn't tell them. They had to tune in to me as much as I was tuning in to them. So our tracking time was our quiet time, our sacred time together. Just me and the dogs, mutely working in the field practicing our telepathy. It was so natural and so peaceful. I felt like an Indian girl!

CHAPTER 37

Zozzo Delivers

From his arrival in 2003 up to May 2004, I completed Zozzo's schutzhund titles. First his Sch 1, then his Sch 2, and finally his Sch 3. Because he excelled at tracking, we also completed his advanced tracking title (FH). The judges' comments were always very complimentary to his work ethic, accuracy, and presence. He was definitely a dog that could take me the distance! We then began to prepare for national level competition by expanding his training experiences with harder tracking and stronger, faster decoys. We spent a week in Florida training with one of my favorite mentors and tracking in the hardest conditions known in this country. Zozzo far exceeded my expectations by rising to the challenge without hesitation! From there we ventured up to Kentucky to train with another world champion competitor and coach. He saw all kinds of pressures from tracking difficulty to decoy presence and threat. So far, I could not find a flaw in this dog, and I was quite pleased. Our path continued to move forward toward our ultimate goal. But we never quite got there.

As well as things were progressing with Zozzo at the time, Tori's emergence in my life seemed to create a powerful metamorphosis. Almost overnight I lost interest in my quest for national level schutzhund competition. Instead, I catapulted into French ring with total conviction. I was already cross-training some of my schutzhund dogs into this new sport, but schutzhund dogs don't necessarily do well in the ring events. The demands of the two sports are very different with vastly opposing psychological pressures, biting expectations, endurance requirements, and work motivation. The dogs who excel in either sport are specifically bred for that sport. Schutzhund penalizes the dogs for fighting the decoy, whereas ring dogs are expected to. The schutzhund phases take no more than ten minutes each and are all scripted exercises that never deviate. The French ring test at the highest level can take a full hour to complete with entirely random exercises. The two sports are night and day regarding scoring, decoy purpose and function, and the dog's ability to think for itself. We begin teaching the ring 3 exercises to puppies at a young age, which I refer to as "formatting." So a cross-trained dog from another sport would miss out on this early programing and certainly be at a big disadvantage.

So you see there are significant differences in the physical and psychological demands and expectations of the dogs. My hopes of successfully transitioning my schutzhund dogs over to this new sport were not necessarily realistic. And this included Zozzo. He was happy to bite the suit, but he would not understand the necessary critical thinking component. Schutzhund dogs are not required to think, reason, and make independent decisions like ring dogs. He would not excel in my new sport and may not even make it all the way through the levels. My change of direction would mean that Zozzo would not achieve his true purpose. Even though I was ruthlessly in pursuit of my own ambitions, I also considered what was best for the dogs. And knowing where his true strengths lie, I began to consider parting with him.

The schutzhund sport dogs only bite a sleeve placed on a single arm. No other bite locations are permitted. In ring sports, the decoys wear a padded bodysuit and the dogs are expected to bite anywhere on this suit. If the ring decoys detect the dog will only bite the arms, they will use this deficiency against the dog, causing them valuable points.

A part of me wondered if I was running from something. I thought I wanted to compete at the national level, but the closer I got, the more

I ran from it. Competing at that level is tremendous pressure on the handler as well as on the dog. The exercises must be meticulously dialed in with incredible precision and perfection. I wasn't sure I wanted to nitpick every little detail just for another half point. I knew myself, and I already knew what this does to me. Remember the shadow side of Nick and Trixie? It most likely would bring out my "oppressor" character. And I already knew I did not enjoy that part of me.

But I could also be running from the "I'm not worthy" tag. And what if I did succeed? The "fear of persecution" tag could get triggered and make it a truly unpleasant experience. I had the perfect dog to achieve my goal, and for some reason, I was still afraid to go for it. The specific reason doesn't really matter in hindsight. What's important is that we learn to see these tags in the moment and be better prepared to act on them the next time it comes around. So maybe I had finally learned from my experience and knew my limitations. Or maybe I was avoiding fully committing and enjoying the success I deserved. We'll never know.

With the free will that God has granted us, we do get to pick whether we want to address our available learning and growth. It is totally up to us. It is in our best interest, however, to clear tags as quickly as possible, because the messages will only get louder each time they show up. The K9 guides don't judge us for not accepting their gifts. They know that we may not be ready and are prepared to come as often as necessary. So even though I was parting with Zozzo or Nick or Öskar once again, there was no judgment, and he would find a way to deliver his message another time and another way.

The good news was that I was able to get Zozzo into the hands of a capable trainer and competitor. In the end, he did realize his full potential by partnering with her to multiple national events in 2005. They had an exciting podium placing at the 2005 Malinois Nationals in Atlanta, placing second overall! In 2006 they represented the United States on the World Team in Hungary at the Belgian Shepherd World Championships (FMBB) and placed respectively midfield. I was so happy for him and proud of them both. I knew I had missed out on a terrific opportunity, and I knew that was my choice. But I am so happy that he was able to give someone else that experience even though I wasn't ready. He far exceeded my expectations as a "national caliber" competitor by successfully competing at the world level! Well done, Zozzo!

Luckily, I maintained breeding rights on Zozzo after I sold him, and he sired two litters for me. His first litter in 2005 was with my powerhouse Apachi (whom you will learn about next) with incredible results! These pups had his size and power and their mom's tenacity and fire. They were great competitors and legends all their own. I was very proud of them. The legacy of Zozzo lived on in his babies. And Öskar moved on once again.

I hope you have enjoyed the blessings from Öskar. It is now time to turn our attention to one of my favorite K9 spirit guides!

My heart was beating so fast, trying desperately to get my attention! I was trying not to cry. I was trying to be brave, to be an adult about this. I wanted to stand fast on my mark without wavering or showing any weakness. My father would be so proud that I was like him!

SECTION 4

Oeragon

(oy-ya-gaan)

"Oeragon"

Oeragon is our third Core Four spirit guide. She is a very different guide, at a more elevated level than what we have worked with so far. Her message and lessons will be different from what we have learned already. We are jumping ahead on the spectrum to a more advanced being with exhilarating powers. As you can see from her image, which takes my breath away, she carries quite a bit more stature than the first two.

Please notice the intensity of her eyes as this is her most recognizable trait. The matching intensity of her energy also bleeds off the page as it seeks to connect with you. Her jawline is more firmly clenched as she breathes through her nose like a predator would just before launching at her prey. In contrast to what we observed in Öskar's image, Oeragon's image portrays a holding of breath. It's almost as if she does not need to breathe. As if she embodies so much life force that breathing would somehow leak it out!

Her eyes will vary between squinty and wide-open depending on her approach with you. The wider the eye, the more she is encouraging you to absorb or take a broader look. The narrower squint reveals a concentrated, laserlike focus, reflecting her desire for you to narrow your focus, your attention, or your direction. Her ears are erect and forward, simultaneously receiving and projecting. This represents your ability to fully embody your own divine soul and project it effectively into the world. Her energy is so focused you will not see her pant as she draws in divine wholeness and funnels it outward into a concentrated stream of consciousness.

I chuckled when she gave me her name because at first I spelled it incorrectly and all I could see was "Oregon" (like the state). I thought surely I had heard wrong. That seemed like a plain name for a spirit. She delicately pointed out that I had spelled it incorrectly. After she coached me on the spelling and pronunciation, I started to see that her name was not plain at all. Rubbing my nose in my own ignorance a little bit more, she whispered, "It means 'origin' in my language." And by origin, she meant divine source. Wow. That is a powerful name! I would also like to point out here that when she speaks to me, her voice is very distinctive, weighted, and elegant, much like the vibe I get from her picture. Her presence and her energy are quite magnificent and very hard to describe in human terms. I don't believe there is anything on earth for me to compare it to.

Oeragon resonates with the black panther as her spirit animal (her guide form). This mystical, intelligent predator is known for its fierce protective abilities with alluding deep wisdom and knowledge. The cat's characteristic piercing stare with its bright yellow eyes set deeply into the beautiful black coat even gives other predators reason to keep their distance. They are revered and feared by all the other big cats because of their unique, mystic, and ominous look. The gaze of the black panther is so deeply intense, it is as if she sees right through you and into your soul. Black panther symbolism regards them as shape-shifters with natural psychic power and magical skills. Their unique vibration even offers protection in the spirit world. Oeragon wishes to share her mystic power with you. If she has selected to work with you, it is to connect you with your God-self. Her energy will easily elevate you to a higher level of awareness.

Oeragon's personality is identical to that of the basenji dog breed, representing her angel form. This sphinx-looking dog is extremely loyal, intelligent, quiet, and thoughtful yet reserved. You can't always read her thoughts as they run deeply within her soul. The confidence and poise of the basenji are equivalent to that of the black panther. This breed was revered as a status symbol among the ancient Egyptians. She does in fact carry herself like the royalty that she is. You may feel as if her intense, steady, quiet gaze could burn a hole into you, but it is merely her attempt to get you to connect with her on a deeper level. Her presence indicates it is time to be loyal to yourself because your higher vibration is calling. Don't waste time and energy on meaningless connections and commitments that don't serve your higher being. Still your mind and focus inward, and hear the calling from your source. It is time to elevate your vibration, and she will show you how.

The blend of both animals lends a calm, focused, confident presence that stands guard patiently waiting for the moment that you are ready to reclaim yourself. Oeragon carries your divine presence for you until you are ready. Her burning gaze acts as a beacon calling you to it, back to your divine self. Calling you back to the version of you in the eyes of God versus who you think you are on this earth plane. Her presence takes your breath away because she mirrors your true God-self. When you actually see her in all her magnificent beauty and power, you are really looking at your own divine soul! She is a mirror of *you!*

Her amplified power agitates your need to be clearly seen and understood, to radiate your vibrant energy into the world, and to regain your connection with the Almighty. With her help, you will identify and dissolve superficial masks of illusion-encasing beliefs you hide behind, beliefs you tell yourself but aren't true. Terminating these old blockages is critical to heighten your awareness and grant you freedom to begin your journey of sovereign transformation! If you accept Oeragon's invitation, your masks (your cocoon) will dissolve and your evolution into the divine butterfly will begin! You will find your way home to the version of you in God's eyes. So welcome her! Embrace her! Allow her to work through you and for you. Enjoy the magical journey of discovering yourself all over again!

Oregon is possibly the most strikingly beautiful K9 guide of the group. I've been honored to experience her twice! I am excited to share her with you, and I hope that you find her as amazing as I did. But before I introduce her, let's take a look at her message.

A Message from Oeragon

Beautiful eyes, golden eyes, panther eyes,
burning fire from within, scared to come out.
Terrified of the world, only comforted by me.
She had to be reassured, supported, sculpted,
nurtured before becoming her true self.
Only then could the fire come out, burning brightly
from the deep volcano of confidence,
becoming completely unstoppable.
Glowing in her full energetic presence,
eyes now like lightning!
Alpha from omega as her full being emerged.

Her illuminating eyes burned a hole into my soul.
Intense, extreme, unwavering.
Connecting us together in eternity,
a multidimensional thread between a human and a dog
guiding me toward my own heart and soul.
My second-in-command stood at the ready
to pilot a long-awaited transformation.
But I hesitated and faltered. The opportunity was too great!
The veil held me captive.
Her insecurity was my insecurity!
I failed her on the deepest level of trust.
She will never give up, she will never leave, she will always be at the ready
to guide me on my divine path of ascension
once I am ready and willing!
(An encouraging message from Apachi, June 9, 2022)

PART 1

Apachi

I had a visit from Apachi during my meditation on May 1, 2022, and this is what happened.

I saw a scared, little puppy cowering in the corner. She was very sad and lonely.

I did not recognize this puppy. I wondered who it was.

The dogs were visiting me in my meditations, but I did not know who this one was.

I turned my gaze a little to the right and saw a beautiful black panther pacing in the opposite corner.

For a moment, I was enthralled in its presence and breathtaking beauty!

As I returned my focus to the puppy, it suddenly transformed into a young woman!

"Wow!" I gasped. My heart quickened. How beautiful she was!

I looked back at the panther and asked her, "Who is this puppy that changed into a woman?"

The panther never stopped moving, but she instantly transformed herself into my "Apachi" right before my eyes!

And then she said, "It is you!"

And I cried!

A wave of divine love, joy, and peace all washed over me simultaneously as I heard Apachi's words. I began to weep as I realized the magnitude of the gift I had just received. It was a message from not just Apachi, not just Oeragon, but also from the divine. It was a confirmation of my purpose, my path, and my ability to deliver this message.

Throughout this journey, I have transformed myself, been reborn without ever dying. The guides provided me with the tools I needed to morph from that scared, little puppy or child into a beautiful, powerful woman I never knew I was underneath. This is Apachi's message, and you will understand it through her story as this is precisely what she did. She literally illustrated my path to me when she was here.

Oeragon's message is a little bit different from that of the previous two guides we just met. She represents the next step of our transformation. She illustrates the possibilities available to us once we clear the masks of illusion that the first two guides addressed. So let's meet Apachi!

"Apachi"

CHAPTER 38

The Light of My Soul

2002

Apachi was an incredible dog. Anyone who met her probably still remembers her. She had a presence that commanded your attention. Much like Tori, she was obviously special early on. I was very excited about her potential and anticipated great things with her. And she delivered just that in spades! Our limitless adventure was jam-packed with success! This is probably one of the easiest sections to write because Apachi was one of the most amazing dogs to ever walk the planet. Her intense bright eyes pierced right through me, right into my soul. This unique canine was even more gifted and special than I ever imagined, and I will explain this to you during her story.

She was a Belgian Malinois born in my very first litter in 2002. But she only just left me last year in 2021. I know you are doing the math and wondering how a dog could live that long—nineteen human years. Her story is unlike any I have ever told. So strap on your magic cap, open your heart and your mind, and I will take you on one of the most incredible adventures between a human and a dog. If you can even consider her to be a dog.

Her litter was a special litter here in the States. I purchased her mother while she was in Germany. She had already earned her schutzhund 3 (Sch 3) and had passed all her health checks. I had her bred to a famous male in Germany before having her shipped to the States. It would be the first litter of these bloodlines born in the US. I expected some powerful schutzhund prospects from this combination, and I was not disappointed. This breeding brought me ten beautiful puppies and a lifetime of memories!

Apachi grabbed my attention when she was just four weeks old, although she was not born as secure and confident as her half sister Catori. She was very shy around strangers, and she didn't want them to look at her or touch her. As strangers reached for her, she would duck and dodge out of range. If not on leash, she would attempt to run and hide. She perfectly reflected me as a child. I was terrified of strangers same as she was. I would not speak, and if pressured, I would hide behind my mother. I remember this version of me very clearly now. But I did not make that connection until Oeragon showed me. Beautiful, isn't it?

To help her get through this fear, I provided a flood of diverse, safe experiences. I meticulously exposed her to various training clubs, dog shows, and dog stores. I desperately wanted Apachi to move past this, and in a way, I had to move past it as well. I was having to trust her to blossom into the dog I could see behind it, much like she could see me for who I really was.

Everything else about her was so perfect! She was very intelligent and learned her exercises quickly. She had a very hard, full grip on her toy, and this was an important trait for schutzhund dogs. She had an incredible nose and showed potential talent for tracking at just eight weeks old. I found her to be very intense, focused, and super easy to train. She was willing to do anything for food or play. Despite her insecurities, she was always wagging her tail and staring a hole through me like she was reading my mind! Apachi was focused and committed with me but still hesitant and nervous when anyone new came into her space.

I discovered that the more obedience she learned, the more I could redirect her fear into knowledge. I would put her into work mode, into an obedience mindset, and then have people come up to her while she was thinking about her toy. For instance, a "stay" was a "stay" even if someone touches you. Or a "watch" (giving me eye contact) is a "watch" no matter who is approaching out of the corner of your eye. When she performed the task correctly without being bothered by the stranger while maintaining focus on me and her assignment, she was richly paid with a reward. And above all else, she pleased me, and I made sure she knew it. With this technique, she could pretend that this stranger was not in her space and was not actually touching her because she was so intently focused on me and her reward. It worked perfectly!

And then she did the most brilliant thing! She began to substitute her fear of the unknown into *trust* for me! She began to completely trust anything I asked her to do. Somehow I had earned her undying, unquestioning, unwavering trust in this process. If I asked her to tolerate someone touching her, she understood that she was safe even though she did not like it. So out of respect for me, she learned to endure it. She had figured out a way to integrate this fearful side of her transmuting it into a practical answer that would satisfy me. Her fear was transforming into knowledge and courage right before my eyes! With just a little kindness, understanding, and education, I was able to guide her through this process. It was brilliant, and I was so proud of her!

Remembering how valuable irony is to the guides, let's look closer. If you flip this story, you might notice that she was asking me to trust in her message and in the process of my own transformation!

With her explosion in trust, her already super engaging, piercing direct eye contact become even more intense. It was like she was burning a hole through me so that she would not notice the things she did not want to see. She performed every activity I gave her with this focus. And this is one of the unique traits she became known for. She never took her eyes off me when we worked on obedience. Consequently, she never got distracted by other dogs, people, or sounds. A hot air balloon could lower down over the top of us, and she would never look away from me. There was nothing that was going to break that direct visual connection between us. Oeragon was coming through in all her glory.

This beautiful little girl was excited to work as much as I would let her. She was so much fun because she always gave 200 percent. She never gave up, never got tired, and you could tell that she was completely devoted to me. I took her many places to practice our obedience, signed her up for group sessions, and got her AKC Canine Good Citizen award. We were always together. If I went to work to train dogs, she went with me. As she matured and came into herself, she became my demonstration dog for my training company. She was also my assistant when I needed to work on specific issues with other dogs. With her meticulous training and sharp mind, she was like a remote-controlled car. And because she was so intensely focused on me, she wasn't affected by anything that might happen around us (loose dog, aggressive dog, screaming kids, drunken crowd). I also used her to neutralize dog-aggressive dogs because she would never react to them or their aggression.

If you have ever seen this kind of focus, then you know how truly amazing it is to witness. And it is even more amazing to *feel* it. Apachi and I were psychically bonded, I now understand. She tuned in to every movement and every breath I took. She was probably even monitoring my heart rate and cortisol. It felt like we were attached by an invisible umbilical cord full of energy. Walking with her at my side was like riding the most beautiful stallion in the world. The two of us moved in total unison. I could palpate the power, the energetic connection, and I could feel the gaze of onlookers as they were drawn to us. It was like we whirled around in this energetic bubble that could not be pierced. I found it empowering and intoxicating. With this type of connection, I felt like I could do anything! And this was the gift that Apachi brought with her, the teaching she had to share, and the lesson she wanted me to learn. She was literally showing me the person I was evolving into, just as she did in the meditation decades later! Once I embraced my full God-self (the version of me in God's eye), I would feel this same incredible energy of my own soul in spades!

If I could only embody that beautiful woman, that powerful all-knowing soul that I really was, then I could see my truth. Instead, I was stuck in the larva form. I was still the scared, little puppy afraid to come out. She was here to show me the true connection I had with the divine and encourage me to find it! The power and intensity I felt between us was actually my connection with the divine!

CHAPTER 39

The Butterfly Emerges

Apachi developed into a very beautiful sixty-pound female, solid muscle, light on her feet, with an insatiable desire to please. She worked and worked until she got it right. She was also very sensitive. If she perceived that I was displeased, she would instantly rework the question and offer me a different answer. And this would go on and on until she finally got the right answer and got paid for her brilliance. She never gave up, never got discouraged or rattled. She had so much desire to please me that I didn't have to add any pressure. She pressured herself into accuracy! I took this determination for granted because I thought at the time that every dog worked this way. But this tremendous work ethic is not even remotely common. It's over-the-top extreme and makes teaching an incredible joy! With such a motivated mind, the sky was the limit on what I could teach her. And Apachi was a sponge for learning.

Rather than focusing on competing with her right away, I spent more time developing her individual skills. Back then I taught my puppies "elements" that I could later string together into a full exercise. Eventually I could rearrange elements into a completely different exercise. Once they understood the basic elements, it was easy to reorganize and produce new exercises from those foundation points. Even when she was a baby, I was teaching her what she needed to know for upper echelon competition using this method. All I had to do then was to string together pieces of what she already knew, and instantly she was ready to compete! This allowed me to keep everything fresh and interesting. It also allowed us to seamlessly move between sports.

It was more important to me that she have a well-rounded foundation and for her to feel totally secure in all environments before I put her into stressful situations for competition. Since I suspected I would be doing multiple sports with her, her training program consisted of a wide range of obedience, scent work, and bite work. Essentially, I was training her to excel in schutzhund, French ring, and AKC obedience simultaneously. This turned out to be a very successful approach, and it was a format that I followed for all my future competition puppies. It provided my puppies with a significant "leg up" or advantage in the competition ring.

I even trained Apachi in three different languages: English, German, and French. She easily shifted between all three without skipping a beat. If I told her to stand in German ("Shtay") and then told her to stand in French ("Debout" (da-boo)), she would think for a second and then grin. "I'm already doing that!" she would say. She loved it when I tested her brilliance!

The longer we worked together and the older she got, the more I really loved this dog! Her tracking abilities were incredible! She worked a track diligently without giving up no matter how hard it was. Tracking requires the dog to work out scent puzzles completely on their own, without help from the handler and without getting frustrated and giving up. The necessary dedication to this activity is not something that can be taught. Either the dog is born with it, or it isn't. It's part of their genetic constitution. This willingness and tenacity can be flexed and strengthened. But it can't be implanted after the fact.

Her obedience was a little flashy, especially with her laser focus. She was very precise with her executions and worked like a machine. She absorbed all the information I gave her, memorized it, and perfected it. It was like she was attached to my brain and knew exactly what I wanted from her. Her protection work on the decoy was also very strong. Despite her insecurities with being so close to strangers, she had learned the behavior I was looking for. And she memorized the confidence I wanted her to portray. So that is what she manifested. She may not have felt it completely on the inside, but she pretended it on the outside. Kind of like "Fake it till you make it." An onlooker couldn't really see what I could see because she had integrated it so well. The judges' comments were always that she was "powerful" and a "force to be reconned with" despite her smaller size. It was a secret that Apachi and I shared, and it made me smile.

At home she came into her own with her rising confidence. She also began to ascend within my pack. As she matured, she began to step into her true power and her full self that she modeled for me. She began to own her greatness and her tremendous power that she possessed. This was the power she wanted me to identify with. This was the awakening that she was inspiring me to achieve. Her ability to transform herself from that *shy, insecure, rattled puppy* into this *bold, confident, secure,* and *demanding* adult was the metamorphosis I was headed for. Only I watched from the outside, not realizing it was meant for me. I adored her and was so grateful for her presence and her gifts even if I didn't see them for what they were at the time.

CHAPTER 40

Apachi Shines!

We started competing in schutzhund when she was eighteen months old. Her first trail in northern Indiana was in good company with the mighty Zozzo as he attempted his Sch 1. She breezed through her temperament test with obedience and a traffic test resulting in a nearly perfect score. She was awarded the "Highest Scoring" dog trophy in her category. The next day, we trialed for her schutzhund 1 (Sch1), and she did pretty well. She had a very nice track considering it was her first trial experience and I was pleased. Her obedience was also nice, just as I expected it to be. The protection test was a little bit bumpy because she was nervous. But she managed to pull it together. She earned her first two titles with respectable scores and a "Highest Scoring Obedience" award to boot. I was very pleased with her effort and her commitment, and we were off to a terrific start.

She achieved her Sch 2 title at a club in Tennessee with even greater confidence and ease. This new level required her to work a harder track laid by a stranger for the first time. The obedience and protection

In tracking the handler is required to remain at the end of the tracking line thirty feet behind the dog. No matter what the dog does, the handler must stay at the end of the line and cannot assist in any way. The handler must not issue commands, tug on the line, or refuse to follow if the dog has ventured off the track.

phases were also mildly more difficult than the Sch 1. Apachi did very well in all three phases and again got excellent marks from the judge regarding her courage and commitment. I was thrilled with yet another remarkable performance.

In July 2004, we switched gears and I prepared Apachi for a French ring trial in Chicago. Apachi had enough foundation with ring that she understood all the exercises and transitioned easily. We reviewed a few things, and off we went. Apachi remembered everything we had practiced since she was a baby and passed her brevet (the temperament test) with flying colors. She won her level with the highest score out of eight dogs. I was very proud of her! The next day we competed for her first working title in this sport, French ring 1. Once again, she produced a very respectable performance, tying us for first place and awarded second place. I was very happy considering she was just coming off two schutzhund trails! Not many dogs can switch gears like that.

This dog just never ceased to amaze me. We were totally in sync with each other, and she completely trusted my leadership. I don't think I have felt that way about any other relationship in my life, human or animal.

CHAPTER 41

Apachi Knows Best

Apachi was now two years old, and I was contemplating breeding her. This meant that we would take a short break from her planned competitions so she could have her puppies. My biggest hurdle with this was in deciding what dog to breed her to. She had so much to offer; she was so intelligent, focused, intense, and committed. The only thing I wanted to improve upon was her genetic self-confidence. After much debate and discussion with other breeders and stud dog owners, I eventually picked a dog from Belgium that was currently living in New York City.

When Apachi came into heat, I loaded her and a couple of other dogs up and drove to New York. I met with the stud owner at a Brooklyn city park, hoping to do the breeding there. But Apachi had other ideas. She apparently did not approve of the dog I picked out for her. It took me two days to realize this. He was not a handsome dog, and he had rather chaotic energy. On paper they looked like a good match, but Apachi was telling me there was no way she would have "swiped right" on his ugly mug! She would stand for him as he mounted, but she would not allow the breeding to happen. She just had this look on her face like "Over my dead body, Mom." We tried everything to get this breeding to succeed and nothing worked. I was completely perplexed. This was her first breeding, but not his. I certainly had never had this happen before and wasn't sure what to make of it.

After much discussion, we decided to shift our focus to a son of this dog. He was not currently titled or proven like his father, but his training was showing tremendous potential, and he would be competing in French ring soon. They brought this dog to the park so I could meet him. He was very handsome, much better looking than his sire, and very flashy! He heeled next to his handler, front legs kicking out with a tremendous spring. He had gigantic energy and power and was a very happy, confident dog. The owners did some obedience and bite work with him so that I could see his qualities. I really liked what I saw, so I approved him as a step-in.

When I brought Apachi out to meet him, her demeanor totally changed! She went goo-goo for this dog and literally melted at the sight of him! I had never seen anything like it. We had our breeding within seconds. And this was the first time I realized my dog had her own standards about who she would breed to! It turned out that she had very good instincts. This breeding gave us some incredible puppies that became legends in their own right!

CHAPTER 42

Embracing New Growth

Pregnancy certainly agreed with Apachi. I think in her eyes, she was put on this planet to be a mom. It was easy to see that she was excited and proud. She just *glowed!* But before her pregnancy started to show, I decided this would be a good time to do something fun with her. We ventured into the AKC obedience ring for the first time together. Even pregnant, she easily qualified in all three of her required legs for her Companion Dog (CD) title. She seemed to be on cloud nine, just floating around the ring. Other dogs took notice, and many tried to meet her. There was a very magnetic attraction about her. Fortunately, she didn't have any trouble staying focused with all those pregnancy hormones oozing out of her!

The AKC exercises were short and easy compared to what she was used to doing. The only things she had to become accustomed to were being touched by the judge during the "stand for exam" exercise and the close proximity of so many other dogs and handlers. But she quickly adapted, and by the third show, she was winning her classes with very few mistakes. I could not have been prouder! Once again, she had mastered her own fears, gathered herself up, and completely manifested the picture that I was looking for. It was truly amazing how she could just step into herself, letting go of old fears that didn't serve her, and fully embracing the part of her that I pushed her to find. As a dog owner, as a trainer, and as a mentor to any living being, nothing is more satisfying than to watch the butterfly come out of the cocoon! And this was exactly what she wanted for me!

We could now check off one more goal from our list of many that I had planned for her. Before her puppies were born, she had two schutzhund titles, a French ring title, and an AKC title. So for the last half of her pregnancy, she got to relax and be spoiled, sleeping in my bed at night and eating as much as she wanted. This gave me a chance to spend a little bit more time with her baby sister, Catori.

Time passed very quickly, and before I knew it, her due date was approaching. The whelping box and the puppy room were ready. I began to monitor Apachi's temperature several times a day. Just before giving birth, the mother's body temperature will drop significantly as the hormones shift preparing for birth. I had been through this many times with her mother, so I was prepared and anxiously awaiting these special babies. But Apachi didn't follow the rules and decided to throw me a curve ball!

One night while she slept in my bed, I woke up to a wet spot, a rather large wet spot. I found it odd since Apachi never peed in the house, much less in my bed. I thought maybe she had just lost control of her bladder with all the puppies in her belly and surging hormones. Of course, I also wondered if it could have been amniotic fluid, but she wasn't showing any signs of labor. Twenty-four hours pass and there was no temperature drop and no labor. I found this to be very odd and called the vet to get his impression. He was not concerned and just told me to keep an eye on her. The next day, everything fell into place as she went into labor.

Apachi pushed those babies out like a machine gun. One puppy came every thirty minutes like clockwork. She never struggled and seemed to enjoy every moment of it. She fully embraced the process of new growth and birth without resistance or fear. This was a fitting symbolic image for what she was secretly inspiriting me to do. All the puppies were healthy, and she was very happy. Ten beautiful puppies were born in the fall of 2004. Born from the father that she had chosen!

This bunch of puppies was pretty intense to say the least. As they grew, so did their energy and intensity! Apachi did a wonderful job feeding and nurturing them, cuddling with them, and preparing them for the world. She did a much better job than her own mother had done with her. She was a real natural. The puppies all went to great homes and most of them to working or performance homes. They all managed to carve out their own place in this world following in the huge footsteps of their legendary mother. In fact, one of her daughters achieved AKC Obedience Trial Champion (OTCH) distinction twenty times! Another female who was also an OTCH was invited to compete at the Crufts Obedience Championship in England! This was quite an honor since American dogs are rarely invited to this prestigious specialty. Many of the males from this litter went on to become police, security, and sport dogs. There were so many great puppies in this litter, and nearly all of them were larger than their mother!

CHAPTER 43

The Dichotomy of Sisters

Apachi adored being with her babies, but I could tell that she was anxious to get back to work. She was concerned that her place in my heart might be erased by another dog if she was absent from her post for too long. After her puppies were weaned and left for their new homes, we resumed our work together. With her talent and precision, we nearly picked up exactly where we left off. We returned to the AKC ring and began to pursue her Companion Dog Excellent (CDX) title. For us this was the easiest competition that Apachi ever had to do. Everything was off leash, and the class consisted of two retrieves and two jumping exercises. These were all the things that Apachi loved to do, so she easily won first place in all three trials.

To go back through her story and see how much progress she truly made is just heartwarming for me. To emerge from that scared, little puppy with a doubtful future into the confident powerhouse that she had become was truly amazing! I am so honored that I got to share such a journey with her, and now to be receiving the precious gifts that she has to share with humanity. It is absolutely breathtaking!

Over the next year, Tori was beginning to mature and her training was progressing well. So I found myself splitting my time between her and Apachi. They were best buddies, always hanging out with me and playing in the yard together. They had two completely different mindsets and energies, however. Patchi was very intense with her laser focus, keenly aware of what was right and wrong. She served as my second-in-command, enforcing the pack rules with an iron fist. If any of the dogs stepped out of line, she quickly corrected them herself or brought my attention to the issue. If I stepped in to correct another dog, she jumped to my side ready to pounce so she could back me up if I needed it. She was always at the ready and eager to be involved. I had to be careful and make it clear that I didn't need her help or else a dogfight would quickly ensue.

Tori, on the other hand, was a little more what I would call "new age." She was a little less connected with the things that were important to Apachi and much more interested in just living life to its fullest. She seemed to have her head a little more in the clouds and was more oblivious to structure and organization than her sister was. Tori's focus was more about getting as much joy out of life as possible so she was less focused on details and more focused on the vibe of experience!

Writing about these two girls and recognizing this stark difference between them really accentuated their distinct purposes in my life. I suddenly realized what they were trying to show me. How these two parts of me (the gifts of Anthea and Oeragon) needed to be blended with each other. Some pieces needed to become more prominent, and other pieces would require more of a backseat placement. Looking back on them, I can totally see the mirror images of me that they each reflected. Hindsight is twenty/twenty of course. But I wish, oh do I wish, I had seen and heard what they were trying to tell me back then. Are you seeing any similarities in your dog(s)?

CHAPTER 44

Tying Up Loose Ends

A year passed since Apachi's first litter, and it was time to breed her again. This time she would be bred to her childhood heartthrob, Zozzo. She was a mere pup when he arrived in the US, and she had been smitten with him since that day. I doubted she would reject my choice for her this time! Apachi was so thrilled she could not wait! She flirted and threw herself at him every single day she was in heat. "What a slut you are!" I kept teasing her. She would only grin from ear to ear having full knowledge of what she was up to. Her wish had come true. She finally got to breed to her man! And again, she glowed in her pregnancy!

But we weren't quite finished with the titles I wanted to check off her list this year. So while she was newly pregnant, I entered her in her final schutzhund trial of her career. Other than a super slight bulge in her belly, you could not tell that she was pregnant. She worked as she always worked, without skipping a beat. She was such a warrior, enjoying every minute of her job and pouring all her soul into her work. She managed to earn a respectable score for her Sch 3, getting accolades from the judge even when she was sassy and naughty. He admired her "power and tenacity" for such a "little" dog. She certainly had a lot to say as a mommy as she bossed the decoys around on the field.

That same trial she also earned her prestigious FH advanced tracking title. This track is laid by a stranger over varied terrain of grass, dirt, and gravel with several required cross tracks. It is aged three hours or more before the dog and handler are allowed to run it. She aced this track and only lost three points overall! This is a difficult feat as most dogs struggle to just complete an advanced track like this. But Apachi managed to achieve the highest ranking possible from the judge while pregnant!

This girl never ceased to amaze me with her skill, her talent, and her commitment to get it right! I have never found another dog with her qualities since. She also tended to produce these qualities in her puppies, and that's why they were also as successful as she was. The more pressure you put on her to get it perfect, the harder she worked to make you happy. So many dogs would quit under the constant expectation of perfection and performance. (Much like me!) But she seemed to thrive under it, and this is one of the things that made her so special. Again, she mirrored a trait that I needed to acquire!

When her puppies arrived in the summer of 2005, she was just as excited as she was about the first batch. This litter carried their father's size and their mother's veracity. And these puppies were equally as powerful as her first. It was lovely to watch them grow, develop, and become miniature versions of her. She was so perfect with them, enjoying them even more than she had the first group. These babies also found their way into capable competition homes. One of the females from this litter was as large as her father and earned her Sch 3 title eight times, competing at three regional championships and one national championship! This daughter of Apachi was a force to be reckoned with, having the size and power of Zozzo and the tenacity and fire of Apachi! As I have said before, Apachi has excellent taste!

After her mommy duties were over, Patchi was anxious to get back to work. So we dusted off the cobwebs, reviewed the exercises, and prepared to do just one more ring trial together. In October 2005, she completed her second leg of her French ring 1 with another first place finish!

This was our final competition together, and it was bittersweet. She had been such an incredible partner and so easy to work with. I would never find a dog as intelligent and adaptable as she was. Nor would I be able to reproduce that electric connection we had. That level of bond appeared to be a once-in-a-lifetime gig!

CHAPTER 45

Running from Myself

After that, Patchi and I hit a pause in our adventure together. The training that Tori required was obligating me to travel. Instead of taking Apachi with us, I left her at home, and this did not bode well with Apachi. Patch considered herself to be the alpha and this was a violation of pack order. *She* was my second-in-command, not Tori. Apachi would attempt to explain this to Tori in pack terms by challenging her to a fight when we returned home. With this increased tension between the two of them, I started to notice that Tori was also becoming more aggressive to other females. It was a red flag, and I didn't want anything to happen to either one of them. I was tortured about how to handle the situation in the best interest of both dogs, the best solution for the two best dogs of a lifetime!

As other females in the pack began to have puppies and Apachi didn't, she also got grumpy with them. She was picking fights every chance she could with any female she could. Obviously, she felt that her position in my pack was being threatened. None of the other females wanted to fight with her, they were just following my orders. Apachi's tyranny forced my hand. I was sad for her because I knew she felt left out. I just wasn't sure what to do about it. I didn't want her to feel cheated, but I had other dogs that I needed to spend time with.

Part of the issue was that my bond with Patchi was so strong that she was fighting to keep that connection. Whereas I, on the other hand, was beginning to feel that connection dwindle. The static was back in my head, I knew something was about to change, and I just didn't know what or how. A *shift* was coming. What was I to do with Patch now that she had done everything on our list? I pondered an appropriate solution for months. I prayed about it and obsessed over what might be the best thing for Apachi. In my heart, I suspected what had to be done even though I did not want to do it. We had been through so much together. She had taught me so much about myself.

Then, one day I got a phone call from a lady looking for a watchdog for her family. She needed a dog to be part of their family and a companion to her eleven-year-old daughter. She needed a noisemaker that would discourage a burglar, but something that was also safe around the mules. An obedient dog was ideal so they could also take it on trial rides with the mules. She wondered if I knew of any available dogs that might be a good match for her situation. She had seen my web site, noticed I was close by, and thought maybe I could help her.

My heart dropped and my throat clenched as I heard myself say, "I might have the perfect dog for you." What? Did I just say that out loud? What was I thinking? I didn't think; I just spoke. I opened my mouth and out came these words. I had no idea they were coming. It's not like I planned to say it. It's not like I thought it through first and then gathered the words. The words just freaking jumped out of my mouth without so much as a second thought to make sure I knew what I was saying! Nothing like this had ever happened to me before. I was *shocked* as I heard myself say the words. I looked down at my beloved Apachi lying at my feet underneath my desk and thought, *How can this be? Am I really going to give her up?* I was instantly choked up in tears, yet I heard myself continue the conversation. It was like there were two of me! One was the heart saying, "Hold on a minute. Let's talk about this!" The other part of me was a disobedient mouth that made commitments that no one else had agreed to yet! It was oddly similar to when I sold Nick and Trixie.

It felt as though my decision was being made for me, and deep in my heart, as much as it hurt, I knew it was something I needed to honor. I was not prepared for this; it was happening way too fast. I heard myself make plans to drive Apachi ninety minutes away to meet with this family. To let them meet my Patch and to let her meet them.

As the next few days passed, I was still in a fog. Was it all a dream? I wandered through my daze not knowing how this was all going to play out. I felt like someone else was driving my life and I was not in charge. Patch had no idea what was coming. When we arrived at their farm, I was very nervous. They were super nice people and had a wonderful home in the country. Apachi tolerated them just like she does with anybody when she's with me. She focused only on me and ignored their fondling. I ran her through some of her obedience, demonstrated her commands and how they could be used on the farm. Of course, they fell in love with her, and they begged to keep her!

The plan we had agreed upon was for them to keep her over a trial weekend. If everything went well, I would come back to get her, have her spayed, then return her for the final time. But they were so in love with Patch! They wanted to just keep her and get her spayed themselves. My head was beginning to spin! I thought I would have a little bit more time to prepare for this termination. It was like a carousel that just kept speeding up and wasn't safe to jump off! Ultimately, I did have a choice. I could have said no and I could have just taken my baby home. But when doors open this quickly and this easily, I blindly go through. Because I know that I'm supposed to. So in my tortured sense of reality, this was *divine intervention*. This was the next step for us. And this was the *shift* that I had felt coming for quite some time now.

Reluctantly I gave Apachi a huge hug as I tried to hold myself together. Then I turned around and quickly walked out their door before I changed my mind. I could hear her whining and straining against the leash to come after me and my heart cracked in two! It was a long drive back home empty-handed. The tears just flooded out. I tried to shove down the pain; I had to stay strong. I would rather sacrifice my own happiness so that she could be happy. Here she would be the queen of her own palace and not have to compete with any other dogs. The peace would subsequently be restored in my pack. That's what I was telling myself anyway. That's the only thing that helped me power through. I was doing it for her, to give her the best life and not be a has-been in my life.

Was I so afraid of my own light and her invitation to come out and be myself that I cast her aside? Did she represent a part of me that I was so terrified to face that I manifested an out? What do you think? Was I running from something? We'll never know for sure, but we will get more clues.

CHAPTER 46

Apachi's Broken Heart

The weeks went by slowly. I tried to stay focused on Tori, but I thought of Apachi often. I even dreamed that she was here with me. When I was out on my training field one day, I swear I felt her out there with me too. It felt like she was always here, still close by. I wasn't sure how that could be. At the time, I didn't know how dogs' spirits or energies worked. Wouldn't she have to be dead for her spirit to hang around? I suffered through the loss as best as I could. It wasn't easy because we were so deeply connected.

A couple of months after I left Patch in her new home, I got a call from her new family. They were terrified and hysterical! Apachi was fighting for her life! She had been taken to their local vet to be spayed. But he didn't do any presurgical workup so he missed her hidden clotting disorder! I didn't even know about it! She was hemorrhaging from the incisions, and she was currently on her second transfusion!

I dropped to my knees because intuitively I knew what this was about. I had felt her energy buzzing around me. It had not been my imagination after all. Apachi was heartbroken, and she no longer wanted to live if she couldn't be with me. No wonder I had felt her presence so strongly! She was determined to leave if she couldn't be with me. I tuned in to her energy, and I could feel her pain because it was the same pain that I had. I knew how she felt, but she had to be strong. I needed her to stay with this family. They loved her now, and she would be breaking their hearts if she left. I pleaded with her to stick it out, to learn to love them, to be the light to them that she had been for me. We had had our time together and we would probably meet again. But for now, I needed her to stay where she was. I had other things I needed to do. I told her how much I loved her and that I always would.

There was no way I could convey this experience in any logical terms to her new owners. All I could offer them was my ongoing support and prayers. Of course, I asked them to keep me posted and let me know if there was anything I could do. I knew there was nothing I could offer physically, but I was somewhat confident in the conversation I had just had with Apachi. This was all new territory for me, and I was just trusting my instincts like I always do. I just held her in my heart and loved her as hard as I could, knowing that she did not belong to me anymore.

I will pause here and disclose a *huge irony* in the way that Apachi was attempting to get my attention. When I was a baby, I also had a blood clotting disorder called immune thrombocytopenic purpura (ITP for short). This is a clotting disorder that happens when the immune system destroys healthy platelets in the blood, impairing clotting function. It can lead to excessive blood loss and bruising. They don't know why children develop this disorder, whether it is a true autoimmune dysfunction or whether they just aren't able to make enough platelets fast enough. But before the doctors were able to diagnose me, there was some concern that I may have *leukemia*. So I was in the hospital for multiple transfusions as a child. I specifically remember the padded cribs they kept me in. I thought my parents had put me in jail!

I eventually outgrew the platelet disorder, thank heavens. But this hidden message from Patch was not lost on me. It was like she was saying, "Don't give up on me! Fight for me like your parents did for you!" This made it especially hard for me to take a stand, hold my position, and not go and rescue her.

A couple of days later, I heard that Apachi was finally home from the hospital and recovering. And that was the last I would hear from them. I never knew if or how Apachi recovered. I was so thankful she decided to stay with them because I knew she had a lot of love to give. I knew that once she committed fully to her new position, she would give them all of her.

I think it was ten years later (roughly 2016) when I heard from them again. They were looking for another dog because Apachi had apparently passed away last year. She had lived a full life, dying quietly in her sleep at thirteen years of age. She had been a cherished family member and they missed her greatly. When I heard that, I started crying all over again. All those memories came flooding back vividly. God, how I missed her!

There was never, *ever* another dog like Apachi. She was one of a kind and one in a million! Oeragon showed me some beautiful teaching through Apachi, and she still does. Her message is so important for humanity as she invites us all to find our God-selves, to spiritually grow, and to remember why we are here. Oeragon provides a very distinct bridge between man's best friend and a deeper, more elevated level of ourselves.

Apachi wasn't done yet. She kept her promise to me to hold her position with her new family. But now that her natural life was over, she had plans to resume her post with me. Brace yourself for something truly amazing!

PART 2

Nikki

A Temporary Placement

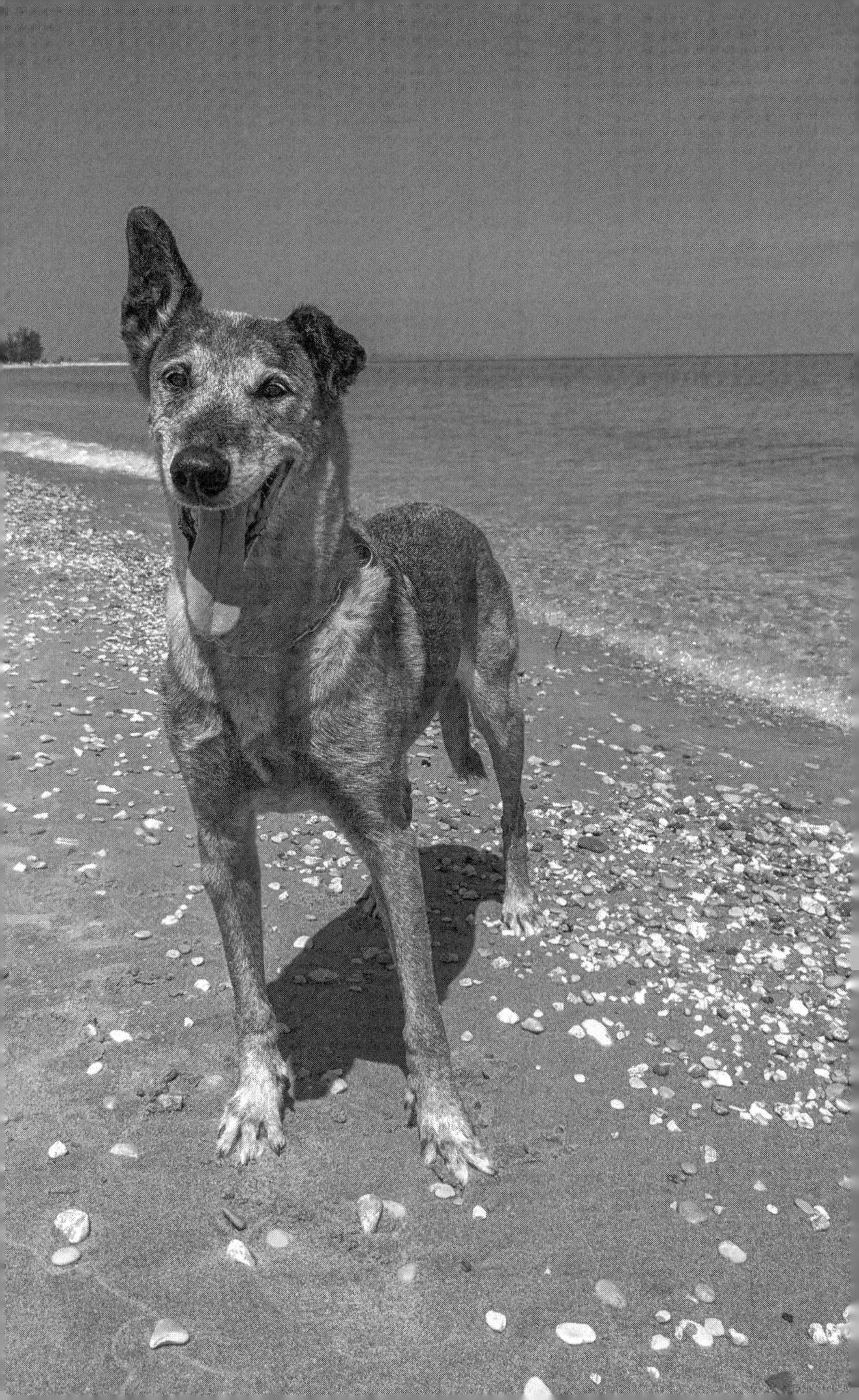

CHAPTER 47

Nikki Isn't Who I Think She Is

Nikki was my pick out of Catori's only litter in 2008. She was a little on the petite side, brave, and a little cocky. She had tremendous desire for food and play. She also loved to fetch and bite. With her compact size, she was very agile and fast. I expected great outcomes from her natural abilities, and I was excited about her potential. But as the other puppies left for their new homes, Nikki seemed to morph into a different dog. She no longer pranced around with the spunk she once had. She was a little more distant and reserved. She enjoyed our games a little, but not as much as she should have. I tried everything I could think of to reach her mind and her heart. This amused her but had no real impact. I realized I was struggling to find my connection with her. I had never experienced this with any of my other puppies. I wasn't sure what to make of it.

We did gradually find a rhythm together, yet it felt somewhat forced. It became clear early on that Nikki had no aspirations for becoming a performer like her mother. Yet I couldn't figure out what she did want to be. I began to wonder why I had kept her. Had I completely misread her? How could I have made such a huge mistake? Where did my special puppy go?

Our relationship felt completely unnatural to me. I had never had to work so hard at developing a bond with any of my puppies or dogs before. Nikki forced me to dig deep into myself and find new commitment and motivation to draw her out of her shell. This little puppy forced me way out of my comfort zone. I had to learn new skills with which to interact with her. But she still just hung back like she was in a waiting mode. She would engage with me somewhat, but it was never fully with her whole heart. She only gave me enough to amuse me, never enough to satiate me.

Despite our struggles, she managed to earn her AKC Star Puppy award at seven months. We busied ourselves with obedience and agility classes. She even joined her mother, Tori, and me on a cross-country trip to New Jersey for some obedience coaching. We gained a little bit more traction in our ever-elusive bond. I just couldn't help but wonder why it was such a struggle for us. Could it be possible that it was time for me to stop competing? It just did not seem to bring me much joy anymore. And Nikki had absolutely no desire to serve in that role. As usual, I was experiencing a faint whisper and an undercurrent in my thoughts. Maybe things were about to change. Was Nikki trying to convey this? Was she the source of the change?

What I did not know in 2008 was that my life was about to drastically change course, setting Nikki up in a significantly different role. I can only imagine what she must have been thinking, knowing in her own way what was before us. She was only biding her time until her role would become more primary. And of course, as you already know, the next year I would lose her mother, sending me into a tailspin.

When Nikki's mother died, she was barely a year old. And in my anguish, I consciously released her from her duties as my companion. I told her she was free to go and join her mother whenever she wished. She did not have to stay just for me; I did not want her. As far as I was concerned, if her mother was gone, I was done. But she refused to leave me. She didn't seem to get the message because she lived a very long life. The one good thing for Nikki after her mother's death was that I gave up trying to force her to become the dog she did not wish to be. I lost all will to train. I dropped the leash and retired from breeding, training, and competition. And this is where Nikki's true role began. She had been waiting for this moment; it was her cue.

Nikki was liberated into her true self at that moment. Her only duty now was to watch over me. She was to hold my energy while I grieved for her mother. She held me tightly until I was ready for the next phase. This was the job she was trying to tell me she was here for. I would also come to realize that this role of hers was only temporary. She would be moving on very quickly, even though she was not leaving. She would be handing over the reins and stepping out of the way in a most magical turn of events.

For a long time after her mother died, I closed my heart to Nikki. I was hurt and angry. I was no longer interested in playing with her. I barely spoke to her, cuddled her, or expressed any sort of love for her. I mourned daily for her mother for the next year. Until that suffering was complete, I had no room for anything else in my black heart. I turned my focus inward searching for my spirituality. I needed to find myself again. I felt lost, forgotten. I was questioning my purpose in life and taking a good, hard look at "Why am I here?" With the dogs, my purpose had been so clear and rewarding, but now all that had changed. I felt naked and alone and off the rails. Maybe I had strayed from my path? What had I missed? I felt like I was only a shadow of myself. Where was the rest of me? I lost all my confidence in myself and didn't know where to turn.

Nikki watched and waited patiently. She stood by me like this was all part of a scripted play. She had the answers I sought, but it was not time yet for me to know. She had no expectations because she *knew*. She was part of the plan, part of the big picture that I could not yet see. She quietly waited while I floundered around in the dark. As much as I tried to push her away, she refused to leave her post. I needed her now more than I knew. She became my constant shadow offering me soft kisses when she could sneak one in. She fully embraced her God-given role as companion and guardian in these precious moments.

CHAPTER 48

A Psychic Dental Emergency

I would experience a profound closure of sorts when Nikki was two years old. In December 2010, I had a rather traumatic dental issue. Ironically, the molar that was now acutely abscessed was the very same baby tooth I had lost as a child. When I was seven years old, this baby tooth had to be pulled. This required me to wear a spacer (braces) for years to ensure that the adult molar would have room to come in correctly. I had only just undergone a root canal on this very molar two years ago. Now this repaired root was acutely infected, necessitating an emergency extraction. All my suffering, enduring years of braces, the scars I still had on the insides of my cheeks, and I was still losing this tooth! It made me wonder whether I was supposed to have anything in that space at all.

Unfortunately, the timing of events prevented me from being sedated for the extraction, and *that* was *not* a good plan as I would soon find out. I was given nitrous oxide, laughing gas, to help keep me calm through the procedure. But there wasn't any gas coming through the tube. I let the nurse know, but she couldn't figure out why. She informed the surgeon, but he became irritated. There was no time to deal with it; he had a very packed schedule that day. So he just ignored it. He numbed my jaw of course, but my anxiety and pain were steadily climbing. I was already anxious with dental work and usually required nitrous just to get a teeth cleaning. I could sense a disaster approaching! I also underestimated my ability to *hear* the incisions as well as the amount of force the surgeon would need to assert in pulling my tooth out. Since I was fully alert, my mind was going into overdrive. I began to freak out. The more I panicked and flinched, the more impatient the surgeon became. I was horrified to realize much too late what a terrible bed side manner this doctor had! The stress, fear, and pain began to culminate. I heard myself hyperventilating as my heart rate soared. I was trembling uncontrollably as my legs began to levitate off the chair. This was undoubtedly one of the most terrifying experiences of my life, yet it should have just been a routine extraction.

    I managed to survive the procedure but felt incredibly violated and traumatized afterward. I could not look the surgeon in the eye as he brought my husband in to explain my aftercare. I just wanted to go home. But I didn't feel any better at home. A horrible sense of grief overcame me as if I had been physically abused! I lay in bed all day and cried; I mean really cried, hard and deep. "Where was this coming from?" I remember questioning. This seemed so off-kilter for the routine procedure I just experienced. It really made me wonder what the significance of that tooth was. I tried to figure out why it had triggered such a deep and profound reaction in me. It almost felt like grief associated with a traumatic death. Was someone dying? I was not currently in touch with my parents. I wondered if something was going on with them. Was there an energetic connection between my tooth and a memory? The explosive emotional release with losing the tooth made me think this might be the case. It also made me realize that space in my mouth was supposed to be empty! I had already lost two teeth from there. I would not put anything else back in that spot.

    Nikki was always close by offering cuddles when I needed them and giving me space when I didn't. I would not discover the answer for my bizarre emotional reaction until September of the following year. It was then that my stepmother emailed to inform me that my father had suffered a massive stroke (on the day of my tooth extraction) and passed away just two days later! No one had attempted to contact me when my father suddenly died at only sixty-seven years of age. Yet my body had felt it and seemed to process it without me even knowing why. That tooth had some emotional connection to my father that had been festering all these years. It represented a big part of the culminating pain between us. As his life was coming to an end, all the puss inside that root came to a head and needed to be freed. The tooth had to come out to release me from that bondage. The toxins, physical, emotional, and spiritual, that were released with the removal of the tooth flooded into my system, overwhelming me into a temporary state of depression. It took many days for me to process and integrate feelings I was experiencing but not understanding. I was vaguely aware that things had changed, but I had no idea what or how until I got that email.

Even after learning of my father's death, it was still a few more years before I actually connected these events and understood their significance! What also surprised me was the amount of grief I then experienced once I learned of his death. I never liked my father as you already know. We had not spoken since 1994 or seen each other since 2000. But a part of me had always hoped that we would finally reunite and repair our relationship. I grieved *hard*—I mean really *hard*—for a whole week after I learned of his death. I had to purge all those emotions I had been holding onto my whole life.

This experience contained two important messages that I have been instructed to share with you. The first one is how connected we all are. Something that seemed so abstract and unrelated (a tooth extraction) was so perfectly connected to my father's departure from this world. I had stored all that deeply rooted pain (infection) from the relationship with my father inside that tooth. When it was finally removed, it exposed all the raw emotion I felt about my father in all its variations over so many years of psychological unrest. All of this came purging out of my body at the precise moment of his death. I then commenced a grieving process even though I did not know why. How incredible is this? We are all so beautifully connected as God's children.

Another important message in this story is of the significance our emotions play in our physical bodies. How emotions can fester and curdle inside us if not released and transmuted into love. Unreleased emotion creates diseases and dysfunctions inside all of us. They also serve to keep us from ourselves. We lose a part of ourselves where these emotions take up residence. And then we spend our whole lives trying to find that part. I was searching for myself because I did not feel whole. I was missing the pieces that had been removed to create the space to store these emotions for so long. Emotions are merely teaching tools. Once the learning is understood, the emotion must be freed and released. Hanging onto emotions makes us sick, unhappy, unhealthy, and unwhole.

Nikki sat lovingly by me as I mourned harder than I ever had before. She had known this was coming and she was ready. It was in her script as she witnessed me recover a part of myself that had been lost for so long. Her role in my life was so different from that of my other dogs. She was ushering me through some tough lessons such as this one necessary for my soul's completion. She saw the stepping-stone it afforded me and escorted me onto it as my soul recovered another part of itself and healed. She was preparing me for the next level, the next step that was soon to come. And she was holding the door open; she was saving a place for someone else.

CHAPTER 49

Avoidance

The years after Tori's death were very quiet. It was strange to not be constantly training and traveling to compete with a dog. For an entire decade I had lived on the road with my pack. It was a shocking shift to suddenly be at home with nothing to do. So I avoided being at home as I threw myself into training and competing with my horse. I was in a state of avoidance and denial. On one hand, I couldn't believe it was all over. On the other hand, I never wanted to go there again. The memories were too fresh and too painful; so many incredible dogs had passed through my hands in a very short period of time. It had been a decade that seemed like a lifetime. It was hard for me to be home where all those painful memories lived. So I stayed away as much as I could, and Nikki just waited.

In 2010 my husband and I began to vacation together for the first time since our wedding in 2000. Having only two dogs now, Nikki and her sister, made it easy to find care for them. We hired a house sitter to stay at the house and be with them in our absence. They tolerated this arrangement but were always thrilled when we came home. Nikki usually expressed her joy with a high-pitched, ear-piercing whine that grated on my nerves. This sound was like nails on a chalkboard to me. Neither of her parents had been vocal like that. But it was a reminiscent characteristic of her grandmother. It was the one thing about her grandmother that annoyed me tremendously. It was my dumb luck that Nikki just happened to inherit it. I tried everything to train her out of it, but nothing worked. I was stuck with it. And to make matters worse, with her high-pitched excitement came her battering ram of a tail! She wagged her tail so forcefully that it left marks in my paint as it hit my walls! It was very nice to be missed, but I could do without the screaming demolition tail!

The vacations sparked a new passion in me. My obsessive self found a new home in coordinating our travel. I became fixated on orchestrating our next trip. It was also nice to leave the dogs behind and experience a life without them. Surprisingly, I did not miss them when we were gone, and I began to yearn for a life without them. I enjoyed the peace and quiet without barking and dog hair. Surprisingly, I would find this escape from reality to be short-lived.

CHAPTER 50

The Swap Out

Leave it to Apachi to write her own story!

A rather strange thing happened, only I didn't know about it until later. It wasn't until I started writing this book that I learned that Apachi had come straight back to me the second she died! Once she had fulfilled the assignment I had given her, and when her physical body wore out, she came back to me. She swapped places with Nikki to complete her mission with me. Apachi spiritually "walked in" to the body of Nikki!

Wait. What?

Yeah, that's what I said! Based on what I was told, what I have learned, the moment her other body ceased to live, Apachi's spirit took possession of my current dog. This is what is referred to as a "walk in."

Do you remember what I told you about
black panther symbolism? They are regarded
as shape-shifters with natural psychic
power and magical skills. Hmmm.

I was aware of this possibility with people, but I never realized it was possible with dogs. This can happen if both spirit beings are willing—that of Apachi and Nikki. We're not talking about a case of possession or multiple personalities here. A "walk in" is when one spirit leaves a body and allows the other spirit to permanently occupy that body and remains for the duration of the life span. The new spirit takes on the personality that has already been established in that body and assumes that life midstream. That's probably why I didn't notice it. Because when Apachi swapped with Nikki, she was assuming Nikki's mannerisms and personality. There were a few subtleties that seemed to change in Nikki around the time that Apachi died. The most obvious one was that Nikki suddenly became very affectionate with me. So much so that she started to literally moan or purr when I would love on her.

The other thing that I noticed was she also became much more bothered by her sister's attempted dominance over her. Neeka, her litter sister, seemed to be completely oblivious to any pack rules or pecking order. She just behaved however she wanted and didn't really care about anybody else. She had no concept of pack order or hierarchy. I remember sensing Nikki's new irritation with her sister, and I could see the puzzled look on her face. It was as if she was thinking, *Doesn't she get it? Doesn't she know that I have higher rank than her?* Neeka was bigger than Nikki, but Nikki had been with me longer than Neeka. So Nikki should have authority. Nikki's or Apachi's expectations were spot-on.

But that was another thing. I had never noticed Nikki keeping track of the rules like this before now. That was something that Apachi always did as the alpha female. In fact, I had wondered when in the world this had changed. Because Nikki had never been a scorekeeper. I also noticed that Nikki's eye contact had suddenly intensified, which reminded me remarkably of Apachi! I had never noticed that about her before Apachi walked in. At the time, I remember wondering if this was something new, or had I just never noticed it before? Additionally, I began to notice how much these two girls, Nikki and Neeka, reminded me so much of their predecessors, Apachi and Catori. Nikki reminded me of Apachi, and Neeka reminded me of their mother, Tori. It was like I had Apachi and Tori back again. Like time had traveled backward somehow. I would have done anything to have them both back again. So I took this as an opportunity to enjoy these two incredible dogs as pets instead of as competitors. I made a conscious effort to relish every moment, and this brought me tremendous peace and joy. I thought I was just imagining it. Little did I know how close to the truth I really was!

So I was perceiving a big change at the time. I just did not know what it was entirely. As I looked back on this unique scenario between Apachi and Nikki, it all made sense and seemed totally plausible. This must have been why Nikki and I never bonded. She was only a temporary babysitter! Even more would be revealed once I developed the skills I needed for this book and Apachi began to speak to me more freely. She explained many unknowns that I will also share with you.

From this point forward, the book will begin to push you a little bit more. It will stretch your current beliefs and your comfort zone and challenge you to expand your own consciousness. It will leap to a whole new level and help you to understand things you never did before. Enjoy the ride and embrace the thrill!

CHAPTER 51

My Black Panther

We already know that Apachi had always carried a special presence. Something I never could put my finger on. It wasn't just me; other people were also drawn to her. She emanated a quality that was greater than that of any canine I had ever met. And there was a reason for this. It wasn't just my overactive, romantic imagination. Her vibration was so much greater than that of a normal dog. What she shared with me also explained why she was so driven to come back to me. Why it broke her heart so terribly when I sent her away that she wanted to end her life.

Apachi and I are very old souls who have walked this planet many lifetimes together. She has been with me many times in physical form, but she is also always with me in spirit form as my black panther spirit guide who has always watched over me. It was with her intense burning gaze that she attempted to *will* me into recognizing who she was and what she was. She wanted so badly for the light bulb to come on so that I would make that connection.

She was assigned the mission of guarding over me until I was ready to start my journey in writing this book. She was the gatekeeper of my journey to sovereign transformation. That's why she was so frantically trying to come back when I sent her away before her time. And that is also why she made a deal with Nikki to allow her to take her place. She needed to fulfill her obligation and escort me into my transformation phase! Wow! I mean wow! Let's just think about this for a moment.

This reveals a whole new light on the meaning and the purpose behind the dogs in our lives. It's no coincidence that we consider them to be angels that watch over us. They truly are angels and guides in physical form. Apachi was the embodiment of one of my guides, my black panther, who served to protect me and assist in my process through all my lives. Even now she sits with me—always has, always will. Our canine companions serve as a unique bridge to our higher consciousness, our higher selves. We saw how Anthea and Öskar assisted us in finding pieces of ourselves that needed to be repaired in the first two sections. Oeragon is the next level. She appears when you are ready to transform into a new vibrational version of yourself, free from your human limitations. She escorts you through your process, providing the tools and opportunities that you require to become a truer version of yourself, more connected to the divine. Just as she was showing me that version of myself earlier in Apachi's story. This guide is very powerful and has the means to achieve her goal as long as you have the will to follow her.

This is huge, folks! We always thought that our dogs were little angels placed here to love us unconditionally. That they were here for us to love, improve our health, reduce our stress, and provide us with unwavering companionship and unconditional love. But it's *so much more* than that! Now's a good time to reread their poem.

A Message from the Core Four

No matter what the circumstances, they were willing to sacrifice their own comfort, their own existence to assist.
Angels without wings, angels without voice, angels in disguise as a quiet, mute best friend who never judged.
Only quietly provoked my spirit into action, into direction, into myself.
In a direction I could not foretell, although it was written, and they knew the way to show me, lighting my path along the way.
Secretly knowing what I needed to get there.

My pack of angels had a big job to get me back to my light.
So I needed an army, and so there were many.
They have been undercover until now.
Now they wish to be known, to be seen, to be heard and loved.
We have always loved them, but now we know why.
We have always thought we could hear them, but now we know that we actually did.
We always thought they should have wings, and now we know they do!
We always thought they looked and seemed familiar, but now we know they are!
They are back! They are here for us!
Embrace your guardians, embrace your angels, embrace their message, and learn to hear them!

I know this may sound far-fetched to some of you. The rest of you are just jumping right in with me! You probably have never heard anything like this before. But surely I have earned some *confidence* with you given all that I've already shared. Surely you will lend me enough *trust* to embrace the message as they have delivered it. Remember this is not *my* message. It's a message from these K9 guides that desperately want to share their gifts with you. So no matter how you feel about what I've said so far, and maybe about what I'm going to say, please keep reading, processing, and absorbing. If that's not possible, please just enjoy a beautiful story about some incredible dogs. Because it's about to get even better! Let's return to our story at the point where Apachi walks into Nikki.

CHAPTER 52

Apachi Comes Home

In 2015 I noticed a change in Nikki. We had returned from Alabama and Nikki seemed unusually clingy. She was much more affectionate than she had ever been, and I remember thinking how odd it was. She climbed up in my lap as I sat in the recliner, pushed herself into my chest, and lovingly looked into my eyes. Our eyes connected and she began to purr. Dogs can't purr like cats. It comes out more like a quiet moan. I was delighted to see that Nikki had missed me so much. But her sudden affectionate expression was so odd that I took a selfie of us. The photo clearly showed her staring adoringly into my eyes. I wanted to relish this moment! We had had a rough road together in our relationship. And this was definitely a milestone! I noticed from that point forward she seemed more attentive, appreciative, and connected to me than she ever had in the past.

She was now seven years old, and this is the exact moment that Apachi had passed and "walked in" to Nikki. I didn't really register the significance of these events. Even years later, after finally hearing of Apachi's passing, it still didn't dawn on me that Apachi was back. It wasn't until I began writing this book and began receiving information from the K9 guides that I understood. I realized that Apachi's spirit had assumed Nikki's body. That's why she seemed to change so drastically and also seemed more familiar. For the remainder of this book, I may refer to her as Nikki in general but as Apachi for more significant points. Just realize that from here on out I am referring to the same dog!

I wished I had known then what I know now. One of the prevailing regrets I had was that of Apachi and Tori missing out on the relaxing lifestyle that Nikki was now enjoying. Knowing that Nikki was really Apachi would have brought me much peace. I also would have cherished every moment with her even more! It explains so much about why Nikki was so content to just be and had no interest in performing. She was simply waiting for the point in which Apachi would return and take over.

This also explains why Nikki did not want to leave me in the end. She was really Apachi. And Apachi could not leave until the precise moment I was ready to move into my next phase. Then and only then would she consider leaving her post. Doing the math, it is comforting to recognize that Apachi and I actually had another seven years together. Thankfully those seven years were much more privileged and relaxing for her than the first four. And seven is a magical number!

I also believe that it was Apachi's urging that spurred me to purchase our first RV in 2016, the year after she returned. She did not want to be left behind as Nikki had been when we traveled. She had every intention of going with us! As the obedient soldier that I am, I did as I was instructed. I began to feel a deep urge to buy a travel trailer, and my sole reasoning was to take the dogs with us on our trips. Within a month, we got our first trailer. No more house sitters. Now Apachi could just come along.

2016 began a whole new chapter for us as we began traveling quite frequently in the RV with Nikki and her sister. She got to travel with us on many adventures to Michigan, Ohio, Kentucky, Pennsylvania, Virginia, West Virginia, Georgia, Tennessee, Arkansas, Missouri, Alabama, Florida, Kansas, and even Colorado. She adapted quickly to this lifestyle and rather enjoyed visiting new places and being out in nature. Nikki kept all the squirrels in our campsite under control and enjoyed frequent walks and hikes that she never got at home. She was also quite content to hang out in the RV while we spent the day riding our mountain bikes. She and her sister were very quiet and obedient. They were usually the most well-behaved dogs in the campground.

Apachi was a definite improvement, and it was so nice to have her back. But she had arrived at the latter half of Nikki's life expectancy. She would quickly become a geriatric, bringing new challenges to our relationship.

CHAPTER 53

Aged Wisdom

Aging was difficult for Nikki's body. Not only had she been exposed to her mother's mold sickness in her womb, but also to the ever-increasing amounts of it in our house and her kennel over her first ten years. It was beginning to take its toll on her body. She was losing bladder control at an alarming rate while simultaneously becoming insatiably thirsty. I was constantly having to monitor her water intake and managing her frequent bathroom breaks. The mold was irritating her skin so she itched like crazy. She would scratch at her ears incessantly, causing hematomas that would have to be drained. Her final hematoma at ten years old permanently damaged her left ear. This same insane itchiness caused her to chew a hole in the tip of her tail, spewing blood all over my house as she wagged it! Of course, I had no idea what was causing all this at the time, but I so wished I had. I kept her on a special diet with human-grade food thinking maybe she had food allergies. Her descent into old age was a rough one for her and me. And it was definitely new territory for me. I was required to be much more attentive and to anticipate her needs less they result in a mess in my house. It took a bit more energy and focus than I anticipated.

Geriatric dogs offer their own unique rewards, but the more we began to travel, the more I began to fantasize about not having any dogs. How nice it would be to live without any dog hair, urine, or vomit.

A life without scooping poop and sleeping in without interruption seemed all too attractive. I began to look forward to those days as Nikki aged and required more care. I told everybody I knew that I was done with dogs and when Nikki passed away there would be no more dogs. Most people expressed their surprise, knowing my history. I think my husband completely ignored my proclamations, expecting me to renege on them. But I was completely serious, and they would see. I yearned to travel and not worry about caring for animals anymore. How liberating that would feel! And I began to anxiously look forward to it!

Don't get me wrong. I still loved my Nikki with all my heart! But this was the first time in my life that I was caring for a geriatric dog. The last half of Nikki's life was quite special and magical, and I wouldn't trade that time with her for the world. It was nice to have a calmer dog around that had "been there, done that" and wasn't surprised by the world. But in the back of my mind, I found myself always wondering, *When will it be?* Every time I found Nikki sleeping deeply, I rushed over to put my hand on her chest just to make sure she was still breathing. The older she got, the more her deep sleep resembled death. It put me a little bit on edge because I just didn't know when or how it would happen. This uncertainty was a little more unsettling than I anticipated.

Of course, the biggest thing that I learned from this was to just enjoy the *now*. I soaked up every little moment that Nikki looked at me with her adoring eyes. I enjoyed every little moan and groan as she delighted in sharing space and affection. I learned to enjoy every annoying solicitation for affection that Nikki bestowed upon me because I never knew when it would all be gone. Because of this unknown, I was much more willing to roll with the punches, to roll with the uncomfortable times, and to tolerate the messes. It taught me to be a little gentler, a little kinder, a lot more forgiving and compassionate than I had been in the past. This experience brought through new pieces of myself that I had never explored before, and for that I was grateful! Over time, my heart seemed to heal from her mother's death, and it gradually began to open again. It can be hard to find your vulnerability again after such a tremendous and painful loss.

Nikki seemed to understand this and to just wait patiently for this transformation in me to occur. She could sense exactly where I was spiritually and lovingly just waited for me to be ready to love her. Even if it took me ten years! After all, she was now where she belonged—back with me. She was very content to enjoy her peaceful life with me every minute that she could. She would just stare at me with those powerful eyes, watching intently just like old times. Reading my thoughts and my energy and hoping that I could read hers.

CHAPTER 54

Nikki as Queen

When Nikki was ten and half years old, her sister tragically died and left her an only child. Nikki relished in having her alone time with me. She became even more spoiled, getting all the attention from both me and my husband and not having to share it with anyone. She got all the cookies that she wanted and any toy that she picked out in the store. She had the bed to herself, and we even indulged her with fancy orthopedic dog beds and blankets. She was a bit pampered as she crept up on eleven years of wisdom. After losing her sister, I relished every moment I had left with her; I knew the clock was ticking for us. Nikki got a lot more kisses and cuddles and she readily accepted all of it. She became more assertive in asking for affection by flipping my arm up with her nose so it landed precisely on her head. It was cute but could easily become annoying when I was busy. But of course, it's one of the first things I missed when she was gone.

As her age progressed, Nikki's vision and hearing began to fade. She was perfectly content to just sleep all day. We occasionally played an easy game of fetch, but I generally limited her running and jumping to avoid unnecessary injury. She certainly didn't require much activity now before she got tired.

She continued to travel with us as our professional companion. She was so easy because she was so experienced and knowledgeable at this

Oeragon

point. She slept the whole time we drove, whether it was two hours or twelve. She behaved like an old professional at each campground. She wasn't excited by much and relished in her quiet, observing years. She just sat patiently at camp watching all the comings and goings. She was content to just be wherever I was.

PART 3
Call to Arms

CHAPTER 55

Cosmic Shift

2020 was a profound shift for the entire planet. None of us could have foreseen the events that were about to happen and the realities that were about to change as the impending virus approached the world in February. By March, most of the United States was on lockdown. This left me lots of time at home with Nikki to contemplate life, the world, health and wellness, and the true meaning behind it all. I was fortunate that I had this time to share with Nikki while others were desperately adding dogs to their household. We shared our very simple days together stuck at the house while my husband continued to work. We enjoyed hanging out in the yard, going for walks, or relaxing on the porch. It was also during the lockdown that I stumbled upon something quite miraculous.

I was out in the yard with Nikki when I saw her attempt to pick up something that looked like a dead animal. But she reflexively dropped it as if startled. Immediately intrigued as to what might have triggered this response, I ran over to her. She was now staring at the thing from a distance, nervous about it and not wanting anything to do with it. This was odd for her because normally she chased animals in the yard. I cautiously approached what appeared to be some sort of animal in the grass. I stooped down to get a better look.

At first, I just saw what appeared to be a scared, stunned, half-grown baby squirrel just lying there looking at me. I could see its rapid panting and even the blinking of it eyes. So I knew it was still alive. But why didn't it try to run? As I attempted to sort out the details, my brain seemed to move in slow motion. Yet I got a vague sense there was something very special about this creature. Lying next to the squirrel baby was another lump, another squirrel. Only this one appeared to be dead and somewhat engorged. All around these squirrels were pieces of a nest, and some pieces were even intertwined within the squirrels. My brain was still struggling to catch up to what my eyes were seeing. But on a much higher level, I already knew. I hunted around for a stick that I could use to investigate why the squirrel wasn't moving. Nikki got a little closer just in case I needed her help I noticed. Even with me poking around and making loud noises and sudden movements, the squirrel made no attempt to flee or protect itself in any way. Having given up on my brain altogether, my intuition was loudly suggesting that there was something different here.

With some further cautious investigation, I realized why that squirrel didn't try to run or even move. The live baby was attached to the dead baby! It was a *conjoined twin,* and as much as I could tell, they were joined at the spine. Do you know what I mean by this? In layman's terms, this was a Siamese twin. This would mean that neither squirrel would ever be able to walk or even leave the nest.

Judging by their size, they appeared to be half grown. And with all the bedding from the nest lying on the ground around them, I realized that their weight must have finally outgrown the nest that was meant for much smaller babies. They must have tumbled all the way down to the ground as it gave way. They had apparently never left the nest as their mother continued to feed them. A deep sadness rushed over me. I had never seen a Siamese twin in person. I was in shock and a little horrified just as I'm sure this baby was after surviving such a fall. I also couldn't shake the profound sadness, like an impending force field, that washed over me. I wasn't sure where it was coming from. Was it from the squirrel? Did it have something to do with COVID? It reminded me of the mysterious sadness I felt when my tooth was pulled. Only this was much deeper and felt grander somehow. I was amazed at how quickly it washed over and through me.

I had no idea what to do for this squirrel. My eyes teared up as I realized there really was nothing that could save this poor creature. I said a prayer for him and asked for his forgiveness because I did not know how to help him. Then I set him to the side and out of harm's way, letting nature take its course.

That sadness stuck with me for many days. But it was two years before I truly understood what significance it had. This squirrel held a very specific symbolism for me in my own spiritual progression. It signified a pivotal point on my journey. This Siamese twin exemplified two different parts of me that I was not yet aware of. The dead half represented my old self, the person that I had identified with up to this point. The alive half was my new self that I had not yet met and was still a little terrified to come out and be fully visible. It also represented me, right here and right now, as I continued to carry around the burden of old pain, beliefs, and habits that no longer served my soul. I needed to let go of this unconscious weight that pulled me down and prevented me from moving forward.

At the time, I could not see any of this, but I could *feel* that it was there. It was a message in a bottle waiting to reach shore. The overwhelming sadness I felt was a grieving of sorts for my old self. It was the part that I was the most familiar with so I was sad to see it go. Oeragon, Apachi, and Nikki knew exactly what was going on. This event triggered my next phase. It signaled the beginning of the changing of the guards!

You see Oeragon's job was to guard over me until I was ready for the next K9 guide, Héric. Her job was to let Héric know when I was ready. The appearance of this twin signified that I was ready for that transition to begin. I was ready to transition into my new self and ready to shed the antiquated half. A cosmic switch had been flipped, not just for humanity but also for me. This was the very moment I began to wake up to my higher self, my purpose, and my calling. Apachi was now nineteen years old. (Nikki was twelve years old.) She saw the signal and sensed its meaning. Oeragon signaled to Héric that the time was nearing to get ready. I was beginning my preparation. It was a call to arms for me and everyone on my team!

Of course, cognitively I had no idea that any of this was going on. I just knew that the world felt different. I again felt like a big change was coming, but I had no idea what. It would be two years later that the full impact of this squirrel would be unveiled and only after I had fully begun that sovereign transformation that Apachi was waiting for. For now, I just kept being. I kept living and doing the only things I knew to do. But I gradually became more and more unsettled physically and spiritually. It was like an itch that I could not scratch. Many things were very uncertain for me, and COVID had amplified this.

CHAPTER 56

An Old Awakening

As 2020 came to a close and my physical therapy practice continued to struggle, I found comfort in helping an old friend. She needed some help at her dog training facility. I never thought I wanted to train dogs again, and honestly it wasn't something I was passionate about anymore. But it seemed to make sense right here and right now. It wouldn't hurt to fill my vacant time and put my old skills to good use. So in December 2020, I did what I never thought I would do. I returned to the world of dog training. It had been eleven years since I abruptly retired, eleven years since the death of Tori. Part of me wondered if I still knew how to do this. But it all came back so quickly and vividly. Of course, what I did not anticipate were all the vivid memories that also came flooding back! The memories were so fresh and sharp that it felt as if those glorious days were only yesterday. There were so many memories I had forgotten that were instantly reinstalled in my mind. It seemed to spark a new light in me, and I enjoyed it more than I thought I would. Working with dogs is so much easier than working with people, and this I had somehow forgotten.

I spent the month of December doing more dog training than physical therapy, and it seemed to light a fire in me. I missed this stuff! I missed watching the light bulb go on when working with a young puppy. I missed laying the foundation for a remarkable relationship. I missed the anticipation of what could be in the beginning of something new. And for the first time in over a decade, I began to consider adding a new dog to my pack. But who was I kidding? I really enjoyed my quiet time with my geriatric princess.

Just after Christmas that year, we took our first trip to Florida in the RV. Nikki got to view the ocean for the first time in her life, and sadly it would be the only time. She was now twelve and a half years old but showed no sign of giving up, no sign of illness, no sign of being ready to leave me. She was living her best possible life and loving every minute of it. I don't think she knew how lucky she was to be a snowbird for the last chapter of her life. None of my other dogs ever got to experience something so regal. She seemed to enjoy the warm weather and the longer walks in the middle of winter. When we took her to the ocean, she had a puzzled look on her face like "Is this it? Is this what all the hype is about?" She didn't seem all that impressed with so much water and not a squirrel to be found. On the other hand, I felt like I was on the edge of the world standing on that beach. I had forgotten the magnificence of the ocean. It took my breath away, and I wondered why it had taken us so long to make a trip like this.

Ironically on several occasions during this trip I fondly thought of Apachi and Tori and wished that I could have shared such a beautiful experience with them. It didn't quite seem fair that they had to work so hard in their life and not get to enjoy such beautiful things like this. But here was Nikki. She didn't have to work at all but got all the glamorous benefits. It just didn't seem fair. Of course, at that point, I didn't know that it was actually Apachi that was experiencing these beautiful memories with me. That knowledge would have brought me so much joy! But I was thankful that I got to share this beautiful experience with Nikki nonetheless.

It was while on this trip that I got an urge, or maybe a prod, to get a new puppy. My initial curiosity about the possibility suddenly morphed into something stronger. I tried to stuff it down. Why would I add chaos into my calm? This subtle hunch grew until I couldn't shake it. I recognized that feeling deep down in my gut. The feeling that had always guided me in the past to find all those magical dogs. Oh no! I had no choice. I would have to obey my gut, my intuition, my calling. I had been through this so many times before. Ignoring it does not work. Trying to rationalize why it is *not* a good idea to get another dog never works. This urge absolutely peaked by the end of our trip. I mentioned the idea to my husband expecting to get some pushback. I was surprised to find him open to this abrupt change of direction. He didn't offer any opposition or even his usual devil's advocate. He just kind of shook his head and said, "What can I say? I knew you weren't done with dogs."

Well, even if he wasn't surprised, I was completely surprised by this turn. I had been telling myself for years that I was not getting another dog. When Nikki was gone, it was all over. But the familiar excitement inside me was rising. I had forgotten that feeling of anticipation that I always got when I felt the push. All the cells in my body light up in response to its keen awakening. It brings a unique sense of awareness that is indescribable as all my senses are heightened. I felt the familiar surge of new possibilities brewing.

This new puppy that was waiting for me would elicit a deliberate sequence of events. She would steer me in a completely new direction in my life that would take me by surprise. The energy was moving, and I could feel it! The K9 guides were meticulously moving everything into position. All I had to do was to hear the calling and respond to it. By this time, my next spirit guide, Héric, had already incarnated in a puppy and was looking forward to connecting with me. Oeragon, Apachi, was pushing me to find her while Héric was softly calling out to me. It was almost time for us to unite and begin a new journey, and they were getting me ready.

I began to perseverate on the various details of this new puppy. I spent significant time and energy in contemplation. Nikki sat quietly next to me throughout all of this. She continued to be her calm self, lovingly returning my gaze as I tried to explain to her what was about to happen. She didn't show any recognition for what I was saying as I talked her though the possibility of adding a new dog to our home. She just did what she always does and solicited more petting. I told her to enjoy her quiet moments as the only dog in the family for the next few days because it was about to change. She was going to have to share her space with another dog again. She just stared at me like she already knew.

The biggest question I had to answer was this: *Which puppy is joining us?* I had no idea if it was to be a purebred, rescue, registered, or mixed breed. There were so many unanswered questions. I didn't have this many questions to cipher through in the past. I always knew what breed I wanted. Usually the only questions I had to answer were male or female and from which country. So this was a lot more territory to nail down.

Also, I felt a sense of urgency that I couldn't describe. As we began to make our way home from Florida, Nikki slept soundly in the back seat of the F250 while I feverishly scoured the internet to get answers and find direction. Once we returned home, I continued my frantic search. I could not sleep at night, compulsively scrolling through puppy listings, litter announcements, and Facebook groups. I knew I did not want another Malinois. I certainly did not want a noisy sheltie; I had already had two. A hard no on a border collie because I really did not like the OCD mentality of my one and only. It would be nice to try a new breed that I had never experienced. But which one?

I investigated fox terriers, Jack Russel terriers, Chihuahuas, mini-Aussies, schipperkes, heeler cattle dogs, and Dutch shepherds. Ugh! I also investigated two new breeds: the mudi and the Lancashire heeler. They weren't the answer either. What about designer mixes? I could experience two breeds at once! I had never had a corgi. They were the perfect smaller size that would make traveling easy. They were also a herding breed with similar drives to the Malinois. Yes, this breed lit a switch and felt congruent with my needs!

Once I narrowed down the breed, I was like a dog chewing a bone. I just could not let it go. I could not sleep, eat, or work. I had to find this puppy. This is how I get when I am being called.

The timing became my next focus. This puppy needed to come home soon. I couldn't wait for a planned litter or a future birth. This puppy was calling me *now*. Nikki kept me company throughout this process. Even though she didn't show it, she was monitoring my progress and providing psychic nudges. I found a couple of litters of corgis, but they were too young and wouldn't be ready soon enough. I found some older puppies that were ready now, but they weren't right either. At one point, I thought I had finally found the right puppy and even placed a deposit. Feeling satisfied that I had achieved my mission, I was finally able to drift off to sleep. But in the middle of the night, I was awakened by a sense of panic because I realized I had made a mistake! I had to start my search all over again!

So out of bed I sprang with Nikki hot on my heels, and back on the internet I went. Surely there was something I had missed. I decided to dig a little deeper. I got the sense that the puppy was nearby. But I was having a hard time finding a suitable litter anywhere close. The pressure was building, and the timing was critical. My husband and Nikki slept soundly as I dug in deeper and dove into the underbelly of the WWW. I cruised all the puppy ads for my area, joined all the corgi groups on Facebook, and still could not find what I was looking for. It took the next four days of frantic searching, posting inquiries, requesting recommendations from people that I knew and those I didn't, constant searching, and fixating on this project before I finally got a lead.

For some reason, I knew this puppy needed to be a tricolor. This puppy needed to be almost all black with white and brown accents. I was not sure why this was so important, but I was only looking at tricolored puppies. I would not understand the significance of this until this puppy turned eighteen months old!

According to some helpful answers to my query in a Facebook group, there was a corgi breeder forty-five minutes away from me that was highly recommended. I could not find anything on her webpage or her Facebook page about available puppies or litters. So I contacted her privately to see if she had anything, holding my breath for her reply. As luck would have it, or *divine design*, she had a litter of puppies that were already eight weeks old! Bingo! And she had one female puppy that was a black tricolor. Double bingo! That checked all the boxes as long as the temperament fit.

Finally, I had a good feeling about this one so I went down for a visit. The mother of the litter was a beautiful black-headed tricolor. She had a black body, head, and ears, a beautiful white collar around her neck with some splashes of white and brown on her face and legs. She was *gorgeous!* She greeted me as I entered the kennel with a very warm welcome, a quiet disposition, and a submissive yet confident approach. Ahh, this was exactly the type of energy I was looking for! And she was the perfect size, not too big. I also noticed she had a gentle yet firm approach with her babies. After raising so many litters of my own, I grew to understand how important the mother was. I placed more significance on her quality than that of the father for my own breeding program. So this was a good sign. I felt like I was in the right place!

I engaged her breeder in some general questions about the genetics of the litter, the health of the parents, the philosophy of her program, vaccination, and deworming protocols—all the typical things I look for in a breeder. I also played with the puppies of course, especially the little tricolor female that I had my eye on. As I played with her, I realized how much she reminded me of a Malinois puppy. She was quite feisty and brave. I was really surprised by her mouthiness and the quality and power of the grips she had! It was reminiscent of my own Malinois puppies.

I was actually pleasantly surprised about how much I liked her all together! I think I might have finally found what I was looking for! Pricing, purchase agreement, and pickup date were all discussed, and I would return next week to pick her up. And just like that, my problem was solved, my itch was scratched, and I could finally rest! The yearning in my gut was gone! The order had been filled. My fire had been replaced by a soft glow in my heart and excitement about a new adventure.

I returned home to inform my husband that we were going to be adding a corgi to our family. He was all too familiar with this process and my innate ability to follow my instincts. I then turned my attention to Nikki, but she only smiled. She was pleased that I had managed once again to locate my next guide. Now I could finally rest after so many nights of frantic searching. I could finally relax. Nikki curled up right next to me as if she was just as exhausted as I was, and we both took a long afternoon nap.

The final K9 guide of the book is about to make his appearance in my life, and it will simultaneously complete Nikki's purpose and story. Let's meet him!

As a dog owner, a trainer, and a mentor to any living being, nothing is more satisfying than to watch the butterfly come out of the cocoon! And this was exactly what she wanted for me!

SECTION 5

Dämeon Ja'Laȓon Héric

(Dä-mon-ya-la-r̃on Er̃ik)

"Héric"

I am delighted to introduce you to our final spirit guide for this book. His name is unique and rather difficult to pronounce: Dämeon Ja' Lafõn Héric (Dä-mon Ya-la-ĩon Erĩk). *He is a masculine energy, and so far, he is the first guide to have a three-part name.* It took me a long time to learn how to spell and pronounce it, and I still stumble over it. Luckily, he has granted permission for me to refer to him as Héric for short. He explained that his name means "divine doorway into all dimensions and all lifetimes." Those between here and there, now and then, and the known and forgotten, because there really is nothing that is unknown to us.

Once again, his image perfectly portrays his energy and purpose. The wide-open eyes serve to receive all visual input through all dimensions. The short, stout nose of the pug matches the rigid beak of the eagle and serves as a dimensional compass tracking where he is, where he is from, and where he is going. The open ear of the bird allows for nonfiltered auditory recording, whereas the cupped ear of the pug serves to soften the acquisition of difficult information. The broad spread of his wings gives him absolute control and precision in his travels. It is with his accurate steering that he can show you exactly what you need to see. The eagle neck is compact like that of the pug. But the aviation expert has a better perspective with his swivel neck and easily zooms in on all aspects of situations, not just the obvious ones.

This powerful guide has chosen the bald eagle as his spirit animal (his guide form), which signifies his ability to soar effortlessly between the physical and the spiritual world. With him the opportunity is ripe for powerful connections to your own unique soul within multiple dimensions as well as directly to the divine. His broad wings help you to easily expand your consciousness beyond limits and into spiritual awakening. Riding the wings of Héric will enable you to easily expand your awareness into new and exciting directions. His energy exudes total freedom and elation because he knows no boundaries! This wise eagle grants his sharp vision to us so that we may see with the clarity that he does. We can see far, and we can see through like never before. This bird of prey also gives you the courage and confidence to receive and deliver messages from the divine, messages for you or for humanity.

When Héric appears to you or calls you, he is inviting you to experience a divine spiritual awakening that will carry you effortlessly into clarity and connection. He offers you the energy, the tools, and the ability to expand your awareness into new realms of consciousness.

The personality of this spirit guide (his angel form) matches that of the pug dog breed. This breed's sole purpose as a lap companion allows Héric to focus closely on his human charges without expectation for anything else. Héric doesn't like to waste energy with frivolous human activities and games. He prefers to conserve his intention to sharply focus on the truly meaningful soul work he has to offer you. This breed also provides additional traits of intelligence, arrogance, and a sense of smug all-knowing that seems to suit him. In fact, the Frank the Pug character in the *Men in Black* movies sums up this persona quite perfectly. From my experience, this spirit guide is definitely not cuddly despite its association with a lapdog. Héric has explained to me that eagles are to be admired from afar! So his canine form loves to be admired but is not fond of physical touch. This has certainly proven to be accurate with all three incarnations of Héric in my life.

This impressive guide offers experiences to elevate your divine enlightenment, expanding your consciousness to become more connected with your own soul as well as with God himself. He was the first to explain that the guides all have "job titles," and he very proudly announced his title long before anyone else. Héric is the *guardian of past-life integration*! With his help, you may become more aware of other lifetimes where trauma needs to be transmuted into love and light in order for your soul to heal and continue to expand. Utilizing his gifts can create immeasurable ease in your current path and bring your soul into full alignment with your purpose. It was with his advanced gifts and tools that I was able to progress so rapidly on my journey.

Although I was hearing Héric's messages and I was channeling his words for months, I had not actually "met" him. I had never been fully in his presence. I had shared space and felt the incredible energy and the love of all the other guides early on. But Héric had held back and waited for the perfect moment to show himself to me. It wasn't until after I finished writing this book that I got to experience him, and he was every bit as impressive and breathtaking as I was instructed to write in these pages.

He appeared during an ayahuasca ceremony that I attended as a celebration for completing the book. While everyone else was off on a dramatic trip remembering all their pain and fear, I was taking a beautiful journey with this powerful angel guide! Initially my dog Gigi appeared before me. But just like in my vision of Oeragon, where the panther turned into my dog, this time my dog turned into her guide! In my vision, Gigi morphed into her expansive, breathtaking, beautiful, powerful, protective, guide self. I was instantly brought to tears as I felt his loving, kind, protective energy. In my vision, I collapsed at his feet because his energy was so great that I could not hold myself up. I wept with divine joy, love, and completeness. I felt so *whole* and so *real* in that moment like I have never felt before. And I was *safe*. In his presence, I felt safer and more protected than I had ever felt in this lifetime.

As I lay there before him completely humble and gracious for his gifts, he reached down with his wing arms and cradled me. My physical body lying on my mat responded and my heart suddenly rose up off the floor and into the air. My knees flexed upward involuntarily so that my body was in the shape of a *W* with my arms hanging out and down to the mat I lay on. I was not sure what was happening, and then I felt him lift me! He catapulted us upward into the heavens, through many dimensions, back to my divine source, and into ascension. He was delivering me from my past, from my pain, from all my brokenness, into the complete version of me the divine had made! I wept as the pure joy poured over me. I wept as all the things that no longer served me were all removed instantly. He spoke to me and explained that there is no need for humanity to suffer. It is not necessary for us to relive our pain, to know where it comes from, or to understand it in order to be relieved of it. He can show us how to let it all go and shed all that karma that holds us back! And at this moment, I truly understood his gift. I could see how he had directed me in my process, lent his tools and gifts to me, and walked me through it step-by-step so that I moved rapidly to this very moment. This was an incredible wow moment, folks. The revelation of humanity no longer needing to suffer blew me away! You will read more about this process in the coming pages. But I had to come back and add this experience to the book because it was just too incredible to leave out or to save for later!

That aside, when Héric has chosen you or you are drawn to him, multidimensional integration may be necessary and available to you. There is a need for you to reconnect with your galactic soul and embrace your ancient wisdom that has been locked away and forgotten. It is time to free this part of you, reconnect, and remember who you really are in the eyes of the Almighty Creator. Héric's presence offers an opportunity for your awareness to expand beyond measure using the tools he has to share with you. If you are willing, it can be a very magical, liberating, and safe experience. Just imagine instantaneous healing from old baggage and pain that has held you captive all your life! His spontaneous healing gifts allow your soul to soar like the eagle as it was intended! Héric wishes for humanity to realize our full potential with our spirituality!

All this certainly makes total sense based on my own experiences. The upcoming pages will demonstrate this very process in my life. The current incarnation of Héric appeared to me just as the gates to my massive transformation were beginning to open. He patiently waited for me to be ready. With his guidance, I explored my soul's history and collected the missing pieces I needed through this lifetime and others. Héric ensured that I was protected, guided, and that I did not lose my way. His canine form may look like an ordinary dog, albeit an absolutely adorable corgi, but his spirit works in ways that are not visible to the naked eye. He whispers messages in my ears, broadcasts visions in my head, or escorts my spirit into another dimension as I sleep or meditate. My corgi is not what she appears to be as she sleeps peacefully next to me day and night. She is so much more than that adorable little face. So much more than that mischievous gleam in her eye or playful little bark. She holds the cosmic door open so that I can access all the information that Héric has to offer. We'll begin this section by tuning in to Gigi, who was constantly by my side as I wrote this book. We'll take a look at her story first. Then I'll share with you the other two dogs Héric came in with, and I think it will make more sense to you.

All the dogs in this book up to this point have passed on and no longer share physical space with me except for this one. Héric is a very different energy and a different experience from what we have discussed thus far. This guide is far more complex and advanced, and as a result, this section is going to be a little different from the preceding three. It won't be as much about what we did together because Héric was not interested in any of that nonsense! His stories are more about what I was experiencing and what opportunities came up while he was at the helm. The pug side of this guide is very inactive and not interested in any type of performance. He prefers to just be and does not like expectations placed upon him. Remember his eagle side prefers to be adored from afar and really does not enjoy being touched. So affection is not something he is likely to seek out or work for. And as you probably already realize, this is very different from the dogs that you have read about thus far.

There is one final piece that Héric wishes for you to know before we move on. He says it is important for you to understand the "brilliance in the orchestration of mankind"! Your unique spiritual path provides specific opportunities for you to complete your soul's learning and growth here on earth. Everything that happens in your life does so for a specific reason. The mystery of your life is to understand the meaning and purpose behind your experiences. This is the overwhelming theme throughout this book. What gift does each experience bring you? What learning and knowledge can you gleam from it? I have learned that all my hard knocks have a purpose in this way. Instead of getting angry or frustrated, I have learned to ask, "What message does it have for me?" The sooner I hear the message and integrate the learning, the sooner I can move on and forward. Héric is here to help all of us locate the pieces of us that are missing, that hold us back and are necessary for us to become the complete version of ourselves. As a loyal servant to God and to you, he is happy to assist in your process and awaken you to your true identity! Here is his message.

A Message from Héric

Eagle eyes and falcon ears perched high above
with laser precision and focus.
Wings to elevate, illuminate, transmute
the lives of past, present, and future.
Hovering, observing, guarding, and protecting
the spirituality of his charge.
Sharp attention on his duty of spirit, not of flesh,
arriving at specific moments on the timeline,
rippling between dimensions,
at a threshold for enlightened awareness.
Raising the curtain, opening the door
to full transformation and integration.
Your guardian awaits for the exact divine opportunity
to nudge you forward on your journey,
dissolving the veil of illusion in each lifetime.
Ready to escort you precisely through the portal to *enlightenment*,
loving, knowing, and bestowing.
Soar with him far beyond the heights of the mighty bald eagle!
(Delivered by Gigi, June 25, 2022)

PART 1

Gigi

Héric has been with me three times now. He has been a tricolored sheltie, a blue merle border collie, and now a tricolored corgi. As with all the other guides, his energy was the same in all three dogs. Each of his visits happened to coincide with a very difficult section in my process. As you will see, his time with me brought some incredibly transformative opportunities. With Héric's help, I could rapidly move through difficult or sticky lessons. My experiences with him were so much deeper and more life changing than anything I experienced with the other guides. Each subsequent visit also provided me with deeper learning and growth than the previous. There was obviously a strategic peeling away of layers for each staggered visit. I think you will be able to see just how different my experience was with him as compared to any of the other guides. So let's take a look.

CHAPTER 57

The Gift of Gigi

January 2021

Let's resume the story about the puppy that Nikki brought me. Once I was able to connect all the clues and locate the correct puppy, I busily prepared for her arrival. It had been a very long time since I had welcomed a new puppy into the fold. I would have to buy all new equipment (leashes, bowls, collars, toys, crate, baby gates) since I sold all my stuff when I retired. I told Nikki she was going to be getting a new little sister, but I only got a blank stare. I can only imagine what she must have been thinking, since she had actually orchestrated the entire transaction. I decided to name the puppy Gigi, or rather I was given this name to call her. I am never really sure how the names I pick come about. It's like they just appear in my mind. However, I do prefer for all my female names to end in *i,* in case you have not yet noticed.

This special little puppy turned out to be an absolute treasure! There was no doubt that she was a *divine gift!* Nikki, on the other hand, was not so convinced. I figured there would be an adjustment period for her. I also underestimated how small this puppy was going to be when I brought her home. She was less than five pounds with no tail and cute, little, perky ears. For heaven's sake, she looked just like a bunny rabbit in the field! Nikki used to chase the bunnies in our yard. So I can imagine the emotional conflict this little creature might have stirred up in my geriatric companion! Gigi would also be an easy grab for the flying predators around here. I would have to watch her closely in the yard so that the hawks did not fly off with her!

Nikki was very uncomfortable about the pup so I kept them separated at first. Nikki wanted nothing to do with Gigi and refused to acknowledge her presence. This was an obvious reflection of how I preferred to deal with uncomfortable situations. I just pretended the people were not there! I could understand her inner turmoil. This puppy certainly did look like prey to her. She was probably very nervous that she might instinctively behave inappropriately and get in trouble for it. So her default behavior was to completely ignore the puppy, not look at her, and stay as far away as she could. That was the only way she knew she would remain in control.

This made Gigi very sad because all she wanted was to cuddle up with Nikki and be her friend. Gigi stood at the baby gate quietly watching Nikki on the other side and submissively inviting her to come and visit. Just as her mother had, Gigi folded her ears down, lowered her head and her eyes, and wiggled her body in hopes that Nikki would accept her. She was so cute and so calm for her age. I was very impressed. She had her hyper moments, but when she was around Nikki, she was always calm and respectful like she was in a state of awe. When Nikki did not want to meet her, Gigi seemed to be utterly heartbroken. It was so sad to watch.

I had baby gates set up throughout the house so that Nikki could be relaxed and protected in her own space without worrying about the puppy invading it. This was always my policy with puppies anyway, so that I could keep a close eye on them. Whatever room I was in, the puppy was with me inside a gate so that I could closely supervise.

I was happy to discover that Gigi was a really easy puppy to train. Crate training progressed very quickly, and within a month, she was completely housebroken. To this date, she has been the cleanest dog we've ever had and still has never messed in the house. She has a lot of food drive so she was easy to teach through motivation and positive reinforcement. I taught her lots of commands and tricks with my typical puppy games. We had a blast getting to know each other.

Nikki watched us from a distance. I used to play all these games with her when she was a baby. I wondered if she missed it. Every day I took the two dogs outside on a leash and walked them together. Gigi was so excited to be so close to Nikki, but the queen was still very nervous about this little puppy being so close to her. She wanted to snap at her anytime Gigi was close enough to touch her. I manually preserved appropriate distance between them using the leashes until Nikki began to relax. Gigi was learning to walk on leash as well as to respect Nikki's space. I kept her safely out of Nikki's reach to prevent any unwanted encounters. The queen needed to feel that I supported her and wouldn't let anything happen to her. It was a process I was familiar with, and I knew to just give it time and patience. Trust sometimes takes time to develop, much as it does with myself.

By the beginning of the third week, Nikki began to relax a bit more. She didn't automatically look away now if the puppy looked at her through the gate. So I began to include Nikki in my training sessions with the pup. With both dogs on leash, I placed Nikki on her place box and Gigi on a different one. I've done this lots of times as a professional trainer. I require them to stay on their place boxes until they hear their names. It teaches them the value of their names because they are only allowed to come off their box when they hear them. We practiced several rounds of calling one dog to me while the other stayed. The dog then had to return to their own box when instructed. The game reset when I called the other dog. It was a great way for Nikki to experience being around the puppy in a controlled environment. Gigi had to really concentrate and think about what she was doing so that she would get her treat. Nikki had to practice trust in my leadership and see that I was looking out for her.

By the end of the third week, they were able to tolerate being next to each other with each of them on their own place box. Nikki also began to tolerate the puppy touching her while on our walks. These were good signs of progress, so they were ready for the next part.

The next step was the hardest part for Nikki because she would have to tolerate the puppy in her space while lying still. I remember that day clearly as I had Nikki lie down on the floor of the den. I then brought Gigi in on leash. Gigi became excited when she saw the big dog was within her reach. She started to wiggle all over and folded her ears back in that familiar submissive pose that she was so good at. I placed Gigi in my lap as I sat on the floor next to Nikki. I restricted Gigi's movements so that she did not climb all over Nikki and overwhelm her. Nikki was trembling with nervous adrenaline. She really wanted to bolt, but I asked her to stay and trust me. The three of us sat together for ten to fifteen minutes. I wasn't sure exactly what I was waiting for, only that I would know it when I saw it. And then the most magical thing happened.

Gigi could sense how nervous the old queen was so she kept low and slinked over my leg, up between Nikki paws, under her chin, and gently pulled herself up around the side of Nikki's neck. She very cautiously made her way up to Nikki's one good ear (the only ear that was still standing). This clever little puppy began to gently lick the inside of the tense dog's ear as her little butt began to wiggle. My jaw dropped! I had never observed such a gentle, kind, intuitive gesture from such a young puppy. It instantly softened the old lady. Nikki's tension seemed to melt like butter. She stopped shivering, her face softened, and she lowered her head so that Gigi could reach her easier. And in that moment, she seemed to suddenly accept this puppy, and the conflict she had been struggling with dissolved instantly. Behold the incredible power of Héric!

Within the next few days, their bond strengthened as Nikki became accustomed to having an energetic puppy in her space. Gigi followed her everywhere like a little shadow and Nikki seemed to look out for her. Their relationship began to blossom, and I realized I was witnessing something very beautiful. I grinned from ear to ear as the beauty of their friendship began to overcome me. Nikki had missed having another dog around even though she didn't want to admit it. And her ability to accept this new puppy into our family without showing any jealousy, only complete understanding, was a beautiful sight and quite touching. I suddenly understood how important this was for Nikki, for her to experience a "sister" that did not bully her. One that she could truly enjoy being around and share her final year with. Nikki had never had any puppies of her own, but it was obvious she would have been an incredible mother.

CHAPTER 58

Nikki Takes a Tumble

These two became inseparable very quickly. Gigi wanted to be wherever Nikki was. In fact, I would frequently find them cuddling together, providing abundant picturesque moments for me to record. Nikki was never jealous or bossy. She was very kind and patient with the puppy. She stood her ground gently if the puppy stepped out of line. And if she had to issue a more serious correction, she would apologize afterward with a sweet little kiss on the nose. She whined with her apology as if to say, "I hate it when you force my hand!" It was precious!

Soon I could walk them both outside in the yard off leash. Gigi had to learn not to nip at Nikki's feet when she wanted her to play. Nikki was an old lady and didn't appreciate being harassed so she gently disciplined Gigi as necessary. I allowed her to do this because she had a natural understanding of just how far to take it and when to drop it. I only interfered if I needed to back Nikki up. Gigi loved to chase Nikki as her big sister gracefully loped through the yard or chased her jolly ball when I threw it. Gigi didn't have any interest in actually doing any retrieving herself. She thought it was much more fun to herd Nikki while she did the work.

Even with her advanced age, Nikki floated over the ground like a gazelle. It was like her feet never touched the ground. One day I was casually tossing her ball and, in her zeal to catch it, she injured herself.

I couldn't see exactly what happened, but she took a rather dramatic tumble headfirst over the ball. When she got up, her left front leg didn't seem to be working. It was just hanging from her side. She couldn't quite get it underneath her to bear weight on it. It almost seemed like she didn't know where it was, or she couldn't control where she put it. I was immediately concerned so I called her over to me to get a better look. Nothing appeared to be broken, and she wasn't showing any sign of pain as I examined her. She did not seem to understand that she had hurt herself either, because she kept trying to get me to throw her ball again. The Malinois breed is terribly accident prone as a rule, so this wasn't the first time something like this had happened. Typically, she responds very well to a little bit of downtime in her crate. So once I made sure she was comfortable, I put her in her crate for a little rest. Gigi was frustrated, of course, that their romp had ended so quickly.

After a couple of hours, Nikki was better able to keep her leg under her and walk. She still seemed to be favoring it a bit but continued to show no sign of distress. By the next day, she was 90 percent better. The injury certainly didn't slow her down any. She could still run just as fast on three legs as she had on four! But I refused to play with her anymore for fear of exacerbating her condition. I didn't want any permanent injuries to rob her freedom during her final year. Silently I feared that her old age was finally catching up to her.

CHAPTER 59

Gigi's Spirit Emerges

When Gigi was three months old, I began taking her with me to work, whether I was training dogs or treating patients at my office. Her training was very solid, and I could send her to a cot where she remained until told otherwise. She liked to watch me work with the other dogs as if she were taking notes. At my office, my patients all loved her and thoroughly enjoyed her visits. She stayed on her cot in the corner of my room, but she was less interested in these sessions. She usually just slept and sometimes snored. This gave everyone a little chuckle. She was such a social butterfly, fully embracing her role as mascot that she took very seriously!

I was amazed to discover that Gigi also adored children. It seemed like the younger the child, the more intent she was on meeting him or her. She could even sense when someone was carrying an infant and was very insistent on meeting their bundle of joy. She was always very appropriate in her approach with the child. The more unsure of her they were, the more submissive to them she was just like she had been with Nikki. She had a natural ability to read people and adjust her energy to theirs. I saw her do this with dogs as well. I was constantly amazed by her innate skills with all creatures. As she unpacked and revealed her many gifts, I felt validated in my impulsive and compulsive need to find her. She was a true gift to humanity and to me. She felt like a personal reward for all my hard work with dogs.

Through the summer of 2021, life went on with these two precious gifts of mine. Watching them together and the joy they experienced with each other brought a newfound joy to my heart that had been missing for a very long time. Gigi's training continued until we reached her limit. She certainly had a threshold when it came to training. Or maybe it was more like a hard stop! She liked to play games and do tricks if it was fun and a reward was immediately forthcoming. But the moment I attempted to switch gears and get her to perform from a sense of duty, the more she refused. I had seen this with other dogs as a professional trainer and these types of dogs are not easy to teach. If they perceive any sort of pressure, they shut down and stop trying. For Gigi it only took three requests for her to complete a task that went unrewarded before she checked out and it was game over.

It was disheartening to find that Gigi had this firm boundary. There was no negotiation or wiggle room with her. These types of dogs are difficult to manipulate or shape. This is just part of their personality, and it doesn't really change no matter how hard you try. They don't make good competition dogs because they can't handle any pressure. But I have known them to make incredibly loyal companions as long as they are allowed to be themselves. I was totally fine with her just being a pet if she was respectful and met my minimal requirements of an obedient family member.

As much as she resisted learning from me, she allowed Nikki to teach her many things. Nikki's first order of business was to teach her puppy how to be a snob to other people and dogs just like she was! But I don't think it caught on. Gigi loved all creatures and found it very difficult to ignore any of them. As far as she was concerned, she was put on this earth to bring all of us together with compassion, love, and insight. She couldn't achieve that by playing hard to get!

However, there was one rule that Nikki was able to teach her successfully, and it was the one about rude dogs. When encountering a rude dog who was barking, lunging, or growling, Gigi learned to turn her nose up, look the other way, and completely ignore it. This made me laugh. Nikki also taught Gigi how to shoplift at the pet store and where all the best items were located. Her big sister expertly modeled how to travel in the car and in the big diesel truck. She showed Gigi the "camping in the RV" routine. This included waiting patiently in her crate while we rode our bikes. She was to resist the urge to bark at any sounds she might hear. She also taught her how to keep watch sitting around at camp and how essential it was to keep at least one eye on all the squirrels. It was pretty darn cute to watch them together.

I was thankful that Gigi took to traveling and camping so easily since it was and is a big part of our lives. She really seemed to enjoy going new places, exploring new things, and meeting new people. And we really enjoyed our first summer with her and Nikki together. Nikki also seemed younger and more energetic since Gigi had arrived. She wasn't sleeping as much, and I was amazed at how healthy she seemed to be at thirteen years old.

We traveled quite a bit that first summer and the girls got to visit Ohio, Pennsylvania, Michigan, Virginia, North Carolina, and Georgia. They especially enjoyed the great sandy beaches of Lake Michigan, where they both had their first swimming experience. Gigi was a good swimmer, but I don't think Nikki liked it. However, Gigi discovered her joy of digging in the sand far more than any water activities. Nikki's preference was relaxing with me on the beach as we took in the beauty of the horizon and the melodic harmony of the waves.

We had some great adventures that summer as Nikki imparted all her great wisdom onto her new protégé. But the summer would soon come to a close. We would pack up the RV, store it for the winter, and shift our focus to the holiday season. *Can you feel it coming? Can you feel a* shift *about to happen? You might be able to recognize the rhythm by now.*

CHAPTER 60

Seeking Knowledge

It was about this time that I was introduced to a numerologist. I was intrigued and decided to schedule a reading. I had never done anything like this even though I had always been curious about the significance of numbers. I had no idea what to expect, but I was delighted to learn many things about myself that I did not know. For instance, my date of birth indicated that I was a born teacher and motivator. She said I had "Jesus numbers," which referred to my ability to teach large groups of people to help themselves. She also said my numbers described me as charismatic, classy, independent, and curious. Well, I was certainly independent and curious, but charismatic and classy I had never owned. Not so far.

She also told me that I was currently undergoing a significant "letting go" or purging phase of my life and beginning a reincarnation of sorts. That is, a reincarnation without dying. Wow! This would certainly prove accurate way beyond measure in the coming year! She continued to say that my life was restructuring from the "practical" to the "free." And that it was going to become easier to be myself and do things that made me happy, not just things that I needed to do or was expected or supposed to do. I had a big career change coming up, but she was unclear what to exactly. I would learn what this change was only a few months later. She specifically predicted big changes coming my way in the beginning of 2022.

One thing that really surprised me is when she told me that my life was meant to be easy after forty-six! Somehow, I had missed that memo! That would have been the year I opened my own physical therapy practice! I did not *need* to work, but I still felt like I had to. One point she made that I already knew was that my numbers indicated I was a very, very old soul and very wise. I had always felt that about myself, and it was reassuring to hear it. The most important thing she revealed that day was that I had lived my whole life to get to this point, for this very moment. I would hear this again and again over the next year. Do you know what I mean by that? This very moment in my life was so significant that everything happened in my life just to get me to it. By now you know more about me than most of my family and friends. So you can appreciate the full weight of that statement. But this moment also ignites the events in the remainder of my life. It's a new jumping off point, the start of a new beginning. A point from which "the real me" begins to emerge. Surprisingly, everything she told me proved to be true without a doubt as the next year played out.

During our conversation, the numerologist encouraged me to learn to meditate, which I did shortly thereafter. Ironically, the mediation skills would give me a fitting foundation for the next phase that was to come. It was all very good information, and even though some of it did not make sense at the time, it all turned out to be astoundingly accurate! I just couldn't see it yet, but dots were being connected and experiences were being lined up. I was approaching the "ready" and about to take launch. By the end of this section, you will see exactly what I mean by this!

CHAPTER 61

Nikki Prepares Her Departure

At the end of October 2021, I was sitting on the couch contemplating how we were going to handle the Christmas holiday this year now that we were down to two dogs. Usually at this time of year, I begin to consider family obligations and I wasn't sure if we would be gathering since COVID lockdown last year. In case we were, I began to consider a plan for handling both dogs. I really didn't want to get the RV out again this year, so maybe we should get a hotel room? Amid my pondering, a foreign thought pushed its way through.

You won't have to worry about me for the holidays.

It appeared to come from Nikki. She was sitting next to me on the couch. I turned to look at her in total disbelief. "What do you mean?" I asked. First off, I was not expecting my dog to talk to me like that. So I wasn't sure if I had heard right. Second, she appeared to be in perfect health so I wasn't sure why I was hearing that. Since I couldn't really tell where it came from, I just ignored it and continued to consider possible options for the holidays. Although I found the whole scenario somewhat overwhelming and decided to table it for the time being.

Gigi had her first birthday a couple weeks later (November 14). I got her a special little birthday cookie, and one for Nikki so she didn't feel left out. We had a cute ceremony just like we did when Nikki turned thirteen. We posed Gigi with her cookie to take the obligatory FB photos. She endured this process but not without expressing her annoyance. Nikki was accustomed to posing for pictures. She had done it her entire life and accepted her duty graciously. When Gigi was finally released, she turned her attention to devouring her cookie, and that was when I heard,

"*Oh good. I'm so glad she's completed a cycle (around the sun). Now it is time for me to go. My job is done.*"

It took my breath away. *What?* I remember thinking. Why was I hearing that? It was in Nikki's voice again. She was completely healthy and happy without issues or complaints. I looked at her quizzically as she enjoyed her party favor. This was becoming a familiar occurrence. I remembered these same conversations with her mother, Tori, some twelve years ago before she died. A sense of dread began to creep in.

I wanted to remain optimistic and not create something that wasn't real. We had so much going for us and so much to be thankful for. I really wasn't anticipating a big change right now. I tried to put that thought out of my head and go on pretending nothing was wrong. That night we went to bed as usual with Nikki sleeping at the foot of the bed and Gigi in her crate.

The next morning, I got out of bad as usual expecting to hear the familiar *click-click* as Nikki's nails hit the wood floor behind me when she let herself down from the bed. But instead, I heard a sprawling *thud!* I whipped my head around in my sleepy daze only to find Nikki spread eagle on the floor. I was perplexed. What had happened? Were her legs asleep? She looked really embarrassed but seemed to be alert and awake and otherwise OK. No sign of pain. Maybe she got tangled up in the sheets somehow? Once I got her up on her feet, she walked around OK so I brushed it off. *Can you feel it? It's a whisper.*

Following our usual routine, I went to get the puppy and let them both out the back door. After giving them enough time to potty, I opened the door to bring them back in. Gigi came as usual, and then I heard Nikki start to come up the steps but abruptly falling back down.

What the heck? What's going on with Nikki? I stepped out the door to get a better look. I could see Nikki struggling to get her feet underneath her and trying with all her might to muster enough control to pull herself up the three short steps. She managed to get it together before I could arrive to help. Again, I was scratching my head thinking how weird this was. I heard a little voice in my head say,

This is it. She will not last long.

Again, I was startled by my thoughts and tried to push them out of my mind, leaving room only for positive options. As she moved through the house, she seemed to be OK. She kept her legs squarely under her and did not fall. She ate her breakfast and curled up on the couch as per her usual routine. I couldn't shake that little voice. I knew something was up, but I did not want to deal with it. We went about our day as I prepared to go to work, and Nikki seemed to get a little better. She had no other issues the rest of the day.

The next day was like a repeat of the previous. Only this time, Nikki could not get herself up off the floor when her legs gave out. She looked so confused and embarrassed that she needed me to help her, maybe even a little scared. Like she really didn't want to be a bother and especially didn't want me to see her like this. *I could feel the shift just as I did with her mother.* I could no longer ignore the voice or pretend that I did not know what was happening.

Nikki was preparing her exit, just like she said. The tears welled up in my eyes and I snuggled up to her and hugged her as tightly as I could. My heart began to strain as it had so many times before for all those that had passed before her. I knew our time was drawing to a close. I could feel it. I wasn't ready to let her go. I had grown so accustomed to having her with me; she was my cocaptain. The dog I had told to go away and leave me alone was now the dog that I did not want to leave! I decided I'd better call the vet and prepare him for the possible progression of events. Because this day was *not* like yesterday. This time she steadily declined as the day progressed.

It was now Tuesday, just two days after she had announced that it was time for her to go. As you already know, I cannot stand to see them suffer. If they want to go, I will certainly let them go even though it kills me, breaks my heart in two. I knew our time was drawing near to a close. By the end of the day, she had progressively worsened until she could no longer stand or walk. I had to carry her outside and hold her up so she could potty. At this point, I knew it was time and we began to say our goodbyes. She had waited as long as she could. Thirteen and a half years was a very respectable age for a Malinois.

It would be an easy transition for her to just be released from this old body that had worn out its welcome. I hung onto the precious seconds, the precious memories. The feel of her coat in my hands, the lick of her tongue on my skin, and the smell of her in my nose. I hoped that I could hold on to the sound of her bark and the thud of her happy tail wage as it met the wall. I tried to memorize it all so I would never forget. She had secured and trained her replacement. She ensured that I was in good hands with Gigi and that my path was on track. It was time.

CHAPTER 62

Apachi Hands over the Reigns

I decided to do a meditation with Nikki to connect spiritually with her. Ha, the irony of that now! I don't have to meditate anymore to connect to her, and I really didn't back then either because I was hearing her as clearly as day. But I wanted to do something special for her to show my appreciation for her companionship and service. In the meditation, I connected with her spirit and used mental pictures to show her what was going to happen the next day when we went to the vet. I don't know if this helped her. She probably thought it was unnecessary since we were already psychically connected. But it allowed me to feel *useful* instead of helpless. I did another meditation with Gigi to explain to her what was about to happen with her sister, so that she would not be frightened when she realized Nikki was gone. And yes, I do realize the major irony in this since Gigi's guide, Héric, is the guardian of past-life integration and the ultimate expert on death and reincarnation!

I spent Nikki's last day on this earth totally devoted to her and never left her side. She seemed a little nervous and didn't want me out of her sight. It was so sad and so hard to see her feel so helpless. She had such an incredible life with us. There were so many adventures that we shared. She taught me so many things about myself. I was so grateful that I got to spoil her rotten and love her as hard as I could even though she always wanted more.

I carried her out to her yard, her field, for one last visit. I thought maybe she would want to say goodbye to a place she had enjoyed so much. But I could tell she was in more pain than she was letting on. She didn't have any interest in seeing her yard. She just wanted to go back inside and cuddle on the couch. If I had known at that point that I was really saying goodbye to Apachi for a second time, this would have been so much harder! I am ultimately thankful that I actually didn't know. And this is a perfect example of *divine design* with a purpose!

Just three days after Gigi's birthday, Nikki was gone from our lives. Just as she had told me. She was ready to go and so she went quickly. Gigi got to say her goodbyes and she seemed content with that. We were all very sad, but we were also very thankful. Grateful for all the gifts that she had given me—all the insight, intuition, and spiritual growth that she had led me to.

As much as I claimed I wanted to be done with the dogs, I was so eternally grateful that I still had a dog to love. I was so very thankful to whatever force outside of me that had pushed me so hard to find Gigi. Losing Nikki was much harder than I anticipated. She had stood by my side the longest of all the dogs I had ever owned. I was eternally grateful that I had Gigi to hold my heart during this loss.

Gigi seemed to mourn for exactly seven days, and then she suddenly snapped out of it and returned to her normal, cheerful, inquisitive self. I wish I could bounce out of it that fast. Even a year later, I still miss her very much. All those annoying habits she had are now so endearing and very much missed. Gigi never even looked for her; it was as if she completely understood what had happened. It is always the humans that struggle.

Nikki/Apachi/Oeragon is a very special spirit that has been with me before in many lifetimes and in many forms. As much as I have tried, it is so difficult to describe our connection in human terms. She continues to be a part of my life as I receive her messages for this book. And I now visit her in the spirit world when I need to feel her energy again. If you are fortunate to have an Oeragon in your life, you will understand how truly unique and amazing they are!

After Nikki's sudden passing we all tried to resume our lives. In a way, her passing was a relief to me. Caring for her occupied space in my energy field that I never realized until she was gone. Once she had moved on, I felt lighter and freer in a way. In contrast, Gigi was such a breeze. After all the years of managing difficult dogs, aggressive personalities, special diets, and unsocial temperaments, it was nice to have a dog that didn't require anything special. She was such a gift in that respect as if I had somehow won the lottery. To me she was a reward in and of herself.

Nikki was certainly right; we didn't have to worry about her for the holidays. There wasn't any stress for me because Gigi was easy to travel with and got along with everyone. For Christmas that year, Gigi was invited to celebrate with the family. None of my other dogs had ever received a personal invitation like that. And it didn't take long for her to work her way into everyone's hearts.

Just two months after Nikki's passing, we returned to Florida, this time with Gigi. I pondered that only one year ago the itch to find her had only just begun. And now we were here together mourning the loss of our friend who had made it all possible. It made me miss Nikki even more. Facebook kept posting memories of her, and each time they popped up, I paused to reflect on her sweet spirit. I was so thankful for her love, devotion, and gifts. I was especially grateful for the gift she had pushed me to find and then left me with, Gigi.

But before we get too deep into Gigi's story, I would like to share Héric's other incarnations with you. His other two incarnations systematically brought me closer and closer to my current spiritual level. They each brought specific and progressive healing gifts and spiritual opportunities preparing me for this moment. Let's meet our next two guests, Mo and Kona.

PART 2

Mo

This story brings us back to my twenties in Memphis, Tennessee.

CHAPTER 63

My First Experience with Héric

Mo was a very special dog to me. He arrived in my life during a period of chaos, instability, paralyzing insecurity, and spiritual unrest. I had no business buying a dog during this time of my life, but once again, I had that unshakable calling that I could not deny. My attempts to ignore it resulted in a very detailed dream where Mo came to me and told me to find him. So I did. All I remembered from the dream was that he was a black Shetland sheepdog. I searched the local paper and found a breeder with a small litter of three puppies. He was the biggest puppy and for some reason I never even looked at the other two. I knew he was the one. In my dream, I named him Kokomo, so I called him Mo.

He looked a lot like Gigi except he was a black-headed tricolored sheltie with a beautiful thick coat. I suppose this was the reason that Gigi had to be a tricolored corgi as well. They looked so much alike! I had not made that connection when I was searching for Gigi. Mo ended up being a bit large for his breed, closer to the size of a border collie. His personality was almost identical to Gigi's as well as his lack of interest in doing anything obedience related. Just like Gigi, he would lose interest and stop cooperating, making it clear that performance was not his destiny. I was OK with that since I also only wanted companionship. And he was the perfect companion. He was obedient and loyal. He did not need a leash because he never ventured very far and always kept an eye on me. He loved to play fetch and was an expert Frisbee master much like Gigi. He also shared Gigi's disdain for affection and cuddling. As much as I desired it, he refused to sleep in the bed with me. As soon as I invited him up, he would jump right back down. The hard floor was more his style. It was like he was allergic to cuddling. I could never sneak one in. Affection was the only thing missing from our relationship. I longed for something soft to curl up to, but that was not his purpose and he made it clear.

I was a very young adult in my early twenties when he came into my life in the fall of 1990. I had just returned to Memphis after a life on the road racing my bicycle. I remember how lost I felt both emotionally and spiritually. Physically I felt I had nowhere to call home. I had no security or safety net. I was terribly broke, living paycheck to paycheck on minimum wage. I couldn't even afford the liability insurance on my car, much less the new transmission that it needed. So I rode my bicycle everywhere. I lived month to month, and I had no real plans for my life or any ambition for the future. I felt like I was drowning, lost, and alone.

Héric could see what was happening and that I needed help. The dream was a message for me to find him. My mother and I had managed to find a residence together pooling our resources to afford rent. I only had minimal clothing, no furniture, and I slept on my massage table. Our temporary home had a little bit of an unfenced yard. There were random furniture pieces left in the house from the previous tenant before her death. Neither one of us had any real possessions. I only kept what would fit in my car since I never knew when I would be moving again. I worked full time at a local bookstore using my bike for transportation. These were spartan times for sure. But for the time being, I was content to just live in the moment.

Spiritually there were greater wisdoms at play. Héric carefully organized the specific support system that I would need approaching a very chaotic, heartbreaking, terrifying period of my life that I could not see coming. And this is what he alluded to when he said it was important to understand the "brilliance in the orchestration of mankind." Let's take a quick look at the events that transpired during Mo's visit.

CHAPTER 64

Behold the Next Seven Years!

Mo was with me for seven years. And during this brief period, I endured some intense, traumatic events. Most people will only experience one of these in their whole life. But I would encounter all five at record speed!

While I had him, I experienced two devastating breakups with serious boyfriends. The second one scarred my heart for several decades to come. To say the least, I was left with some serious emotional baggage. My ability to feel and express love would be locked down as a result. For the sake of simplicity, I won't go into detail about these relationships and how they affected me. I think everyone has had their own version of this experience and might already be painfully familiar with how it feels. Instead, I will focus on the more unusual and profound components of this period.

One such example is that of my father's arrest and conviction that also forced me to make a life-altering decision about him. Thankfully, I found my way back to college and graduated with a professional degree. But in 1994, I was diagnosed with a serious ailment that would result in complicating impairments. And finally, in 1996 I suddenly found myself moving to a different state, changing the trajectory of my path!

Yeah, like I said, this was no ordinary time in my life. I needed big-time help to get through all of this and survive!

When you consider all these events in such a brief period, it can really explain the message and the purpose of Héric's visit. When people have told me that I needed to write a book, it was usually when I shared one of these stories. These five events were so impactful that I could have written a book about each of them. But what is so fascinating is that even though these horrendous things happened in my life, I found my way through and still turned out amazing! This is because quietly in the background, Héric was orchestrating the pieces that held me together and got me through.

There are so many conversations we could have in this chapter; I could write a whole book on each event. But for the sake of staying on topic, let's get right to the chase. With Héric now in my life, my vision began to sharpen up a little bit. Obviously, I became a bit clearer on a path because I finally committed to college and chose a profession. For the first time in my life, I could visualize a direction, and I felt a calling to become a physical therapist. After being adrift and uncertain what my future held, it was comforting to settle into a purpose. This was only possible with the calming guidance of Héric in my life. Héric drew me back to myself and the direction I was to go. He subtly reminded me of who I was. As they say, when you are in line with your divine path and purpose, doors open easily and you move through the process quickly. Mo was not just a quiet companion that kept me company and offered passive support. He was patiently directing my spirit in ways I could not detect consciously. So let's take a closer look at what I mean.

CHAPTER 65

Karma Comes Knocking

Shortly after acquiring Mo, my mother and I had to find a new place to live, and we landed in a duplex. We somehow always managed to find a place even though we had very little means between the two of us. It was while we were in this duplex that I remember trying desperately to fix my relationship with my father. He was now living in Texas and working as the administrator of a psychiatric hospital. He was reluctant to improve our relationship despite his training as a family counselor and psychotherapist. I suppose this is one reason why his marriage to my mother did not last. I asked him to commit to a scheduled weekly phone call so that we could at least practice regular communication. He agreed and for the first two weeks called me as scheduled. I can't remember what we talked about or whether we were making any progress. But I do remember that by the third week, he missed his call. As you can imagine, I was furious with him for breaking his agreement. I was not the least bit surprised that he had once again disappointed me. How could I have been so naïve as to think he was capable of change? I tried calling him on his cell, in his office, and at his house with no luck. For the next three days, I continued to try to reach him by phone. I finally got his secretary on the other end. When I asked her where my father was, she got very nervous and sounded like she was whispering into the phone. "Heather, I hate to be the one to tell you this, but your father has been arrested."

Well, at least I guess he had a good excuse! There was a part of me that was relieved he was being held accountable for something by someone. I thought that maybe now he would be forced to deal with himself, to mature, and to become a reliable adult for a change. At least I could hope that this might be an opportunity for positive growth for him.

The next few months were confusing and difficult as we dealt with his arrest and his impending trial. I don't want to reveal the nature of his crime, but I will say that he feared for his life in Texas. Protesters had gathered outside the jail demanding the death penalty. He was convicted, but fortunately of a much lesser crime. He was sentenced to prison, but only for three years in a white-collar prison. All his assets were seized to pay the fines incurred for his crime. His wife lost their home. In a way, I felt that there had finally been some justice after all this time for how he had treated his own family. As they say, he had made his bed … I was totally OK with everything he was now answering to. Above all else, I really held out a little hope that he and I would eventually be able to have a true father-daughter relationship when this was all over.

But currently I had my own drama and my own battles to fight. I could not be distracted with the karma that he had created for himself. That was all on him.

CHAPTER 66

Alternate #7

Returning to college was difficult financially because of actions my father had taken involving my social security number before his arrest. But I wasn't about to let his poor choices stop me. Héric and my other angels cleverly found ways to unlock many doors in this process. Every time I reached a blockade on my path, it was easily dissolved by my angels. Héric made sure of it. I worked very hard for the next two years to catch up. I attended classes full time year-round while working three part-time jobs. I was more determined than ever to finally finish college.

By now I had moved into a one-bedroom apartment off campus. This building was so old that the floors were slanted. By today's standards, it probably would have been condemned. But it was all that I could afford, and it was my sanctuary. Poor Mo was shut in the apartment for long hours alone with nothing to do but wait for me to return. And he never complained. He only saw me in the evenings when I came home to study, eat, and sleep.

Within eighteen months of this arduous schedule, I had all the required credits to apply to the University of Tennessee medical school. I finally knew that I wanted to be a physical therapist! But applying for the physical therapy program in the early nineties was quite competitive. The state schools only took in-state students because they had so many applicants. Luckily, I had a state school with a physical therapy program just ten miles from my apartment! More than three hundred students applied for the class of 1994, and only 150 candidates were called for interviews. Sixty applicants were accepted for each class. I was a nervous wreck about getting in. I didn't really have a backup plan in case I didn't. I had lived the last two years so completely focused on this moment that I really wasn't sure what would happen if things didn't go as I hoped.

So I was ecstatic when I was called in for an interview! Surely this was a good sign. I took it as confirmation that I was finally on the right path. But in the end, I was chosen as alternate number seven. I was heartbroken to say the least. Why would seven people give up their opportunity to go to physical therapy school? It just did not seem realistic that I was going to make it into the program this year. This was a huge speed bump I hadn't seen coming. I had no fallback plan so I needed to get a job and start paying some of these student loans off. I was not a quitter, and I was not a complainer. I just had to do whatever it took to get through this. So I pivoted and began searching for full-time employment.

I managed to find a job at the university campus as an accounting clerk in the accounting department. Even though the campus was only ten miles from my house, it was too far to walk, there were no accommodations for me to ride my bike, and I couldn't afford to park on campus. The city bus would require two transfers and would be a forty-five-minute ride. This really wasn't economical. Once again, Héric twirled his little wand and found a solution for me. One of the ladies in my department at my new job drove within a mile of my apartment on her way to the office. I walked that one mile to a street corner where she picked me up and took me into work. Brilliant, wasn't it? Everything works out and clicks into place when you're moving in the direction you're supposed to go. *Yup, just wait for it!*

I happily worked dutifully at my new accounting position on campus for the next six months. I was very thankful for the income and the distraction. As time approached for the 1994 class to begin, I was surprised by a phone call from the dean of the program. She was calling to offer me a position in the class after all! (Bingo! Back on my path!) What? Had the impossible happened? I could not believe it! Why would so many people turn down this opportunity? Because I was supposed to be in this program, right here, right now! That spot had been energetically reserved just for me! Héric made sure of it.

I had a lot of hard work ahead of me and more loans to get approved, but at least parking and health care were included with tuition. Resigning from my job, I had to prepare for a very intense two years ahead. But I could never have imagined just how intense it was going to be, especially for me. The program would offer little time off and no summer breaks. But I was completely ready to fully commit all my time and focus to complete this mission. I was 100 percent invested, more than anything in my life before. What I could *not* foresee was another major event that was to transpire within this one and how it would shape the rest of my life!

School was indeed intense. We were in class from eight to five every day with additional studies at night. This made for a very long day. There was no time for a job or social life and no time to spend with Mo. He barely saw the light of day with a brief walk twice daily. As usual he never complained, just watched me as I studied. It was a tough pace to sustain, even for someone as driven as me. I was on a tight budget with my student loans so I lived on a shoestring allowance with no money for going out. I packed a bagged lunch and pretty much ate the same foods every day. I had no time to make creative meals. I only did what was quick, easy, and cheap. Times were tough for sure, but I didn't really seem to notice. I was so intently concentrating on my goal. I relied on my laser-sharp focus of the eagle to keep my eyes on the prize. Everything else I ignored. This approach served me well, especially with the roadblock that I was about to experience!

CHAPTER 67

Medical Disaster

As the first year of PT school was nearing an end, we were going to have the first and only break throughout the entire program. We would have a five-week break before the start of our second year. I was so relieved that time to rest and recoup was on its way. I really needed a break and a mental health check. I had been pushing very hard over the last three years and it was taking its toll. It was all starting to catch up to me. I could feel burnout creeping in. But I had to hold on. I had to stay focused and keep it together just a little longer.

On one of the last days of school before Thanksgiving, I stopped in the women's restroom between classes. After using the bathroom, I stood from the toilet to pull my pants up when suddenly everything went black. My limp body dropped to the floor like a sack of potatoes as I began having a seizure. There was another student in the restroom who frantically went running for help. The ambulance was called, and the school was notified.

As my body lay there in a crumpled mass on the cold floor of the stall, I saw someone I recognized. She was beckoning to me. She acted like she knew me. But she was up on the ceiling! What was she doing up there? She was asking me to follow her. I remember feeling a little confused and conflicted about what to do. She waved at me again. I seemed to know her; she looked familiar. I sensed that I trusted her.

What the heck, I thought as I decided to follow her. I felt myself drift up to the ceiling and move in her direction. Briefly I turned back and saw my body lying alone on the cold floor. I felt sad. But then my focus was abruptly shifted back at my friend. I suddenly noticed she looked like one of my teachers! And then I floated after her. Up and up into the rafters.

I awoke in the back of an ambulance to a rather annoying finger prick. "Ouch!" The next thing I remember was a strange woman going through my purse and asking me all kinds of questions. The ambulance was not a smooth ride and the bed I was on was shaking and vibrating from the rough road. I had a terrible headache, and I was not in the mood for twenty questions. She informed me that they were taking me to the ER. I started to protest thinking about Mo at home alone. But I did not appear to have a choice in the matter.

Thank heavens I now had health insurance. This was the first time since leaving college in 1989 that I was insured. Once again, I was in the right place at the right time. Being in this college program had paid for my insurance coverage! Héric had thought of everything, and I had the care that I would need for this very emergency. My school was also adjacent to one of the best neurosurgical practices in the nation, the Semmes Murphy Clinic. I just can't make this stuff up! Do you see all the little miracles here?

After some testing, it was determined that I had a ganglioglioma in the left parietal lobe of my brain just above my ear. This is a rare type of brain tumor that is usually benign. But they needed a biopsy to confirm that. My options were to do a biopsy then possibly a craniotomy. Or I could use antiseizure medication to prevent further seizure activity and continue with school. I didn't like to take drugs and the idea of having two brain surgeries was not all that appealing either. The school was involved because I was about to participate in clinical rotations as part of my program. They were going to require proof of medical stability before they would allow me to continue my program.

I chose to undergo a craniotomy to remove *and* biopsy the tumor, and I just so happened to have a five-week break that would allow time for such a procedure. Hopefully, this would give me enough time to recover before returning to my rigorous schedule. Or so I thought. So the five weeks I was planning on to rest from school, I would instead be recovering from brain surgery! I certainly did not see that coming!

Even though I wasn't expecting this turn of events, I really didn't have time to question it. I'm not a "Why me?" kind of gal. I put my goggles on, dialed in my tunnel vision, and dug in deep to get myself through it. I *had* to get through this. I *had* to succeed. I *had* to finish school. There were no other options for me. There was no safety net to fall back on. *I was all on my own,* and I *had* to make this work. So I did.

CHAPTER 68

Blinded by the Darkness

I was very anxious about the surgery, and it took all my willpower not to chicken out. Despite my well-thought-out plan to schedule this big surgery during my five-week break, nature had its own calling. The day before my surgery, Memphis was struck by a horrific ice storm! The city came to a standstill as it tumbled into darkness. The power lines fell from the weight of the ice, and there was literally no light or heat in the city. A heavy, dense fog also set in, making it extremely difficult to get around. Without streetlights and traffic signals, it was unbearably disorienting when driving. I remember what a bizarre feeling it was to be so lost in such a familiar place. Was this a sign from the universe? Most definitely, but I did not have time to ponder. I was grasping at straws to stay focused and committed to going through with this. I could not possibly handle anything else on my plate right now! So I really didn't care what meaning it had.

Hospitals were forced onto their backup power as the linemen worked feverishly to get the power back up again. The hospitals and hotels were the first to be restored. But I was without power for almost a whole week. Unfortunately, this also meant that my procedure would have to be delayed. Now instead of having the full five weeks to recover, it was going to have to be squeezed into four. I could only hope it would be enough.

My craniotomy was now scheduled for the day after Valentine's Day. My boyfriend and I enjoyed a nice dinner out at a fancy Indian restaurant, which was probably not the best idea. I doubt I drank enough water, and I'm sure the meal was quite salty. This would prove to be a problem for the next day. In today's world, you are instructed on exactly how much water to drink the day before your surgery. You are about to find out why this is!

My mother came down from Indiana for the surgery and stayed at my apartment so she could take care of Mo. I had never had any kind of surgery before, and I was much more terrified than I was letting on. If I did not have someone to take me to the hospital, there was a big chance that I would have just chickened out completely. My surgery was scheduled for first thing in the morning. I remember my mother and boyfriend being there as they took me into preop. And the last thing I remember was the anesthesiologist trying to get a vein in my hand. Such a painful area to poke and prod. "Why don't you …" I began to suggest before the lights went out.

Again, that lady appeared, dressed in white and calling to me. She wanted me to follow her. It seemed very important although I could not understand why. Everything was so vague. Like there was a part of me that knew a lot more than I did. I rose to follow her and was startled that my body was not with me. I turned to look and noticed that I was on the operating room table. Oh boy, I did *not* want to see this! Brain surgery is not something you want to watch. Thankfully, my attention was drawn back to my friend. She encouraged me to stay focused and that we needed to hurry. She gestured for me to follow her again. So I did. We floated up into the ceiling of the operating room.

CHAPTER 69

Spiritual Counsel

I'm going to deviate from my typical process and instead take you into the future at this point. Because twenty-eight years later I would discover the meaning of the surgery and the visitations. It was during an astrological reading in 2022 that I learned this tumor had developed because of my internalized anguish around my father. Two decades of built-up anger, pain, and frustration had created a lot of energy. My body internalized that energy into a focal point in my brain, having no other creative outlet to flow it into. This energy had to be released by removing the tumor. Harmony would then be restored through my energetic system once the blockage was removed. The surgery itself also provided a convenient exit strategy that I had planned ahead of time. Basically, I knew how difficult and unpleasant things were meant to be for me up to this point in my life and I had planned a way out in case it was too much.

It was a "check-in station" where I met with my guides, regrouped, and decided if I wanted to continue with the path I had chosen. So it was one of my guides that came to get me and took me into counsel with all my other guides to discuss my experience so far. I was also reminded at this point of my purpose for being here. I was reminded of the very special message that I came to Earth to deliver personally to humanity. They also reminded me that it would still be some time before I would be able to act on my obligation. I was to continue my path, continue cleaning up loose ends, recovering lost soul fragments, and accumulating experience and knowledge. I would be called when the time was right for me to begin. And we now know that happened during COVID lockdown with the conjoined squirrel.

I was then given the option of continuing my path according to plan or to abandon my post and leave for good. This crossroad was an opportunity for a repurposing of sorts or a death. I decided to stay and fulfill my destiny, fulfil my obligation, and complete my mission. Receiving that reminder was all that I needed to spiritually refocus and reconnect with my higher self. Consciously I was still in the dark and had no idea what was going on. But spiritually I knew all. And ever since that surgery, I have had trouble sleeping. Ever since that day, my soul has been waiting for that call to action. For almost thirty years I waited, sleeping with one eye open. I didn't want to miss the signal. Consciously I was just trying to survive. I had a deep-rooted drive to keep moving forward no matter what.

The surgery lasted five to seven hours and the notes indicated there was an arterial bleed that complicated the procedure. Because I tend to overprepare, I had donated my own blood just in case something like that happened. This long surgery gave me ample time to visit with my spiritual counsel and take a break from being human. It was a respite that I desperately needed. But it must have been a nerve-wracking experience for my mother, anxiously waiting for it to be over.

The first thing I remember as the fog of the anesthesia began to clear was a violent urge to vomit. I had not even opened my eyes before I requested a bucket. The dry heaves were vicious because of dehydration from my meal choice the night before. Vomiting was not a pleasant experience with a head wound! It caused a rapid increase in pressure inside my brain that had just been cut open. I begged for it to stop, afraid my sutures would all burst open.

I spent three days in the hospital following the surgery. It took that long for me to realize that I could not read. I stared at the calendar posted on the wall in my room having no idea what it was. They brought me menus so I could choose my meals, and I didn't know what they were. Friends brought cards by, and I could not read them. I just pretended I knew what they said as I stared blankly at them. I'm not sure why it took me so long to realize that I couldn't read. My surgeon did not seem very surprised when I told him. The tumor was in my dominant hemisphere in the middle of language and mathematic processing centers. I guess he just assumed it would come back once the delicate tissue healed. But this was a devastating impairment to a full-time student!

By the time I was released from the hospital, my mother had gone back to Indiana and I was alone in my apartment to care for myself and Mo. The horseshoe incision in my skull just above my ear was thankfully not very big. They had to saw through the cranial bones and peel them back to reach the tumor. These pieces of bone were now held together with absorbable sutures. But I could actually hear these bones move against each other every time I took a deep breath. The only experience I can relate it to is when your ears are clogged and you can hear the inside of your skull every time you breathe. This constant rubbing sound was a maddening experience. And it persisted for several weeks until the bones finally fused.

I was still pretty weak from the anesthesia, and I lived in a second-story apartment. Getting up and down the stairs to take Mo outside for potty breaks was a little difficult in the first few weeks. My girlfriend took me shopping for groceries and I almost collapsed before I got to the checkout. Things were rougher and tougher than I anticipated, but I tried to remain optimistic. I only had four weeks to put this behind me and prepare to return to school. I focused most of my energy on recovering my ability to read. Luckily, I discovered that if I wrote something down, I could then read it. I used my short-term memory of what I had just written to tell my brain what the words said. I hoped this meant that I would be able to take notes and at least read what I had written. But this only solved part of my problem.

There was still the challenge of keeping pace with the textbook reading assignments. The university had a service for blind students that converted written words into an audio recording. But the audio was in a painful computer voice. So even though my reading assignments were transferred to cassette tapes, they were so painful to listen to that they just put me to sleep! Unfortunately, it wasn't much help. I defaulted to my own strategy in attempts to teach myself to read again.

Three weeks after returning to school full time, I was taking a test when I discovered I could no longer do basic math either. I could not remember how to add and subtract or multiply and divide in my head, all of which were required in my program. I had been a math major in high school so it was particularly disturbing to lose all this knowledge so quickly. Where did it all go? I was devastated as I fled to the bathroom in tears. The depth of my predicament had finally hit me. And my reality was just a little bit too much to bear in addition to the baseline stress of the program. What was I going to do? My insurance wouldn't cover the speech therapy I desperately needed, and I couldn't afford to pay out of pocket. So I reached out to my school dean. The school agreed to limit my exams to one in a day to reduce my stress level and account for my increased cognitive burden. I would also be permitted to take my exam in a quiet room if I needed it. Some professors were supportive. Others were condescending and snarky. I felt guilty in asking for help, like I should be able to do this all on my own without any special considerations. But I was more desperate than ashamed and would accept whatever assistance I could get.

Naturally, I was terrified, but I didn't really have time to be. I had to figure out how to get through this and graduate. There was no other option besides graduation for me. I never even considered withdrawing from the program on a medical leave. I just knew that the clock was ticking and that if I didn't get this done now, it was not going to happen. So I pushed forward with every ounce of determination that I had. And I found a way to get through it all somehow. Unfortunately, it would take another twenty years for me to fully recover my ability to read on a functional level. But I managed to regain enough ability to survive school. It just took me longer to read because I read *backward*. For bigger words, I had to guess what I thought they were and sound them out to determine if the sound of the word looked like the shape. Then I had to decipher if the meaning of the word fit the context. It was a frustratingly slow procedure. But I had no other choice. I survived like this well into my career and into middle age.

Twenty years down the road, I would heal myself fully and recover the ability to ready naturally completely by accident. This switch got flipped when I began to listen to audiobooks in the car. My brain used this exercise to rewire itself without any conscious effort on my part as it rerouted old broken pathways into new functional highways! After several years of listening to audiobooks, I was magically transformed from a visual learner into an auditory learner! I was quite surprised one day when I could finally read without guessing the words. Everything had come back! There was a light at the end of the tunnel after all. It was just that the tunnel was so long that I could not see it! My faith in the process carried me through and I experienced another tiny miracle!

CHAPTER 70

Last Chance

After my surgery and while I was still in PT school, my father was released from prison and came for a visit. I was hoping to start a new chapter with him. I desperately needed him to be proud of all I had come through in these very tough years all on my own. I was hoping to have a pleasant experience and that our relationship would move forward into healing. But the reunion was awkward. He seemed anxious, which put me a bit on edge. He hadn't come to support me or acknowledge all that I had overcome. Not once did he say, "Great job!" But he did ask me a very strange question. "Would you say that you love me?" What? Well, no. At this moment, I did not. He had given me no reason to. Nothing had changed between us. So I hesitated, shrugged my shoulders, and muttered, "I guess," as I rolled my eyes.

What nerve! That's all he had to say after what he put us through? It's not like he was proclaiming his love for *me*. He just wanted to know if I loved him! It was like dealing with an insecure child constantly needing to be reassured. It really put me off and I had to leave the room to gain my composure. Mo was there listening to it all. So he followed me out of the room when I left. I then heard my dad talking to someone. Who could he be talking to? I hoped he wasn't using my phone. I had a basic phone service that charged me for each call out that I made. Yeah, I mean I was on a very tight budget!

I returned to see him replacing my phone back in its cradle. I asked him who he was talking to. He would not tell me. The rest of the conversation consisted of him complaining about other people. Not once did we discuss our relationship, if he had learned anything about himself while incarcerated, or how sorry he was for being a terrible father. He demonstrated zero accountability for his actions and choices that led to his arrest. Everything was someone else's fault.

And that was it for me. I was *done!* This was the last straw. If incarceration had not driven a serious message home to him, nothing would. And I needed to shed the dead weight. I kicked him out and told him never to contact me again. Being his daughter, he knew I was serious. His family line was notorious for kicking people out and erasing them. It was a genetic skill that came very easily. He did not put up a fight, and that infuriated me even more. He was such a coward. No wonder he could not be the father I needed.

Six months later, I was speaking to a member of my church. She was a psychotherapist who had worked with my father at a local psychiatric hospital where he was the assistant administrator. I had also worked there in the accounting department during my early college years. So she and I were well acquainted. We happened to be discussing him and his bizarre behavior. Apparently, I was not the only one who had noticed it. I could tell she was reluctant to share this, but she mentioned she had received a rather strange voice message from him. He had called her to tell her that his daughter really *did* love him. She said he sounded strange, somewhat manic, and she had no idea why he was telling her such a thing. I was shocked! He had called her that day in my apartment! Neither one of us could decipher his state of mind. Or if she could, she would not say. This was all just too much for me to handle in addition to school and my reading disability. I was glad to be done with him.

I never spoke to my father again after that fateful day in 1994. I saw him at a couple of family events and kept my distance. Sadly, all he would have had to do to get back into my heart was to say he was sorry. If he had only shown some interest in repairing our relationship, some interest in actually being a father to me and being accountable for his actions, I would have welcomed him back. But he was incapable, I would later discover. Such character would require much more strength, morality, and dignity than he could muster.

CHAPTER 71

The Pieces Finally Come Together

I did make it through school somehow, by the grace of God, and I was thankful for that. There were some in our class who did not. So I was proud that I could hammer through so much hardship and still graduate! The next step would be to pass the grueling board exam, and I did have my concerns about that. My reading and comprehension skills still weren't 100 percent yet. I had the greatest difficulty when I felt stressed or pressured under time. If I began to doubt myself, it escalated quickly into a fight-or-flight survival response. My fragile nervous system defaulted to primitive protective responses when complex thought was impaired. This is common for the head injury I was dealing with. My brain was still healing from the surgery and new neurons had to be formed for my brain to function correctly. The old routes didn't work anymore, and it had to figure out how to access the information that was now cut off. So when pushed or pressured, my body automatically defaulted to the sympathetic nervous system for preservation and triggered a panic response. The moment I sensed that the thought train I was riding was suddenly out of track, the panic button was triggered and my instinct was to run! It was sheer panic with no escape. And the more I panicked, the less I was able to read or comprehend.

The exam was five hours long and I was likely to become fatigued in addition to stressed. I wasn't even sure I could retain all the information I needed to pass the difficult test. Thankfully, it occurred to me to request special assistance based on my temporary medical disability. My surgeon provided the necessary documentation, and I received the assistance I requested. I was given a private room in which to take my exam, and I also had a person sitting nearby who could help read things to me if I began to panic. It helped just knowing that I had a backup. But I never ended up using my crutch. I was able to complete my exam in the allotted time without any help, and thankfully I did pass on the first try. It was unfortunate that there were many students who did not pass. I knew I had a lot to be thankful for, and I was very appreciative for all the angelic gifts and human assistance that I received to make it possible.

Let's just take a moment to review what happened in the last two years. First, I had a brain tumor that I did not know about but would require medical attention. Second, I didn't have medical insurance before getting into the physical therapy program. Third, I got into PT school on the first try as the seventh alternate. I happened to live only ten miles from one of only two state PT schools. The PT program only had one break for the entire two-year schedule, and I discovered I needed to have brain surgery just weeks beforehand! Because I had the medical insurance provided by the school, I was able to afford the care I required. The physical therapy school also happened to be right next door to one of the nation's leading neurosurgical groups.

Think about how many moving pieces had to all come together at an exact moment for all this to be possible. I was not in Memphis by accident. I had not decided to become a physical therapist by accident. I did not get into physical therapy school after seven other people declined the opportunity by accident. It was not coincidence that this school included medical insurance as part of the tuition. And it was no coincidence that the very school I chose literally sat next to the neurosurgical practice I would need. These are the miracles in life that we sometimes do not see. This two-year period alone would have been reason enough to need extra spiritual support. Héric was here for a reason. Even though I felt very alone in these two years, I was never actually alone. I always had Mo right next to me patiently waiting, patiently watching, and standing guard over my soul. He helped orchestrate the beautiful miracle moments that were necessary for all these pieces to come together. And everything turned out just fine. Remember Héric's message about the "brilliance in the orchestration of mankind"?

I just wanted to make sure my readers appreciated all the subtleties of the story. In the moment, these miracles may not always be obvious, making it challenging to just trust and understand that there is a reason for everything in life. There was a reason I had the brain tumor. There was just as much a reason for why it needed to be removed and why it needed to happen exactly when it did. There was a reason my experience through physical therapy school was so much more complex and difficult than the rest of my classmates. I never asked, "Why?" I just trusted, followed, and kept moving forward. I did not understand then that it was *faith* that kept me calm. It was *faith* in the process, *faith* in a higher power, and *faith* in my ability to trust myself. This to me is the true meaning of *faith*. I never prayed that my obstacles would be removed or made easier for me. I knew that all was as it should be. I was not given any task that was too great. On some unconscious level, I knew all this even though consciously I didn't know how or why.

CHAPTER 72

A Resurrection

The part of my life that occurred after the surgery has always seemed very different and separate somehow. I often referred to these years as my "bonus" years. It felt like a new beginning and an extra experience that quite possibly might not have happened at all. This second half of my life has felt like a closure of sorts, tying up loose ends while revisiting some previous experiences. For instance, I managed to recycle three of my favorite experiences after the surgery: dog training, bicycle racing, and horseback riding. Only the second go-round, I took all these a lot further than the first time. It was like I got a second chance or a do-over. The reconnection to cycling is what catapulted me into the next chapter of my life.

After graduation I accepted a position with a home health agency in Memphis. I worked sixty-hour weeks to begin paying off my school debt. I was certainly enjoying a more laid-back version of life if you consider sixty-hour weeks to be laid-back! But I found myself lonely, especially on the holidays. With my mother living in Indiana with her mother and brother, I often spent the holidays alone. A single day off work was not enough time to make the eight-hour drive up to Indiana. Memphis wasn't really a happy place for me either. It contained so many bad memories of family, ex-boyfriends, and sadness. Everywhere I went, I recovered bad memories and experiences. These haunted me and seemed to keep me spinning in the same old rut. I yearned for a fresh start. I desperately needed a place without memories.

I decided to move to Indiana, where my mother and her family were. It would be nice to be around family for the first time in my life! I had always lived so far away from my aunts, uncles, and cousins. I longed to be part of something, to know what family really felt like. My own dysfunctional family had been a rather unpleasant experience. It would be good to be around a happy one. So I decided to make a change. Initially I planned to make this move in the next five years. But Héric pushed me to do it in just three months! There were apparently some pressing connections that required my presence in Indiana sooner. So I made all the arrangements and packed us up for a big move that would set the stage for the next part of my journey.

Ironically, moving to Indiana brought new opportunities and experiences, but none of them had to do with family. For one, I quickly climbed the ranks with the company I hired on with. I went from staff physical therapist covering multiple nursing homes in a day to outpatient clinic director in a matter of months. Additionally, my exercise blossomed from general fitness to race-ready cycling. As it turned out, Indianapolis had a rather large road racing community. There were plenty of group social rides as well as training rides available weekly. I quickly regained my fitness and eased back into a familiar way of life on a bicycle. This was my "home." The bicycle was where I was connected to myself, confident, and successful. It was my comfort zone.

Early on, I connected with a group of cyclists that I enjoyed spending time with. It was with them that I began to mountain bike for the first time. The more I rode, the more I enjoyed it. But I quickly outgrew my group of recreational riders and branched out on my own to explore more serious riding. I ventured to West Virginia, Utah, and Arizona to experience more challenging mountain bike trails. And it wasn't very long before I found myself entering my first mountain bike race. In the beginning, I mostly raced the local trail races in Indiana, Ohio, and Illinois. I found that I was pretty good at it, better than I had been as a road racer at least. So I got more serious with my training and added races to my calendar.

This was something I never thought I would do. I had never been drawn to mountain bike racing before, but I found it exhilarating and completely different from anything else I had ever done. It was much more fun than the road racing I had grown up with! I loved being on the trails and riding in the trees. It was so grounding compared to riding on hot, hard pavement. The mountain biking community was also much more focused on being in the outdoors as well. Most competitors camped in a tent at the start line and brought their dogs with them. The whole experience rejuvenated my ravaged soul!

I was delighted that this environment welcomed Mo and that he could so easily join me in my quest. He fit in at camp, but with his heavy coat and small feet, he was not a good option for a trail dog. So he was happy to hang out at camp when I needed him to. He was an absolutely gorgeous dog. Many people were drawn to him, approaching to say hello and maybe sneak a pet. But he was not the least bit interested in other people or dogs. And you already know how he felt about affection. He made this clear to strangers when he avoided their attempts to pet him by expertly skirting out of reach. He'd look past their adoring glances searching for me. He was very loyal and would never leave me. But eventually he had to. *Can you feel it? Here comes another one, another shift.*

CHAPTER 73

Mo's Shift Comes to a Close

I remember I went with two friends to a mountain bike race in North Carolina. We took our camping gear and went in their SUV. Mo had trouble getting into the vehicle, which I thought was strange. Usually, he had no issue jumping up into the car or onto the bed. But now he seemed to have a weak back leg requiring me to lift him into the vehicle. I thought maybe he had pulled something so I wasn't worried about it. He was obsessive about his Frisbee, so it was certainly possible he could have a pulled muscle. *But deep in the recesses of my subconsciousness, I felt the subtle rise of significance.*

Once we got home, he was no better; in fact, he seemed to be getting worse. By the time I got him to the vet, he could barely stand up with his hind legs. They did some x-rays and a neurological exam and couldn't find anything wrong. We were referred to a university veterinarian hospital for further testing. This was a teaching hospital, so they wanted me to leave Mo with them all day to be studied. I was reluctant, but also desperate to get answers. So against my better judgment, I left him in their care. I imagine they had all their students come in and examine him like a lab rat. By the end of the day, their only recommendation was to do a very expensive myelogram. No one would speculate what was going on with Mo, what the myelogram might show or rule out, and what course of action might be required. I found them completely useless from a grieving pet owner's perspective. The experience left me without answers or hope. And Mo was progressively worsening. I felt like time was running out.

We returned to our vet hoping to get some support and he finally theorized that Mo most likely had a progressive spinal disease. There would be no cure and he would eventually be completely paralyzed in his back end. I was devastated! My little buddy had always been by my side through so many tough times in these last seven years. The thought of losing him at such a young age was unbearable. He was such a good dog, and I wasn't sure if I could go on without him. But I was about to find out.

Within another week, Mo was completely paralyzed and bladder incontinent. I now had to carry him. I was horribly sad, and he seemed just as upset. I could only imagine how confused he must have been, unable to control his body. I always considered myself to be a strong person. I mean look at what I have already been through. But it is totally different when you must be strong for someone else. I was suddenly feeling very weak. This was much more than I could emotionally endure. It broke my heart to see him like this, reduced to immobility and incontinence. He deserved better. I was going to need to make a hard decision soon. The kind of decision that no one wants to face. I just could not bear to see him like this. It was hard to tell if he was in any pain. If he was, he did not let it show.

On a Friday morning, we made our final trip to the vet together. I knew it was time for us to part ways. This was a grueling decision for me, and I felt like my heart was being ripped in two. Mentally he was still all there. Physically his body had abandoned him. It was time for me to continue on my own. He had done his job and gotten me through some really tough stuff. His shift was over. There would be no more games of Frisbee. There would be no more camping trips or walks in the park. I would miss my cocaptain ushering me to a race. And he would not be there waiting for me to come home or to ride back into camp.

I bawled my eyes out all the way to work. Then somehow, I pulled myself together and got through my day. I felt empty inside, like I was the walking dead. I did not tell anyone what had happened. And as soon as I left work, I packed up all my stuff and drove three hours north to a campground where we had spent many weekends together. I spent that entire weekend in total silence, mourning the loss of my best friend. I did not speak to another living soul.

Today there are many options for dogs with Mo's condition. I see these dogs running around on carts everywhere, happily adjusting to a new way of life. And I wonder how our life would have been different if that had been an option for us. But this would not be our final goodbye as you already know. It was merely a break in the current. Héric would be back.

Of course, there is always a reason for why they come and why they go. I've already rather graphically described to you the reasons why I needed Héric in my life during this time. But there was also a very specific reason for him to step away and very quickly. Time was approaching for me to meet my future spouse, and he knew this. But for me to make the connection in time, I would have to drastically change my lifestyle. Mo knew that his presence would hold me back from that opportunity. I needed to be freed up so that I could travel and race a lot more than what I was doing now. And that's exactly what happened after his death.

My grief threw me full throttle into a vicious cycle of training, traveling, and competing. I did not spend a single weekend at home, and some weekends I even had two races. I spent a lot of time in Ohio racing with a team out of Cincinnati that I eventually joined. I enjoyed the members on the team because they were fun to be around, very serious about the sport, and willing to travel to bigger races. And right now, I was especially looking for a *grand adventure*. I wanted to live big and play hard! So I needed people in my life that I could experience that with. This group filled that order in spades. But what I did not realize was that it would be with this team that I would meet my future husband!

PART 3

Kona

A Dog of a Different Color

Héric (via Mo) provided me with a baseline introduction to my own enlightenment and the first step to my expanded consciousness during surgery. He worked ever so patiently within my comfort zone. We will now see how his support elevated to the next level as he made magical things happen through Kona.

Let's continue our story.

CHAPTER 74

A Familiar Dog

Héric was not gone for very long after Mo died. The months after Mo's death were a blur. I felt I was avoiding the pain of being home without him by finding ways to stay away with all my travel and racing. I cannot remember a single weekend at home after he died. I was somehow excelling at a career yet also enjoying a life on the road on the weekends. I was also enjoying all my freedom without having to worry about caring for a dog. It was only a matter of months with my rigorous training, travel, and racing routine that I met my future husband. It seemed that must have been the urgent matter for which Mo created space. But once I had connected with my soul mate, Héric began planning his return.

I was still in the same apartment when Mo left. I still had his empty crate sitting in my bedroom. The wounds from his passing were very fresh. My new boyfriend lived in Ohio, so we commuted back and forth the first year. It made no sense to add a dog to my life with this current state of chaos. But this does not mean it wasn't meant to be. Sometimes the most irrational options are the most *divine callings*. Once again, a dream nudged me into considering another dog. I don't remember specific details, but it prompted me to get out the newspaper and begin sorting through the puppy ads. This time I knew I was getting a border collie.

I struggled with whether it was appropriate for me to add a dog, given my current amount of travel. But the more I pondered it, the more

I was pushed toward it. And when spirit calls, I follow. Even if it doesn't make sense. I really did miss having a dog, but I felt like my heart was still connected to Mo. Would I even be able to bond with a new dog? I guess it really didn't matter what fears and excuses I offered. I was being called again and I had to act. Whenever I get these impulses, gut feelings, or deeply connected instincts, there is nothing that can stand in my way of following them. It would be an early test for my new relationship. I wasn't even sure how my boyfriend felt about having a dog around. Or how he would react when I showed up with a new dog. All these questions would be answered, but I had no intention of discussing it with him beforehand. This was my decision, my calling, and it wasn't up for debate. Yeah, I was a little bit ornery like that. I guess it was also a means of preserving my independence within a new relationship. Whatever the rationale, I was suddenly catapulted into the hunt for a new canine companion.

After only a brief search, I found a border collie breeder with a litter of puppies a couple of hours from me, and I headed out to meet them. I had never owned a border collie before. I figured this breed was a great option for my current active lifestyle. It would be nice to have a dog that could run along with the mountain bikes, too. So I was excited to be experiencing a new breed with new possibilities.

I arrived to look at the puppies and was surprised to find that this breeder was an actual sheep farmer and used her dogs to work the farm. I found her eight-week-old litter of black and white puppies to be very cute but very active. Being around them made me question my calling. I suddenly remembered how much work it was to break in a new puppy. I felt a sense of hesitation creep in. Ugh. All the crate and potty training that would be required. Was I really up for it? Almost as if the breeder sensed my sudden drift in commitment, she suggested an alternative. She also had a seven-month-old male puppy available. He was a beautiful blue merle color with one blue eye.

I had always wanted a blue merle. This recessive coloration is a marbling of white and black giving these white dogs spots or swirls of blue-gray tinge that often coincided with blue eyes. He was beautiful and quite friendly! As I began to weigh the pros and cons of each option, it seemed it would be a lot easier to deal with the seven-month-old than an eight-week-old puppy. I was not very drawn to any of the younger puppies. Given my hectic schedule, it seemed a no-brainer to choose the older puppy. So I decided to bring the unique one home. I named him after Mo when I registered him as Kona Mo Blue.

When I brought Kona home to my apartment, it became obvious that he had never been inside a house. Stairs and carpet were both new to him, and he was terrified of both! This didn't really worry me because I figured he would eventually settle in and adjust to his new surroundings. He did adjust somewhat, but he was always strangely affected by "normal" things. Crate training went pretty well, but according to my neighbors, he would sometimes bark, whine, or howl when I was away. So this new dog offered some extra challenges that I wasn't expecting.

We quickly set about getting to know each other. I had to teach him his name, to walk on a leash, to not potty in my apartment, and to keep his crate clean. He didn't have any issues with chewing things up and was compliant when I told him to leave things alone. He was a pretty quiet fellow, not vocally inclined like most dogs. One thing I quickly discovered was his OCD nature toward anything fetch: ball or Frisbee. In general, I was impressed at what an easygoing young dog he was. He would fit in well with the mountain biking crowd. Luckily, he fit perfectly in the back seat of my two-door Nissan 240SX and was a good traveler. Most importantly, my new boyfriend seemed to like him too, so I decided to keep him as well!

Somewhere along the way, I noticed a nagging question in the back of my mind. Could Mo have come back to me in this dog? The dates did not match up in that Kona would have been conceived before Mo died. I wasn't sure how dogs' spirits worked back then. Was it even possible? But then again, I did not know then what I know now. Kona had a familiar feel to him, something I just couldn't put my finger on. I eventually dropped the thought because I figured there was no way I would ever actually know. Yeah, ironic, right? Unknown to me, there would be a recurring theme during Kona's visit, one of *unpredictable uncertainty* and *redirection*.

CHAPTER 75

Winding Curves Ahead

Shortly after I acquired Kona, I found myself unemployed because of a poorly planned job change. For the first and only time in my career, I was out of a job. During these six months, I struggled to find work. I feared I would lose my car and be kicked out of my apartment. It happened to be a rare occasion when physical therapy jobs were scarce. Medicare was undergoing a major restructuring that left therapy companies on edge. This created a temporary hiring freeze. It was innocent bad timing on my part to leave one job and not have the next one completely secured. There had always been such demand for physical therapists that I typically had three or four jobs to pick from at any given time. Unfortunately, this just happened to be one of those exceptions to the rule. So things were tense in my life for a bit.

This provided more time to spend at home with Kona, and I was thankful for the company. I had more time to ride my bike so I did lots of training. And I literally had to *ride* this uncertainty out. Luckily, the drought only lasted six months and I was able to get back to work. But with the extra free time to consider my future, I decided to change direction with my career. Instead of taking another job with a company, I opted to work for myself! I became a self-employed contractor for the state. It was great money and I got to totally control my own schedule! My patience had paid off and I was being sent in another direction. I would more than double my previous income and be my own boss! Héric was back at the helm! Things were looking up once again!

After a year of long-distance dating, my boyfriend moved to Indiana, and we got an apartment together. Shortly thereafter, we were engaged to be married. Things were certainly looking up and life was good! Being my own boss gave me more control over my training, traveling, and competition schedule. I was fitter and more competitive in mountain biking than ever before in my athletic career. I traveled to races all over the region and even raced in national events. In 1998 I completed my most impressive season ranked as the number one woman in my region. I was winning all my local events, but I also challenged myself with national series events where I could compete against the pros. In 1999 I hoped to finish the season well enough to category-up to a professional license. But the year did not go as planned. I began to feel poorly. With each demanding race, I got weaker and weaker. I was having tremendous difficulty sleeping and was susceptible to frequent colds that invariably morphed into bronchitis. My body was in trouble, and I was running on fumes!

At the peak of my difficulties, we traveled to Red Wing, Minnesota, with Kona to compete in one of the NORBA (National OffRoad Bicycle Association) national championship events at the Welch Village Ski resort. This was a challenging course on the side of a ski mountain. There were many grass climbs in full sun, which easily taxes the legs and invites quick fatigue. This course was not ideally suited to me, and it would be hard. But I had put in the training, and I was ready for the challenge.

The night before the race, I could not sleep at all. My brain would not turn off and I couldn't find the switch to force a reboot. Later I would come to understand how devastated my nervous system was causing it to become locked into sympathetic overdrive. My body had lost the ability to switch gears from fight or flight and relax into rest and digest. It was maddening! I was miserable that night, fitfully tossing and turning as my fiancé and teammates slept blissfully nearby. They all awoke rested as the alarm rang at 5 a.m., but I had not slept a wink. Even so, I was determined that this would not stop me. I could push through this because I was tough. Somehow, I would find a way to deliver the performance I knew that I was capable of.

However, as much as I tried, my body could not cash the check that day. I gave that race my all, pushed as hard as I could. I felt like I was generating massive amounts of power on the climbs. But my competitors just kept passing me. It was like I was going backward instead of forward. I was giving it my all but steadily drifted to the back of the pack. I couldn't understand it. I was heartbroken and devastated. Instead of solidifying my rankings, I tumbled downward on the charts. I did manage to finish, although I am not sure how. This would be one of my final attempts to race, before I became so sick that I was forced to retire. My body had given all it could to my cause. But there was a limit to its abilities in my compromised state. I just did not know it yet.

As the fall of 1999 approached, I could no longer ride my bike, much less train and race. I tested positive for Epstein-Barr virus and cytomegalovirus. I was extremely fatigued and weak and had severe insomnia, frequent migraines, unrelenting vertigo, and malaise. I could not even follow a thirty-minute sitcom! To complicate things even more, I also developed multiple food sensitivities that made eating very challenging. Direct sun exposure caused an instant migraine and overwhelming fatigue. So I had to stay inside and thus began a very "dark" time for me. I had finished the 1998 racing season at the top of my game. To go from such a distinction into a helpless heap of sickness was incredibly difficult for me. I was a person of action, not suffering and complaining. But I felt helpless to defend myself from this virus. There seemed to be nothing I could do about the sudden spiral into powerlessness. And this, I would discover, was another example of *divine design!*

These powerful viruses ravaged my body and forced me to abandon my current values in life: the exercise, travel, competition, and astounding work ethic. My life was reduced to the bare necessity activities required to just take care of me. It was frightening not knowing when or if I would ever feel better. I could only tolerate working a few hours a day, but I never had to stop working completely. I was so blessed that I had transitioned into self-employment permitting me the flexibility I required! *(Divine design again.)* I spent most of my time trying to sleep even though I could not. Kona was my constant companion through this very dark time. I could no longer take him for walks or spend any quality outdoor time with him. So we just hung out in the apartment together and he never complained. I was eternally thankful for the quiet compassionate company. He was there for me, ready to catch me over the next few months as I tumbled into the unknown.

****

If there is one thing that I have learned about sudden devastating life events, it is that they happen for a reason. This illness forced me to hit the pause button on life, allowing space for all the invisible pieces to line up for the next interchange. I witnessed the beauty of everything coming to a complete stop in my life, so all the moving pieces lined up at just the right angle. All the necessary components moved into place; some stopped, some sped up, and some spun around. All so that I did not miss this next connection. Kona was there waiting, watching, whispering in my ear, signaling to the other guides, and making sure that everything was ready for this next phase. He quietly held me in my misery, understanding the *divine purpose* that I could not see. He held a space open for something new to arrive. Another massive shift was coming, a very important one that I could not afford to miss! Kona was assigned to escort me to this most important rendezvous.

I couldn't see what was happening or what was coming. I only vaguely perceived my life suddenly taking an about turn, a really *huge* about-face. And what I turned to focus on next was something I was very familiar with. Dogs.

CHAPTER 76

A New Direction from a Powerful Force

It took about a year for me to heal enough to feel like pursuing anything outside of my own self-care. Exercise was still not an option. Just a long walk provoked severe fatigue. I needed something to focus on and sink my passion into to get me through this rugged time. But what was that to be?

At the end of 1999, I happened to catch a *Breed All about It* episode on Animal Planet while cuddled up with Kona on the couch. The breed they were profiling was the Belgian Malinois. I was fascinated. I had never heard about this breed. Its medium size, short, tight coat, athletic build, and exuberant intelligence seemed to be a perfect combination of the German shepherd and border collie. But this breed was still somewhat rare in the US and information was difficult to come by. I began to research as much as I could find on the internet, most of it from foreign countries. I found myself suddenly insatiably obsessed with learning everything I could about them.

This was now the familiar echo of a calling. Only this calling proved to be one of the most intense that I would ever experience. The story of the dog calling me is incredibly special, but she has decided to save her message for the next book. What is important for you to realize here is that Kona, Héric, was present just to make sure this connection happened. It was so important because it would set the stage for the next ten years of my life and provide the opportunity for all the other dogs to come through. If this connection had been missed, this book would not have been possible!

This next dog represented my future with the dogs in all its totality. She was my true beginning of my life with them. It was because of her that I became a professional dog trainer and breeder and competed at the national level. The experience with her would create the unique opportunities for me to interact with so many dogs all at once! If we had not connected, none of this would have been possible. She was the reason Héric had created such a powerful vortex with my illness, causing my life to essentially stop and wait for this moment to happen! I had to get to the portal on time! Compared to all the other dogs that called to me, she turned out to be the most powerful spiritual connection of all of them!

That's all I can tell you about her right now, but I want you to know this much so that you understand the reason that I required Kona's presence at this very moment.

CHAPTER 77

Moving On

Once I walked through that necessary door and found that one specific puppy, the floodgates opened! I got more and more callings from more and more dogs wanting to come to me. Before I knew it, I had four Malinois and my one border collie. We were outgrowing our home that we had just purchased eighteen months before, and I was looking for a bigger one that could accommodate even more dogs. Things were clearly moving in a different direction for me. Exercise was the last thing on my mind, yet I had plenty of energy to spend with the dogs without becoming fatigued! It seemed the more I embraced my new path, the healthier I became. This is yet another incredible example of *divine design*.

But I began to feel that Kona's time to move on was approaching. He had made sure the next few guides had been heard, located, and were in place to deliver their messages. Thankfully, he would remain here on earth this time. He had another job to do, another soul to help. So I sought out a new home for my precious Kona. He would be easy to match because he got along with everyone and everything. Ironically, he would find a suitable home with a young couple that I already knew. He lived out his life in a loving, devoted family of his own. I hope that he brought them much joy and happiness. But sadly, once he left here, I never saw him again.

He had done his job very well and succeeded in his mission. When I look back at how all the pieces had so magically come together at just the right moment, I am overwhelmed with gratitude and amazement. When unpleasant things happen to us, it can be difficult to clearly understand them in the moment. But as they say, "Hindsight is twenty/twenty." I am grateful that I had the wisdom to turn around and look so that I could see the beauty in what felt like devastation! Héric worked magic to connect me to my higher self and allow me to begin to hear the flood of dogs that were waiting.

Now that I have shared all Héric's visits with you, let us return our focus to 2022 and my ongoing opportunities with my current Héric puppy.

Sudden devastating life events ... happen for a reason ... I witnessed the beauty of everything coming to a complete stop in my life, so all the moving pieces lined up at just the right angle ... All so that I did not miss this next connection.

PART 4

The Rebirth

2022

In this part, Héric will provide the greatest level of enlightenment and integration when I decided to get out of the way!

Let's continue our story.

CHAPTER 78

The Wheels Begin to Turn

As we bring our focus back to this little bundle of joy that abruptly entered my life, much like Trixie did, I would like to attest to what a gift she is! Gigi is literally a gift from God. She is the most perfect dog! She has no vices, she's easy to live with, and she is constantly bringing a smile to my face. She seems to know that she is an ambassador to the world and delightfully brings light and joy to everyone she meets! Without a doubt, she was a wise investment!

Gigi, Héric, has been my constant companion throughout my rapid fast-forward transformation in 2022. She was with me for every meditation, every hypnosis, every spiritual reading, and every journey into myself. The learning I traversed was intense, deep, revealing, and completely healing. Héric made sure of it! The remainder of this section will discuss some of this process because it completes the stories I have already shared with you. It also provides the why for all my experiences and explains the sharp trajectory of my life. Héric skillfully and expertly provided the doorway I required to find the answers I sought. I could not have achieved such rapid spiritual growth without his help!

All the stories I have shared already have been somewhat miraculous.

But the journey I embarked upon at the beginning of 2022 would top everything I had already lived through and answer all my questions! Héric would now move mountains as he escorted me into my most important phase of enlightenment and integration!

CHAPTER 79

The Beginning of a New Adventure

Just as predicted, my soul began to churn from deep down inside as 2022 emerged, creating a sense of restlessness and subtle agitation. I became emotionally, physically, and spiritually unsettled. There was something *big* coming. I could feel it. But I had no idea what, when, or where. There was one thing I did know, and that was big events like this require big help. I felt a new push to look outside myself, to search for someone who could guide and direct me through whatever this was. Héric knew I was heeding his push, searching for his human helpers. He sent me clues, psychic feelings engaging my claircognizance, urging me to hang on, help was on the way!

A sense of urgency overcame me, and I felt like the clock was ticking. I felt as if I was somehow behind schedule. I was chomping at the bit, eager to move toward something that I couldn't see, touch, understand, or perceive yet on any level. I was simultaneously terrified and exhilarated much like that squirrel. Everything in my life had come together for this moment, this precise opportunity for all to be revealed. The information I had received from the numerologist the year before was encouraging. It provided some validation of my life so far while suggesting there were still great things to come. But I also sensed a new direction, and I was anxious to unveil those details.

I needed help from someone more experienced and skilled to make sense of it all. I needed clarity and direction. As Héric pushed me forward into my answers, the planets aligned, the dots merged, and everything fell into place. My spirit guides skillfully led me to human assistance that could provide their own tools in helping me to unlock mine. Once I located one human helper, more emerged in his wake. Everything began to unfold in the most brilliant, magical version of *divine design!* I had the help that I needed to make sense of all this and move quickly along my path. Héric had once again succeeded in the very complex task of connecting me to my human angels!

My magical journey officially began on February 2, 2022, with a spiritual reading where I learned I was to write my book *now*. This date is also significant because in numerology these digits represent a "moment of alignment." Additionally, the sequence of twos signifies "angel numbers." So it was a very special day to be kicking off a journey to enlightenment and connecting with K9 angels! I had no idea what this whole process was going to look like when I started. I had no idea that I would be led through a series of events that would ultimately and thoroughly heal my soul. The only thing I knew in the beginning was that I was going to write a book. But I was in for a much bigger adventure than I realized.

Apparently, the guides' first order of business was to lead me through my own healing. This served two purposes. First, it allowed me to experience the full magnitude of their gifts as I unknowingly and blindly ventured through *their* process. Second, it gave me content for this book regarding context and order. As I mentioned in the opening, the guides insisted on a specific order for the book. The importance of this was demonstrated through my own healing process. My root emotional trauma, blockages, or "tags" needed to be healed before anything else was possible. Once I identified and integrated those teachings, I was led into a transformation phase where I finally saw *my true self* for the first time. The final stage birthed me into enlightenment, liberated consciousness, and full integration of my own divine self. All drawing me closer and closer to my Source. Here I will share with you pieces of my process to further illustrate the beauty of the message as well as a possible template for what you may experience.

CHAPTER 80

Journey into the Unknown

By March 2022, I started to get messages in my dreams and in my mediations. I began to identify and process some significant tags, including "No one cares," "I'm not worthy," "I'm not loved," and "I don't belong." There were roughly twenty of these in total. Some of them I was aware of, and others smacked me across the face because I did not know they were there. But the more I dug, the more I found. I allowed the K9 guides, Anthea and Öskar, to lead me where I needed to go. The more healing I received from these tags, the more I could "hear" the guides (clairaudience). With each tag, all the emotional junk stored with it was released. I felt lighter and my mind got quieter. I began to become more aware of my thoughts and how certain thoughts just ran in the background, whether I wanted them to or not. These were usually negative thoughts attached to a tag that needed to be removed. So I meticulously removed them, cleaned out my energetic body of all its waste, and freed myself from my own chains! I had tried my whole life to push away these negative thoughts consciously, and it never worked. The healing tools from the guides provided permanent relief instantly! It was an exhilarating process!

The more I practiced meditation, the easier it got for me to get out of the way and open my mind to the divine. The more aware I became, the more I learned to stay in the back seat and let him drive. The more I realized that I really don't know *anything*, the more I let go of the reins and the need for control. And as I grew into ultimate vulnerability and trust, I began to feel my connection and to *understand*. My newfound clairvoyance allowed me to *see* the purpose behind seemingly irrelevant things.

My meditations took on a life of their own. I never knew what was going to happen when I sat down with the K9 guides. Sometimes I experienced the traditional relaxing meditations that most people think meditations are. But generally, this was not the case. My sessions involved much more active work and explorations. I also didn't know who I was going to be working with from session to session. Sometimes I worked with just one K9 guide; other times all four were present. I've had meditations where I was met by my personal spirit guide; other times it was my higher self who showed up. Later I worked with versions of my soul from previous lifetimes that I had met in hypnosis sessions. Sometimes my meditation got interrupted by the K9 guides with words or passages for the book that required immediate dictation. But the K9 guides were always there, managing the pieces and the process, walking me through their system step-by-step.

On really grand occasions, my meditations were totally hijacked by my spiritual counsel (the same counsel I met with during my brain surgery) as I was teleported into another dimension. Here they attended to me like a NASCAR pit crew removing old, outdated programming and installing new intergalactic tools, skills, and wisdom.

They explained that they were providing me with "knowledge, symbols, techniques, and connections" that were "keys to humanity's understanding." These tools would "unlock humanity's awareness, unlock their armor, and help to bring them back into alignment with their true purpose, their soulful purpose, and why they are on this planet."

Whatever needed to happen happened. I offered myself as a servant in any capacity in which I was needed and allowed the process to unfold in *divine order*. None of it was scary, and I was always safe and protected. I knew I was in the presence of truly amazing entities delicately caring for the welfare of humanity and the planet. Their connection to God was undeniably strong and beautiful. The messages they gave me were healing and uplifting for the world. The need for healing for all of us is tremendous and urgent, which is why I have been given the task and the tools to share the gifts of the K9 guides with the world.

In addition to the meditations, I concurrently experienced an expansion of my consciousness. It began as a sensation of my physical margins expanding like that of a cinnamon roll as it rises in the oven. My body felt like it was spreading out, getting puffier and puffier. Like my skin was bursting outward into a larger-than-life helium balloon version of itself. Later I felt my energy expand around and outside me. It kept growing and reaching until it felt like a massive beacon of light filling my house and then reaching for the stars. In subsequent sessions, my consciousness grew to the size of the planet. And each time I had one of these "growth" experiences, I felt more and more connected to my original source, my divinity. I easily felt the connection among the plants, the animals, the planet, and humans and how all of this is tethered to Source. We are all one. With each expansion, all this became astoundingly clear and undeniable!

My dream state became a classroom. As I slept, I was acutely aware of data being transferred, like computer bytes, streaming into my consciousness. Pages and pages of symbols, some even in color, rolled past my face as I absorbed the information. I was aware that this was necessary information for the book and that I would understand what it all meant, even though I did not recognize the language it came in. There were many conversations with my guides about this whole process. I could hear them speaking to me, see them standing there, and fully understood what I was told. These dreams were so vivid that often they woke me with an urgent need to write, supplying me with specific words to put on the page or a specific organization of the information. I was often up by 2 a.m., wide-awake and ready to write. I just went with it, and I was never tired.

In the beginning, I utilized regressive therapy that revealed many valuable things about myself, my path, and the ancestral entanglement that encased me in my father's lineage. This was also where I first visited my own *soul* and came face-to-face with Archangel Michael! These sessions with my gifted therapist were invaluable and undoubtably essential. I had always had my reservations about doing such work. But the guides encouraged me to toss aside all my fears and trust in the divinely protected process. They now wish for me to share a little bit of my journey with you.

CHAPTER 81

Missing Pieces

One of my first experiences during hypnosis was when I entered a room filled with brilliant white light. As I walked into this room, it felt like I was walking into a cloud filled with amazing energy. The power and the depth of this energy literally took my breath away! It was like jumping into an ice-cold river. Except instead of feeling cold, I felt incredible love, peace, and an energetic vibration that warmed me all over. I began to weep and tremble recognizing that I was *home*. I could not speak as I felt like I was levitating in a bath of love, kindness, and compassion. At first, I assumed I was in the presence of God himself, a natural assumption with such beautiful resonance and love. But when I asked, I was told no, this energy was actually that of myself. It was my light, my power, and my wholeness I felt! How comforting it was to bathe in this heavenly version of my own true self! *So this is who I am! Wow!* I thought. I was blown away! And then I wondered, *If this is how loving, peaceful, and powerful I am, how much stronger is the energy and the presence of the Almighty?* And this brought a whole new perspective to what I *thought* I already knew!

I could then see how far I had strayed from myself and how much I had forgotten. How I had fallen prey to the illusions of fear and pain here on earth that kidnapped me from my truth. But I vowed to never forget this! And ever since that day, I have been able to revisit this space in my consciousness and experience the peace, the connection, the true me I am meant to be here on this planet. Anytime I want to remember who I am, that's where I go.

Another beautiful moment was when I opened the door to a room and found it full of all my dogs! There must have been fifty dogs waiting for me! They were all smiling, barking, wagging their tails, and jumping up and down. A deeply consuming sense of *love* came washing over me like a tidal wave when I opened that door. I became overcome with emotion, and I wept like a vulnerable child in their presence. They embraced me with all their angelic love and spoke to me clearly for the first time in my journey. Their collective voice appeared in my head and told me they have always been with me, watching over me, talking to me, waiting for the time to be right. Making sure I was safe and on my path, anxiously waiting for the right time to let me hear from them. It was the first time I had ever heard them speak to me, and it was validation that I was in the right place!

As I have already shared, I also received my first astrological reading during this process. This session revealed so much about me that was critical for me to trust myself and this process. Having absolutely no knowledge of what I was questioning or struggling with and armed with only the date and time of birth and the city I was born in, this is what the astrologer shared:

> You're here to do a mission and you're gonna stick it out, come hell or high water, and accomplish what you came here to do! You've willingly taken on this assignment that on the surface looks like you've been enduring deprivations, limitations, and living on a shoestring. You live connected to the Source, devoted to serving the truth, the light, and humanity's liberation. This dedication has been so complete, so fierce, that you have been willing to take on enormous sacrifices and be highly disciplined. And sometimes you've questioned it because the source for this sacrifice was completely unconscious! This is who you are internally that no

one sees below the horizon. You have been waiting for your marching orders (to complete this mission) your whole life!

Specific assessments helped me to understand my ability to find the dogs anywhere in the world and my ability to understand things clearly without knowing how.

Your intuition is off the charts! You (have) followed your gut all the time! You've followed your instinct and intuition every single time, not being sure that it was going to produce anything or that it was going to be relevant. But you just had to do it at the time. You have a holographic mind that sees the truth. You understand the meaning of things without taking them apart. You look at something and you just know how it works.

Her words merely echoed everything about me that I had felt and assumed to be true even though I had no proof of it. She validated my core assumption of who I really was and confirmed the blueprint that had always been there. But I would have never been connected to these talented professionals if it had not been for the gifted clairvoyant and mystic who made all this possible. This skillful master served as my trusted mentor through my transformation process. He helped guide me back to myself through my process of discovery and development. He served as a "fact checker" as I began to receive information from the guides. I relied on his experience to validate my experience and gain confidence in my own skills. Our sessions were instrumental in my ability to connect to my inherent tools I needed to hear the guides and fulfill my mission.

These human angels were all part of my evolution, validating my instincts and what I thought I was receiving. They taught me to trust in what I already knew but did not yet fully understand. They gently reassured my confidence or redirected my focus when I needed it without interrupting in my process or in the message. I gradually stretched my wings and gained confidence in my abilities with their help. However, the K9 guides refused to share their message with anyone other than me no matter how psychic or skilled. They insisted on only sharing it with me to prevent it from becoming skewed. My human support staff was only allowed to participate in this process in an objective, supportive role. This kept the message and my process pure and untainted.

As I continued along my journey and with each level of healing, I began to change in ways I never thought possible. My energy changed, my attitude changed, my expectations changed, and my spirit changed. I began to have more control over how I perceived the world and how the world perceived me. I discovered some very painful truths about previous experiences on this planet in this lifetime and others. But I was also given the tools to heal them so they no longer infected me. I began to detect my direct tether to God Almighty himself and to all his creatures. My vision, hearing, and touch changed as my awareness transformed.

Everything seemed new and exciting, much like it would after a rebirth. I was also beginning to understand a different me, one that I had never noticed before. I saw her in mediations, in dreams, and in my daily thoughts. I could see her hairstyle, her glasses, her clothing choices, and her smile! I even felt her energy. She was a very different me that I was evolving into. She was a part of me that had been hidden away my whole life. I was now ready to embrace her and release her into the world. I was becoming a whole new person as I evolved out of my spiritual cocoon!

My transformation was *fast* and unrelenting. But this was necessary before I was able to tap into my tools I already possessed but had buried deep inside my unconscious brain. Now that all the lifetimes of healing had been completed, I could finally have access to everything I needed to share this message with the world! And I could finally unapologetically be me!

CHAPTER 82

Are You My Father?

Before this whole transformation began in 2022, I thought I had done everything I needed to in relation to my father. I wasn't mad at him anymore and had moved on with my life. He was long gone and the opportunity for change had passed. So I figured there wasn't anything left for me to do. Boy, was I wrong! The energy between us had not dissipated just because I was no longer angry. I still had a lot of work to do around our relationship before I was free to move on. And I was about to expose these lingering roots by accident.

One of the most important discoveries I made throughout this entire process was the *why* to my relationship with my father. I want to share this revelation with you because it might resonate with your own learning, and it completes the story of me. The first critical piece I encountered was during my astrology reading. Do you remember how my astrologer described him as a "tyrant, obsessive-compulsive control freak, heavy handed, emotionally unavailable, manipulative, bipolar, and schizophrenic"? This was so comforting to me because it was how I had always seen him. In that session, she also went on to describe his psychological cruelty in his attempts to control us. I had put all that out of my mind and buried those experiences deep in my subconscious to survive. This reminder made me realize that even though I was no longer angry, I still needed to process these memories before I could move on.

But I also learned something truly amazing in that session. Something that brought me comfort about my dad. She told me that no matter who ended up being my father, my experience would have been the same because that father figure was written in my astrological blueprint! Let me rephrase that because it is very important that you understand. *I would have had the same life experience no matter who my father was!* Because my father wasn't just a father in my life. He represented the complete embodiment of all my persecutors from all my previous lifetimes! (And there were many.) He provided a fast track for me to confront, process, and transmute all these experiences in one fell swoop! In other words, I chose to have one massive experience to represent everything all at once. And this was all written in my astrological chart!

This information and realization caused my soul to *move*. It changed me. Suddenly his cruelty was not a personal attack. It was a profound gift he lovingly provided me by being such a terrible person just so my soul could achieve enlightenment! This also meant that he knowingly submitted himself to the inhumanity of his own father only so he could become the miserable person I needed him to be!

This floored me! And at this moment, I was suddenly filled with a tremendous sense of peace and compassion for him. His choices demonstrated the most selfless form of love. I felt the layers of pain, anger, and betrayal deep down inside begin to melt and trickle out of me. I finally understood! But my clarity did not stop there. This ball was only beginning to roll!

Throughout my transformation and healing process during 2022, I learned to rely heavily on my newfound skill of meditation. Not for relaxation but as a tool for connecting to my clairvoyance and uncovering the knowledge I needed. The better I got at it, the easier I could connect with my soul, my guides, and past lives. I could often obtain critical details I needed to complete my healing process. It was within this sacred space that I received one of the most revealing clues about my father. I was told to investigate my father's lineage; there was an ancestral piece that I needed to clear so I could recover a missing chunk of my tattered soul. I found this fascinating. So I began my crusade for this hidden knowledge with a regressive hypnotherapy session.

    I do not know what my readers' beliefs about reincarnation may be. I have already referred to past lives many places in this book. It has never been something that I have ever questioned. I have always just understood and accepted that I have been here before. However, it is not essential that you embrace this concept if it is not something you are comfortable with. I only include it in this book because I find it necessary to understand who I am and why I am here. Please accept the next few paragraphs on whatever level is comfortable for you. No matter what your beliefs, just keep reading. This information is very powerful, important, and might be surprisingly relative to you. Please don't let a scary concept stop you from reading further. Because you are not going to want to miss what comes next!

CHAPTER 83

Ancestral Entanglement

The purpose of my hypnosis session was to specifically address this ancestral clue that was so critical for me to heal. Gigi was close by as my session began. There were three lifetimes that would answer my question so three doors appeared to me. So I walked through the first door and found myself in the early 1800s in an old town just like in the Westerns. I noticed the dirt roads with horse-drawn carriages as well as scantly built wooden structures and walkways. I was a young man up to no good and looking for trouble. I was on foot and did not appear to own a horse. I found myself robbing the local mercantile. Naturally, I was pursued by the merchant, apprehended by the marshal, and thrown into jail for my crime. While in jail, I stewed in anger and plotted my revenge on the store owner who had put me there. As soon as I was released, I returned to the mercantile to retaliate. I savagely beat him with my bare hands out of pure *rage* then set his establishment on fire! It burned to the ground while his unconscious, half-dead body lay inside.

I was a ruthless cuss, angry at the world, and set on destruction. I sounded a lot like my grandfather and my father. I was very uncomfortable with the "me" I witnessed in this life. I asked forgiveness for the violence and pain I had caused others. But I also had to forgiving *myself.* And this is when I came face-to-face with Archangel Michael!

His overwhelming presence felt like warm, bright, white light and took my breath away! His energy was one hundred times greater than that of my own soul experience. His holy being filled every inch of my awareness; I could see no end to him. A sense of complete peace, love, and compassion filled every cell in my body then overflowed and spilled far beyond me. The energy was incredible! I began to tremble all over. My legs shook so fiercely that they levitated off the bed I was lying on. I struggled to speak the words the facilitator instructed. I just wanted to stay in this moment and never leave! It was like a warm, loving embrace of a father offering full protection and safety. Something I had certainly never experienced here on earth.

As I requested his assistance to absolve and dissolve all past transgressions in that life, I began to weep. I could literally feel the forgiving force of one of God's mightiest angels clear out all the pain, fear, hate, and guilt from my energy field! His power was so great I could not contain it within my being, and it seeped out of me as I allowed it to flow through me. If I were not already lying down, I would have collapsed under the immense power that I was feeling. Archangel Michael easily and instantly transmuted all this historical pain into love and light and freed me from the chains that had bound me. I now felt light as a feather!

Once I collected myself, it was time to move on to the next door. I had no idea what to expect next, but I had full confidence in the process. The second life I visited must have been shortly after the first. I was again a man, but this time, I was the patriarch of a very powerful and wealthy family. We owned an enormous parcel of land in what felt like the Texas region. The scene reminded me of the TV show *Bonanza*. My family was currently feuding with a neighboring family over land. My *rage* around the dispute led our families into a bloody, violent battle that could have been easily settled with more peaceful means. But I was thirsty for power and control and anxious to display my authority. I eradicated anyone who stood in my way, and my greed cost many innocent lives. Both sides suffered heavy casualties. Again, this reminded me very much of my grandfather's energy with a strong resemblance to his character. I again called on Archangel Michael to help me forgive and be forgiven, to transmute the learning into love and light, and to leave the negativity behind. I had been carrying all this guilt from lifetime to lifetime. Finally shedding it permitted me to collect more of my divine self, allowing my own God energy to shine through brighter.

The third door was a bit different. I was now a girl and a submissive member of a violent family. I was the only girl, but I had many older brothers. It felt to be in the early 1900s, and I noticed we lived in a poorly constructed wooden structure in a forest. It seems like the floor of this home was slanted and drafty. We had an old-timey automobile with the big wheels, but we did not have a lot of money. I was in my early teens, and I was aware that I had been sexually violated by another family member. I tried to keep it secret because I was ashamed, but my brothers eventually found out. They set out to execute their own vigilante justice on the uncle who had raped me. In their *rage* for revenge, they bound the man and dragged him to death behind our family vehicle! I watched in horror, powerless as a woman to stop it. Somehow, I perceived the learning from the last lifetime had integrated, and I now wanted to avoid violence in this one. I surprisingly did not wish any ill will on this man despite his predatory treatment of me.

From then on, I lived as a prisoner in my own home because, even as a victim, I had brought shame on the family. I was not allowed to leave the house or express my opinion. I was a prisoner in my home. I was internally *enraged* at my brothers and at my *powerlessness* yet never expressed it. This life for some reason held more emotional pain than the previous two. I could clearly see where the tags of rage and powerlessness had emerged. I had to forgive all those who had harmed me directly and indirectly and forgive myself for not speaking up and defending what was right. All this energy had to be transmuted into God's love and light and released into the universe so that my soul would be free to move on. And with divine help it was, and I was finally freed. I felt so light, quiet, happy, and joyous! It was obvious to me that I had been carrying the burden of these lives for quite some time. I was elated to finally be free!

All three characters I visited in this hypnosis session were ancestors in my father's and grandfather's lineage. I learned that I was instrumental in instigating the long line of violence that had created the "redneck gangster" tradition in my family that I so despised now. My grandfather was actually a descendent of me! I started the genetic chain that perpetuated the cycle. His brutality of my father was because of my actions many lifetimes ago. The abuse my father suffered at the hands of his own father created the person he was to me. I was not the victim of him. Rather, he was the victim of me!

It is difficult for me to describe in words the feelings and emotions that came up when I finally *got* this. This *huge* realization pulled all my experiences together and explained *everything*. When I learned the role my father had played in my life from the astrologer, I was able to forgive him. But with this new, deeper understanding of my own part in who he became, I saw our relationship in an even different light. I had actually wounded him! No wonder he was so bitter toward me! Suddenly, the ever-elusive love for my father just came pouring out of my soul! It felt like the pure and sacred love of a mother for her own child. I wanted to cradle him in my arms, love and protect him, and never let him go. Much like a mother would do after discovering her child had been harmed. I longed to say how sorry I was for everything he endured because of me! It was the first time in my life I had ever felt love for him. It was a relief to finally feel the dam open and flowing!

CHAPTER 84

Rage

This hypnosis experience brought such deep understanding and healing that it totally changed me. Once I was able to see the full truth, heal it, and release it, my past no longer held any power over me. My soul was finally free from the shackles that had bound it for many lifetimes. None of the memories I had pondered over my whole life mattered anymore. I was instantly absolved from all the pain, guilt, and anguish I had carried for so long when Archangel Michael transformed all of this into love and light. I was finally free!

I think it is important to realize here that no amount of thought control (saying "I forgive my father"), positive thinking, pretending things didn't bother me, talking about my feelings, forcing thoughts of him out of my mind, etc. had ever provided me with this kind of instant and complete healing! From my experience, I now understand how critical it is to heal the soul energetically from all wounds. I thought I had forgiven my father, but I wasn't even close. I needed angelic assistance to identify and free the ancestral entanglement. The energy had to be transmuted by devoted servants of God in order for me to be completely free.

I was also surprised to learn that I had agreed to carry all the guilt of the family lineage all these lifetimes because I was the only one who was strong enough to endure it. This ancestral entanglement represented genetic karma passed down through the generations until it could be cleared. This was an assignment I agreed to, and it was part of my job this lifetime to finally dissolve it for good. And this hypnosis session allowed me to do just that! The family history finally stopped here with me. This explained why my family's ways affected me so differently from anyone else. I was carrying a much different burden than other members of my family!

This was all incredible information, but I still had more questions after my hypnosis session. So I went back to my meditation with what I had just learned and asked if there was anything else I needed to know. I was surprised to receive a very detailed answer. When my higher self appeared before me, I saw three versions—one for each life I had visited. I knew that's who they were because they looked just like they had in the hypnosis session. They explained to me that they represented three versions of *rage*. The first life was *individual rage*. The second life was *group* or *gang rage*. The third life was *unexpressed, suppressed,* or *inhibited rage*.

This was a powerful message from the spirit world, a warning of sorts. I knew my life had been filled with rage until I was cleansed of it just moments ago. I had always felt it bubbling up inside me just under the surface and ready to explode at the slightest frustration. You might recall some important lessons in this book about this rage. But this message is also for humanity. Rage is a predominant issue in our culture today. It is literally killing us and pulling us apart. We were never meant to be filled with so much savage hate, and our heavenly Father hopes that we will embrace the tools he has provided to free us from the illusions that blind us. I can only hope that my experience can speak to those who need to hear it.

We all have the ability to grow and heal, and this is one thing I am meant to teach you. I bring you the K9 guides and their messages to provide you with the tools for your own healing and awakening. But I am also to provide you with the tools to unlock your spiritual self. This is the true self you are meant to be that will allow the world to heal, reconnect with its true purpose, and allow humanity to save itself from the current downward spiral. I can only deliver the message I was given and trust that it will be received.

I witnessed the beauty of everything coming to a complete stop in my life, so all the moving pieces lined up at just the right angle. All the necessary components moved into place; some stopped, some sped up, and some spun around. All so that I did not miss this next connection.

SECTION 6
Their Gift to Humanity

CHAPTER 85

In Summary

Working with the tools that these K9 guides have to offer is enlightening and exhilarating. I have provided you with a lot of information and want to close this book by tying it all together.

As Anthea so expertly illustrated in her stories, feelings of betrayal, persecution, and inadequacy all created self-doubt, insecurity, and fear. Öskar showed us how a sense of powerlessness and rejection can instill deep-seated rage and rob us of our voice. But these perceived emotions were only illusions that our minds talked us into. That's how two people can have such opposite reactions to the same experience; it's our conscious mind that tells us how to interpret or spin the information into the illusion. Tags were an important part of their teaching because these need to be healed before the illusions are dissolved. Only then will the angelic side of the guides and of *you* come shining through! Only after I removed the blockage to my joy could I feel joy! Only after I healed the memories that stifled my power and my voice could I own them both. Anthea and Öskar demonstrate their important value in facilitating this process.

Oeragon is at a different level from the first two guides. Once you have successfully purged the bondage that controls you with Anthea and Öskar, she will illuminate your light and your power. She will invite you to shed the masks you hide behind, drop the lies you tell yourself, and empower you to finally see yourself fully! She will appear when the opportunity is right for you to reunite with your own brilliant soul. Most of us have never met our own souls. Because if we walked around with the awareness of who we really were in God's eyes, there would be no war or violence; it would be impossible from the elated state of godly love and joy! Remember how Apachi transformed her fear into undying, unquestioning, unwavering trust? She used this trust to transmute her fear. This is how she dissolved her masks. Remember when I described the intense energetic connection that flowed between us? She was showing me the version of myself I would find once I released my masks and trusted in the divine. The energy I experienced between her and me was the same energy that I felt when I met my soul for the first time!

Héric is the crème de la crème of these guides. He shows up for you when you are ready for a big surge into expanded consciousness, spiritual connection, and ultimate enlightenment. It was with his help that I was able to progress so quickly. He escorted me through mystic meditations to heal old wounds, review previous lives, and even explore other dimensions for the knowledge I required. He is so powerful! And he is waiting to share his gifts with you!

It is important to progress in this order, thus the presentation order of this book. This is the order that my journey followed even though I did not know it at the time. The guides will appear in your life or call to you based on the level you are ready for. If you attempt to connect with a guide that is not suited to you, it will be unsuccessful. When I attempted to receive the message from a guide out of this order, I was denied access. So they won't allow you to jump ahead or pick and choose who you work with. Kindly set aside who you *think* you are and where you *think* you want to go, like I had to. These guides know far more than we do because they have a direct connection to God and our soul's records. If you *allow* them, they will carry you through a wonderful process of healing and discovery.

There are more guides that will fill in more of the steps as we go along. But for now, these four wanted to introduce you to the big picture. I guess they represented the beginning, the middle, and the top! I am excited to meet the next bunch and share more messages and healing with you. But for now, embrace a new concept and digest what I have laid before you. Integrate what spoke to you. Soon we will be moving on to specific techniques, processes, and strategies they wish to share.

****

CHAPTER 86

A Revolution of Awareness

My life was tough, intense, and fast for a reason. Remember that everything in it was for the sole purpose of getting me to this very moment. So that I could bring these experiences to you and use them as a teaching tool. I hope the contents of this book, the valuable messages from the guides, how they shaped my life, and the transformation that blossomed from the healing they brought will encourage you on your own journey to ascension. The time is now as humanity is in crisis. The K9 spirit guides are anxious to assist all of us in a revolution of awareness. It is time for us all to heed our calling and become our true God-selves!

Even if you don't have a dog, you can still have a K9 spirit guide, and you can call on them for support. They work with all humankind as God's loyal servants. Part of my assignment is to teach those who wish to know how to follow the steps and progress through their own unique path to spiritual enlightenment. You too can learn to communicate with your K9 spirit guides and achieve oneness with Source.

The K9 guides will be providing a step-by-step process for healing that will include mediations unique to each guide and their message and some sort of workbook to direct you in using their tools. But they did not want me to hold the printing of this book until that was ready. So those tools will be available at a later date. Be sure to follow me @

K9spiritguides on FB, IG, Twitter, and YouTube, and visit my blog page (www.k9spiritguides.com) to stay abreast of new information as it becomes available. The guides frequently push me to post and blog pertinent information they wish to be shared, so be sure to follow me. There will also be future books revealing more of the guides because this is just the beginning! Please drop me a note or a post in social media and tell me which of these K9 spirit guides you have with you now or maybe visited you in your past. You will begin to become more aware of them now that they have introduced themselves to you.

Thank you for joining me on a very special journey! I appreciate the trust you lent me as I revealed something so new and different. I hope this information sparks your own journey into discovery and enlightenment. Cherish the dogs in your life; they are so much more powerful than you realize! Begin to tune in to them and hear their messages for you. Maybe you have an Anthea, Öskar, Oeragon, or Héric with you now. Their healing tools can make life so much easier for you, as they did for me!

Epilogue

View from a Star

I leave you with one final impression. During one of my hypnosis sessions, I found myself sitting on a star. From this star I could see Earth in the distance. As I gazed at the distant planet a feeling of trepidation washed over me. I realized I was contemplating my next trip back. My soul was conflicted about the upcoming assignment; it would be very difficult. Was I up to the task? Was it going to be any different from all the other times? Was the world finally ready for the message I had to deliver?

I had already attempted to deliver my message on multiple occasions. Each time I was violently persecuted for the gifts that I offered. Humanity had not been ready. So many times, I had failed my mission.

Was humanity finally ready? Would this lifetime finally be successful?

So I ask you, have I finally succeeded in my mission?

Acknowledgments

Because none of us are in this alone, it is important to acknowledge those who have contributed to our process.

I certainly relied on the support of my spiritual advisors throughout my awakening.

Without Clayton John Ainger's skillful, clairvoyant, mystic guidance, I would never have fully understood my path. His wisdom catapulted my consciousness, allowing me to connect with my calling. His leadership cradled me throughout an exciting and bewildering time while his meditations provided the medium for my spiritual exploration.

Rania James blessed me with her astrological mastery as she so skillfully unveiled my clandestine path. Her wisdom provided me with a complete understanding of who I had been and who I was becoming. The clarity of her gift lent the courage I required to answer my calling!

Liz Vincent's unique regressive techniques exposed events in this life and others that required my attention. Her vast experience and knowledge were evident in the ease with which our sessions progressed. And with her leadership, I was able to gleam powerful healing that allowed me to move forward quickly on my path.

Joni Hansen's genius numerology reading kicked off my awakening phase with valuable insight into just how my numbers fed into who I was and where I was going. My session with her ignited the fire within and proved 100 percent accurate within the next eighteen months.

All of you enabled me to locate my divine self and my purpose and to connect with my skills with great ease and speed! You are all an incredible gift to this world!

And I want to thank the stars of this book. Without all the dogs who volunteered to be a part of my journey, my life would not have been so magical!

This book is dedicated to my mother, who has always loved me and chose to give me life knowing what a rough road it would be. And then she chose to stick around.
And to my husband, who devoted himself to carrying me until I was able. Even though all this seems far-fetched to him, he has supported me fully throughout my process.
I am eternally grateful to have him by my side.

Since the beginning of time, animal spirits have walked side by side with humans. They have watched over us, guided us, protected us, provided insight to us, even when we can't see them, even when they aren't in physical form.

A message from Stoney, May 7, 2022